A Survey

of

Christian

Hymnody

William J. Reynolds
Milburn Price

Hope Publishing Company
Carol Stream, Illinois 60188

Preface

One likes what has become familiar. Attitudes toward hymns and hymn singing are much influenced by subjective association. It does not follow that hearty participation involves careful thought or conscious insight regarding the substance of the words or music. For most of us the hymn has a sacred aura, and to submit it to careful scrutiny sometimes causes inward resentment. But ministers as well as lay workers involved in academic programs have a responsibility for selecting hymnic materials. If these leaders can be helped to understand the values of hymn singing and the need for exercising careful judgment in the choices of hymns, the intelligent appreciation of students and the spiritual growth of congregations will be increased.

The importance given, in recent years, to the place and practice of hymnody in the worship of congregations representing a wide variety of denominations has increased the validity of this study. The contributions and trends of the present, as well as the heritage of the past, have become matters of interest to many lay people, as well as to students, church musicians, and clergy. It is to this wide spectrum of both leaders and participants in congregational song that this book is directed.

To understand hymns, it is imperative to have an awareness of the historical development of hymnody, as well as a knowledge of the broad scope of hymnic literature and of major trends in religious thought. Prospective leaders need to understand the changing attitudes toward the use of hymns as church history unfolded. The materials presented here are designed to acquaint the student with the scope of Christian hymnody, its historical patterns, the environment from which it emerged, the contribution of significant individuals and specific collections of hymns and tunes that furthered the ever-increasing stream of Christian song.

To illustrate historical development of our hymnody, a careful selection of hymns is provided representing the types and periods under consideration. These illustrative hymns are given in the form in which they appear in contemporary hymnals. Such presentation is more practical for critical study than the reproduction of the same material in its original form. The numbers in parentheses by the hymn titles and tune names throughout each chapter refer to these illustrative hymns.

This selection of hymns is not to be regarded as an "abridged hymnal," but rather as a collection reflecting many facets of contributions to Christian hymnody. Both familiar and unfamiliar hymns will be found. The appearance of a familiar hymn set to an unfamiliar tune is not to imply preference for the unfamiliar over the familiar. Likewise, the absence of many hymns is not to imply that they are of lesser quality or value.

Firsthand experience with the hymns themselves will prove of greatest value in this study. Read each aloud to gain an appreciation of its literary significance as a religious and poetic expression. Sing the tune to gain an awareness of its musical characteristics and emotional impact. Doing both will give effective practice in good tempos and phrasing and will furnish a means of realizing the full spirit of the hymn.

Sincere appreciation is expressed to individuals and publishers who kindly granted permission for the use of their copyrighted materials. Every effort has been made to trace the ownership of all copyrighted items, although exact ownership is obscure in some instances. Copyright acknowledgements are indicated, and this material may not be duplicated in any form without the permission of the copyright owner.

William J. Reynolds
Milburn Price

Spring, 1987

Introduction

What the Words Mean

Hymns provide the congregation an opportunity to express their beliefs about faith and doctrine and the experiences of the Christian life. To be an authentic expression of faith, the beliefs embodied in the hymns must be true, must be based on scripture, and must be in keeping with the accepted doctrines of the congregation. Those responsible for compiling a hymnal have given attention to doctrinal truth and have sought to avoid vague and ambiguous language and expressions that are not in accord with scriptural teaching.

The hymn writer chooses words and phrases to express ideas, feelings, and understandings. Those who sing the hymn appropriate these words and phrases to express their feelings, beliefs, and understandings. When a person sings

> Let all the world in every corner sing:
>   My God and King!

the "my" refers not to George Herbert, but to the person singing these words. When someone sings the stanzas of "Fairest Lord Jesus"

> Thee will I cherish,
> Thee will I honor,
> Thou, my soul's glory, joy and crown.

the "I" is no longer the anonymous writer of these lines, but the singer who is expressing devotion.

Hymns express doctrinal truth about God the Father and his presence in the world; truths about Jesus Christ the Son and his work as Savior and Redeemer; and truths about the Holy Spirit, the Comforter. These are theological expressions. Theology—the understanding of God—is a significant part of hymnology—the understanding of hymns.

Words about God

In singing hymns, the singer experiences a greater awareness of God—his character, his attributes, and his provisions for his children.

The holiness and perfectness of God are seen in the lines of Reginald Heber's "Holy, holy, holy."

> Only thou art holy; there is none beside thee,
> Perfect in power, in love, and purity.

In the same hymn, the writer speaks of the eternal character of God.

> Cherubim and seraphim falling down before thee,
> Who wert, and art, and evermore shalt be.

The hymn "The God of Abraham praise" reminds us of the timelessness of God. Here is the truth that the infinite God had no beginning, and will have no ending. Conceived as the changeless Being, he exists in timeless perfection.

> The God of Abraham praise,
>   All praised be his name,
> Who was, and is, and is to be,
>   For aye the same!
> The one eternal God,
>   Ere aught that now appears;
> The first, the Last: beyond all thought
>   His timeless years!

Joachim Neander refers to God as "the King of creation" in his "Praise to the Lord, the Almighty." "The God of all creation" is the acknowledgement of Johann J. Schutz in his "Sing praise to God who reigns above." The creative work of God is lauded in a recent hymn by Timothy Dudley-Smith.

> The Lord in wisdom made the earth,
>   Our sky and sea and land,
> And gave the furthest stars their birth,
>   Unnumbered as the sand:
>   Beyond all words, all stars and skies,
>   He reigns all-loving and all-wise![1]

Christians sing of God as life-giver, and of his unchanging steadfastness in Walter Chalmers Smith's "Immortal, invisible, God only wise."

> To all life thou givest to both great and small;
> In all life thou livest the true life of all;
> We blossom and flourish as leaves on the tree,
> And wither and perish—but naught changeth thee.

Hymn writers have used descriptive names for God in referring to his attributes. One illustration of such usage is found in Robert Grant's "O worship the King."

> Our Shield and Defender, the Ancient of Days,
> Our Maker, Defender, Redeemer, and Friend.

Words about Jesus Christ

Words expressing praise of Jesus Christ are found in abundance in hymns and proclaim what Christians believe about God's Son. Theodulph's "All glory, laud, and honor" proclaims

> Thou art the King of Israel,
>   Thou David's royal Son,
> Who in the Lord's name comest,
>   The King and blessed One.

The anonymous writer of "Fairest Lord Jesus" compares Jesus Christ to meadows, woodlands, and the "blooming garb of spring," and concludes that

> Jesus is fairer, Jesus is purer,
> Who makes the woeful heart to sing.

Jesus is compared to the sun, moon, and stars, yet

> Jesus shines brighter, Jesus shines purer
> Than all the angels heav'n can boast.

The redemptive role of Jesus involved in his death on the cross is evident in Isaac Watts's "Alas, and did my Savior bleed."

> Was it for crimes that I had done
>   He groaned upon the tree?
> Amazing pity, grace unknown
>   And love beyond degree.
>
> Well might the sun in darkness hide,
>   And shut his glories in,
> When Christ the mighty Maker died
>   For man the creature's sin.

This emphasis is also found in Francis Xavier's "My God, I love Thee."

> But for that thou didst all mankind
>   Upon the cross embrace;
> For us didst bear the nails and spear,
>   And manifold disgrace.

The triumphant resurrection of Jesus from the grave is sounded forth by several writers. Matthew Bridges, in his "Crown Him with many crowns," proclaims

> Crown him the Lord of life,
>   Who triumphed o'er the grave,
> And rose victorious in the strife
>   For those he came to save.

Charles Wesley sings of the joy of the resurrection in his "Christ the Lord is risen today."

> Lives again our glorious King, Alleluia!
> Where, O Death, is now thy sting? Alleluia!
> Dying once, he all doth save, Alleluia!
> Where thy victory, O Grave? Alleluia!

"Good Christians, all rejoice," the Medieval Latin carol, reminds Christians that

> Now ye need not fear the grave:
> Jesus Christ was born to save.

The belief that Jesus Christ was God incarnate—both God and man—is evident in Charles Wesley's "Hark! the herald angels sing."

> Veiled in flesh the Godhead see,
> Hail th' incarnate Deity!
> Pleased as man in earth to dwell,
> Jesus, our Immanuel.

Reference to this truth is found in Cecil Frances Alexander's "Once in royal David's city."

> He came down to earth from heaven,
>   Who is God and Lord of all,
> And his shelter was a stable,
>   And his cradle was a stall;
> With the poor, and mean, and lowly,
> Lived on earth our Savior holy.

Words about the Holy Spirit

Reflected in a number of hymns is the Christian's belief in the role of the Holy Spirit in revealing God's will to mankind, as an enabler, and in convicting unbelievers. This is found in George Croly's "Spirit of God, descend upon my heart."

> Teach me to love Thee as Thine angels love,
>   One holy passion filling all my frame:
> The baptism of the heav'n-descended Dove—
>   My heart an altar and thy love the flame.

The enabling power of the Holy Spirit is mentioned in the familiar Negro spiritual:

> Sometimes I feel discouraged,
>   And think my work's in vain,
> But then the Holy Spirit
>   Revives my soul again.

The work of the Holy Spirit to reveal and illumine God's Word is the reference in Charles Wesley's "Come, Holy Ghost, our hearts inspire."

> Come, Holy Ghost, for moved by thee
>   The prophets wrote and spoke;
> Unlock the truth, thyself the key,
>   Unseal the sacred book.

Some hymns written in recent decades touch upon the need for an awareness of human needs under the moving influence of the Holy Spirit. In Henry H. Tweedy's "O Spirit of the living God," he asks the Holy Spirit to

> Teach us to utter living words
>   Of truth which all may hear,
> The language all may understand
>   When love speaks loud and clear.

Words about the Trinity—God Three-in-One

The three persons of the Godhead are spoken of or addressed in a number of hymns. "We believe in one true God" is a creedal-like statement about God the Father in stanza one, Jesus Christ in stanza two, and the Holy Spirit in stanza three. A similar pattern of stanzas is found in "Come, Thou Almighty King," followed by a concluding stanza:

> To thee, great One in Three,
> The highest praises be
>   Hence, evermore!
> Thy sovereign majesty
> May we in glory see,
> And to eternity
>   Love and adore.

William Whiting's hymn "Eternal Father, strong to save," though not written about the Trinity, reveals a Trinitarian structure as stanza one is addressed to God the Father, stanza two to "O Savior, whose almighty word," stanza three to "O Holy Spirit, who didst brood," and the final stanza to "Trinity of love and pow'r."

To offset the influence of Arianism, which maintained that Jesus was not equal with God, the early Christians added Trinitarian doxologies to their hymns. This practice became an accepted part of the development of Christian hymnody across the centuries. The widely used Doxology of Thomas Ken, "Praise God from whom all blessings flow," was attached to three hymns he wrote for the students at Winchester College, about 1673. The four-line stanza, praising Father, Son, and Holy Spirit, remains as the most frequently sung Christian song.

Words that Proclaim the Gospel

Some hymns speak directly to the unbeliever of the salvation made possible through Jesus Christ. Frederick W. Faber's hymn "There is a wideness in God's mercy" speaks of this salvation. The original first stanza is:

> Souls of men! why will ye scatter
>   Like a crowd of frightened sheep?
> Foolish hearts! why will ye wander
>   From a love so true and deep?

The version of Faber's hymn found in most hymnals uses stanzas four and six:

> There's a wideness in God's mercy,
>   Like the wideness of the sea;
> There's a kindness in his justice,
>   Which is more than liberty.
>
> There is welcome for the sinner,
>   And more graces for the good;
> There is mercy with the Savior;
>   There is healing in his blood.

Joseph Hart's "Come, ye sinners, poor and needy," written in 1759, extends a direct invitation to the unbeliever.

> Come, ye sinners, poor and needy,
>   Weak and wounded, sick and sore;
> Jesus ready stands to save you,
>   Full of pity, love and power.

There are also hymns that reflect the individual's decision to accept Jesus Christ as Savior. Among these are Charlotte Elliott's "Just as I am, without one plea," Lewis Hartsough's "I hear Thy welcome voice," and Horatio Bonar's "I heard the voice of Jesus say." A recent hymn that expresses this response is Brian Wren's "I come with joy to meet my Lord."

> I come with joy to meet my Lord,
>   Forgiven, loved, and free,
> In awe and wonder to recall
>   His life laid down for me.[2]

Words that Tell a Story

Some hymns are written in a narrative style. These are ballad-like, for they tell a story that is complete in the several stanzas. All stanzas have to be sung to complete the story. Several well-known Christmas carols fall into this category, such as "The first nowell" and "While shepherds watched their flocks by night." The events surrounding the birth of Jesus are described in these carols in logical order.

J. Edgar Park's "We would see Jesus; Lo, His star is shining" has a broader scope. The first stanza tells of Jesus' birth, the second of his childhood, and the third of his ministry. The fourth stanza offers a present-day commitment with the final line "Lord, we are thine, we give ourselves to thee." Louis F. Benson's "O sing a song of Bethlehem" has a similar structure as it deals with Bethlehem, Nazareth, and Galilee in three stanzas. Jan Struther's "When Stephen, full of power and grace" tells of Stephen's life in stanza one and his martyrdom in stanza two. The final stanza is one of commitment for the singer, "Let me, O Lord, thy cause defend."

Words Exhorting Believers

While some hymns are addressed directly to God and some to unbelievers, other hymns are sung by believers to believers exhorting them to praise God, to grow in discipleship, to proclaim the gospel, to rejoice in the goodness of God, or to place their trust more completely in God. Among those hymns that exhort believers to praise God are Francis of Assisi's "All creatures of our God and King" and George Herbert's "Let all the world in every corner sing." Some of the Christmas hymns, such as "Good Christians, all rejoice" and "Go, tell it on the mountain," exhort Christians to celebrate and proclaim the good news that Christ has brought salvation.

Paul Gerhardt's "Give to the winds your fears" urges the believer to place faith in God.

> To him commit your griefs;
>   Your ways put in his hands,
> To his sure truth and tender care
>   Who earth and heaven commands.

Trusting in God is the focus of George Neumark's "If you will only let God guide you."

> Whatever comes, he'll stand beside you,
>   To bear you through the evil days;
> Who trusts in God's unchanging love
>   Builds on the rock that cannot move.

Words about Christian Awareness of Social Needs

Not until the middle of the nineteenth century did hymns begin to speak to human needs, world peace, and social justice. One of the first was Henry

Chorley's "God the all-terrible," written in 1842. Combined with John Eller-ton's additional stanzas, it has become "God the omnipotent," with each stanza ending with a prayer for peace. Protesting the injustice of war with Mexico and the possibility of acquiring new territory that would enlarge the area of slavery, James Russell Lowell wrote "Once to every man and nation" in 1845.

Edmund H. Sears's "It came upon the midnight clear," written in 1849, was the first of the carol-like Christmas hymns emphasizing the social message of Christmas. There is no mention of Christ, the newborn King, or any other elements of the scriptural account of the birth of Christ as recorded in Matt-hew and Luke, except for the song of the heavenly host, "Peace on earth, good will to men." Written when war clouds were gathering over the question of slavery, Sears's hymn says

> Beneath the angel-strain have rolled
> Two thousand years of wrong;
> And man, at war with man, hears not
> The love song that they bring:
> O hush the noise, ye men of strife,
> And hear the angels sing.

These lines speak plainly of social injustice. To those "beneath life's crushing load," Sears gives comfort:

> O rest beside the weary road,
> And hear the angels sing.

Among the twentieth-century hymns that have words of meaning regarding the Christian's responsibility to other people are: Frank Mason North's "Where cross the crowded ways of life" (1903), G.K. Chesterton's "O God of earth and altar" (1936), W. Nantlais Williams' "Jesus, friend of thronging pilgrims" (1954), Fred Pratt Green's "When the Church of Jesus" (1960), Erik Routley's "All who love and serve your city" (1966), Elton Trueblood's "Thou, whose purpose is to kindle" (1967), and Timothy Dudley-Smith's "As for our world we lift our hearts in praise" (1968).

Hymns About Our World's Natural Resources

Concern for conserving the world's natural resources in recent years has been responsible for hymns that speak earnestly about ecological situations. Charles Kingsley's "From Thee all skill and science flow," written in 1871, is a forerunner of this concern. His final stanza is quite ahead of his time.

> When ever blue the sky shall gleam,
>   And ever green the sod,
> And our rude work deface no more
>   The paradise of God.

Recent hymns that speak to ecological concerns are Ian Fraser's "Lord, bring the day to pass" (1964), Fred Pratt Green's "God in His love for us lent us this planet" (1971), Brian Wren's "Thank you, God, for water, soil and air" (1973), and Thomas H. Troeger's "God folds the mountains out of rock" (1985).

The Bible in the Hymnal

That God's people should turn to God's Word as a source of song is a response to the Creator. The Hebrew Psalter recorded the songs of the children of Israel, and these were handed down to succeeding generations. The early Christians continued singing these and added their own expressions of praise and adoration recalling what God has done in Christ.

The index of scriptural references in a hymnal reveals how closely related the hymnal is to Scripture. Some hymns were written using a portion of scripture as source text: "A charge to keep I have" (Lev. 8:35); "Rejoice, ye pure in heart" (Psa. 33:1); "Give to the winds your fears" (Psa. 37:5); Sometimes a light surprises" (Hab. 3:17-18); "When I survey the wondrous cross" (Gal. 6:14); "The head that once was crowned with thorns" (Heb. 2:10); "Holy, holy, holy" (Rev. 4:8-11), and others. Some hymns are poetic arrangements of scripture, arranged in regular lines with poetic rhyme. These hymns contain a maximum of scripture for the congregation to sing together. Among these are: "The Lord's my Shepherd, I'll not want" (Psa. 23); "While shepherds watched their flocks by night" (Luke 2:8-14); and "All people that on earth do dwell" (Psa. 100). Other hymns reveal words and phrases from scripture woven skillfully into the fabric of the hymn, revealing the hymn writer's great familiarity with God's Word. A vivid example is "How firm a foundation, ye saints of the Lord." Stanza two is based on Isa. 41:10; stanza three, Isa. 43:2a, I Kings 1:29; stanza four, I Peter 4:12, 2 Cor. 12:9a, Isa. 43:2a, Isa. 1:25a, Zech. 13:9a; and stanza five, John 13:23, Psa. 16:10, Deut. 31:6b, Heb. 13:5.

Biblical Imagery

Hymn writers have often used descriptive words and phrases associated with biblical experiences to enhance their hymn writing. This practice is found most frequently in hymns written during the eighteenth and nineteenth centuries. The use of such word images brings to those who sing the hymn a reminder of the biblical source.

"Alpha and Omega" (Rev. 1:8, 11; 21:5; 22:13) refer to Jesus, the first and last, the beginning and the ending. Charles Wesley uses this terminology in "Love divine, all loves excelling," stanza 2.

"Ancient of Days" (Dan. 7:9,13), a name for God, occurs in "Come, Thou almighty King," stanza 1; Robert Grant's "O worship the King," stanza 1; Walter Chalmers Smith's "Immortal, invisible, God only wise," stanza 1; Matthew Bridges'

"Behold, the Lamb of God," stanza 3; and William C. Doane's "Ancient of Days, who sittest throned in glory," stanza 3.

"Bethel" (Gen. 35:15), the name given by Jacob to the place where he talked with God, is found in Sarah Flowers Adams' "Nearer, my God to Thee," stanza 4.

"Dayspring" (Luke 1:78b-79) refers to Jesus and is found in "O come, O come, Emmanuel," stanza 2, and in Charles Wesley's "Christ, whose glory fills the skies."

"Daystar" (2 Peter 1:19) refers to Jesus Christ and is found in Charles Wesley's "Christ, whose glory fills the skies," stanza 1, and in J.R.L. Stainer's "Daystar on high, bright harbinger of gladness," stanza 1.

"Desire of Nations" (Haggai 2:7) refers to Christ and occurs in "O come, O come, Emmanuel," stanza 4.

"Ebenezer" (I Sam. 7:12) is the name given by Samuel to a place between Mizpeh and Shen where he set a stone and where the Lord enabled Israel to defeat the Philistines. As a marker for remembrance, it meant "hitherto has the Lord helped us." Robert Robinson used the word in "Come, thou Fount of every blessing," stanza 2.

"Fire and cloudy pillar" (Ex. 13:21) refers to the pillar of cloud and the pillar of fire by which God led Moses and the children of Israel. The phrase occurs in William Williams' "Guide me, O Thou great Jehovah," stanza 2, and in Bernard Barton's "Lamp of our feet, whereby we trace," stanza 3.

"Jerusalem" appears in hymnic literature with two different meanings—God's people (Isa. 40:1-8) found in Johannes Olearius' "Comfort, comfort ye my people," stanza 1; and as a synonym for heaven (Rev. 21:2), found in "Jerusalem, my happy home," stanza 1, and Isaac Watts's "I'm not ashamed to own my Lord," stanza 4.

"Mercy Seat" is literally the covering of the ark of the covenant (Ex. 25:17-22). In hymnic literature it means the "place of atonement," and is found in Sylvanus D. Phelps' "Savior, thy dying love," stanza 2, and in Thomas Moore's "Come, ye disconsolate," stanza 1.

"Mount Pisgah" (Deut. 3:27) is a part of a mountain range near the northeastern end of the Dead Sea. From its summit, called Nebo, Moses viewed the promised land. William Walford used this term in "Sweet hour of prayer," stanza 3, referring to a place from which the Christian sees heaven.

"Rose of Sharon" (Song of Sol. 2:1), a synonym for Christ and his gospel, occurs in Bourne H. Draper's "Ye Christian heralds, go proclaim," stanza 1. The sixteenth-century German hymn "Lo, how a Rose e'er blooming" uses the rose as a symbol for Christ.

"Sun of Righteousness" (Mal. 4:2), a synonym for Christ, was used by Charles Wesley in two hymns: "Hark! the herald angels sing," stanza 3, and "Christ, whose glory fills the skies," stanza 1.

"Jacob's Ladder" refers to Jacob's dream of a ladder reaching from earth to heaven (Gen. 28:10-22). The Negro spiritual "We are climbing Jacob's ladder" and the anonymous folk hymn "As Jacob with travel was weary one day" both use this imagery.

"Zion" is used in hymnic literature in at least four different ways. In Benjamin Schmolck's "Open now thy gates of beauty," stanza 1, the term refers to Mount Zion, a place of worship. A second usage refers to God's people. This occurs in Timothy Dwight's "I love thy kingdom, Lord," stanza 5, in Mary Ann Thomson's "O Zion, haste, thy mission high fulfilling," stanza 1, in Paul Gerhardt's "O how shall I receive thee," stanza 2, and in Heinrich Held's "Let the earth now praise the Lord," stanza 3. A third usage is specifically the church, as in Benjamin Webb's "Praise the Rock of our salvation," stanza 1, and in John Newton's "Glorious things of thee are spoken," stanza 1. A fourth usage is as a synonym for heaven, as found in John Mason Neale's translation "Jerusalem the golden," stanza 2, and the American folk hymn "As Jacob with travel was weary one day," stanza 2.

Metrical Forms of Hymns

Hymnic literature has made use of poetic meter and rhythm resulting in a system of symbols and terminology peculiar to this area of study. An examination of any hymnal will reveal a metrical form indicated for each hymn. Except for the three most frequently found meters—common, long and short—these will be shown in a series of digits: 8.7.8.7; 12.11.12.11; 7.7.7.7.7; for example. The number of digits shown indicates the number of lines per stanza, and each digit the number of syllables in each given line. For example, 7.7.7.7.7.7. indicates that each stanza has six lines, and each line seven syllables. The metrical form, 8.7.8.7., shows that each stanza has four lines, and that the first and third lines have eight syllables each, while the second and fourth lines have seven syllables each. The addition of D to these numbers, that is 8.7.8.7.D., indicates that each stanza has eight lines or a four-line stanza doubled. This could also be written 8.7.8.7.8.7.8.7

Three metrical forms of hymns are usually indicated by initials rather than by digits: C.M. (common meter); S.M. (short meter); and L.M. (long meter).

Common Meter. Common meter (C.M.) is a four-line stanza made up of 8.6.8.6. syllables. This is the Old English ballad meter, originally two septenary lines each containing seven iambic feet, or fourteen syllables. This couplet, known as a "fourteener," breaks into four lines of four and three feet, or eight and six syllables. The rhyme is *abab*:

O God, our help in ages past,	(8)a
Our hope for years to come,	(6)b
Our shelter from the stormy blast	(8)a
And our eternal home.	(6)b
(Isaac Watts)	

or *abcb*:

In Christ, there is no East or West	(8)a
In him no South or North,	(6)b
But one great fellowship of love	(8)c
Throughout the whole wide earth.	(6)b
(John Oxenham)	

Short Meter. Short meter (S.M.) is a four-line stanza made up of 6.6.8.6. syllables. It is a breakdown of the unequal couplet combining an Alexandrine and a septenary. This early Tudor meter was called "Poulter's Measure," because of the poulterers' custom of giving twelve for the first dozen and thirteen or fourteen for the second. The couplet of twelve and fourteen syllables breaks into a four-line stanza. Its rhyme is *abab*:

Blest be the tie that binds	(6)a
Our hearts in Christian love	(6)b
The fellowship of kindred minds	(8)a
Is like to that above.	(6)b
(John Fawcett)	

or *abcb*:

I love thy kingdom, Lord,	(6)a
The house of thine abode,	(6)b
The church our blest Redeemer saved	(8)c
With his own precious blood.	(6)b
(Timothy Dwight)	

Long Meter. Long meter (L.M.) is a four-line stanza, each line containing eight syllables, 8.8.8.8. The form follows the iambic-dimeter pattern of the early Latin hymns of Ambrosian tradition. The rhyme is *abab*:

When I survey the wondrous cross	(8)a
On which the Prince of Glory died,	(8)b
My richest gain I count but loss,	(8)a
And pour contempt on all my pride.	(8)b
(Isaac Watts)	

or *aabb*:

Lord of all being, throned afar,	(8)a
Thy glory flames from sun and star:	(8)a
Center and soul of every sphere,	(8)b
Yet to each loving heart how near!	(8)b
(Oliver Wendell Holmes)	

or *abba*:

Strong Son of God, immortal Love,	(8)a
Whom we, that have not seen thy face,	(8)b
By faith, and faith alone, embrace,	(8)b
Believing where we cannot prove.	(8)a
(Alfred Tennyson)	

ENDNOTES

Contents

Chapter One

EARLY CHURCH SONG

Christianity was born within a Jewish environment that existed in the midst of a widespread Greco-Roman culture. When the Christian era dawned, the religious activity of Judaism centered around the Temple and the synagogue. In the four hundred years that had elapsed between the return of the exiles from the Babylonian captivity to the advent of Christ, the Temple had developed an elaborate service of worship. Its ceremonies were under the careful administration of a priestly hierarchy. Obedience to Temple ordinances by the people and sacrificial worship by the priesthood for the people became basic functions. The synagogue seems to have developed during the Exile when the Jews were cut off from the Temple and its services. In the synagogue the scribes read from the Law and explained the Scriptures, and the people sang the psalms. After the synagogue was transplanted back to the Jewish homeland, it continued these practices and eventually rivaled the Temple.

Temple music was elaborate, that of the synagogue more simple. In the Temple, priests and choirs chanted the psalms and portions of the Pentateuch, but in the synagogue the people shared in the musical portion of the service. Instrumental music was employed in Temple worship, while in the synagogue singing was generally unaccompanied.

The Book of Psalms

The Book of Psalms, found in the Old Testament, is thought to have been compiled during and after the Babylonian exile. On the basis of internal evidence, some of the psalms seem to indicate that they were used for public worship, some for private devotion, and some for the celebration of specific events. Singing of the psalms was usually done in a direct manner, but, on the basis of structure, some were obviously sung antiphonally. Scholars are not in agreement on whether or not the psalms were solely, or primarily, intended for use in Temple liturgy.

The Hebrew Psalter and the manner in which it was used provided the musical heritage of the early Christians. The texts reflected the basic concepts of God and his moral nature. They gave evidence of the personal element of religion—individual communion with God. The tunes were seemingly taught and preserved only in the oral tradition. With the psalms so positively associated with the vocal expression of religious experience, it is not surprising to find that, at the conclusion of the Last Supper, Christ and his disciples sang a hymn which historians believe to have been a portion of the Hallel, Psalms 113-118.

Old Testament Canticles

Although the Psalms form the largest body of song from the Old Testament, there are other passages which, by their poetic structure and their context within the scriptural narrative, must also be considered to be antecedents of the songs of faith of later eras. Several of these canticles, as they are called, became prominent as foundation for the odes of the canon in Byzantine hymnody.

The earliest Old Testament canticle is the Song of Moses which appears in the fifteenth chapter of Exodus as a celebration of the deliverance of the Hebrews from Egyptian captivity and of the destruction of the Egyptian army in the Red Sea. A second Song of Moses, recorded in Deuteronomy 32, provided instruction from God to the Israelites as Moses prepared to relinquish his leadership just prior to his death.

Other Old Testament canticles include the Song of Isaiah (Isaiah 26:9-21), the Song of Hannah (I Samuel 2:1-10), the Song of Jonah (Jonah 2:2-9), and the Song of Habakkuk (Habakkuk 3:2-19).

New Testament Hymns

The early Christians sought to supplement their heritage of psalms with songs of their own Christian experience. They desired songs that would praise the name of Christ and tell of his gospel. Three lyric portions of the Nativity from Luke's Gospel were appropriated.

Luke 1:46-56: This song of Mary became known as the Magnificat and is found today as part of the Roman Catholic rites sung in the Office of Vespers. In the Anglican Service it is part of the Evening Prayer or Evensong.

Luke 1:67-80 This song, sung by Zacharias, became known as the Benedictus and is presently sung at Lauds in the Roman Catholic Church and at Morning Prayer in the Anglican Service.

Luke 2:27-32: This song of Simeon became known as the Nunc Dimittis and is found today in the service of Compline in the Roman Catholic Church, in Evensong in the Anglican Service, and in the Lutheran Communion service.

In various places in the New Testament the hymnlike structure of the writing gives the implication that these scriptures were sung or chanted:

> But as it is written,
>   Eye hath not seen,
>   nor ear heard,
>   neither have entered into the heart of man,
>   the things which God hath prepared for them
>   that love him.
>
>   I Corinthians 2:9

> Awake thou that sleepest,
>   and rise from the dead,
>   and Christ shall give thee light.
>
>   Ephesians 5:14

> Now unto the King eternal,
>   immortal, invisible,
>   the only wise God,
>   be honor and glory
>   forever and ever.
>
>   I Timothy 1:17

> God was manifest in the flesh,
>   justified in the Spirit,
>   seen of angels,
>   preached unto the Gentiles,
>   believed on in the world,
>   received up into glory.
>
>   I Timothy 3:16

> For if we be dead with him,
> we shall also live with him;
>   if we suffer,
>   we shall also reign with him;
>   if we deny him,
>   he also will deny us;
>   if we believe not,
>   yet he abideth faithful:
>   he cannot deny himself.
>
>   II Timothy 2:11-13

Thus, the body of Christian song began to take shape from the Scriptures and from the extemporized vocal expressions of the early Christians.

The practice of Christian song is well documented in the Scriptures. It is not known what songs or Scriptures were sung, but, for example, the account of the imprisonment of Paul and Silas relates: "And at midnight Paul and Silas prayed, and sang praises unto God: and the prisoners heard them." (Acts 16:25)

From the writings of Paul come further evidence of the significance of Christian song both as an instrument of praise to God and as a tool for teaching: Ephesians 5:18-19, and Colossians 3:16.

About the manner of performance, Paul writes: "I will sing with the spirit, and I will sing with the understanding also." (I Corinthians 14:15)

Early Christian Hymnody

After the destruction of the Temple in A.D. 70, there were significant developments that directly and indirectly exerted influence on Christian song. The persecution of believers increased, and meetings for praise and fellowship were held in secret. The Gospel spread beyond nationalistic bounds as Gentiles were converted to Christianity, but hostility grew between Christians and the Jews who did not accept Christ as the Messiah. In A.D. 70 and again in A.D. 132 the strength of Jewish nationalism was crushed by Roman conquests. The consequent overthrow of Jewish institutions loosened existing ties to the Jewish rituals and ceremonies. Christians therefore retained only those elements that they deemed appropriate to their needs during this formative period. In the early centuries, the distinction emerged between clergy and laity which later developed into a system of patriarchs, priests, bishops, and deacons. No longer were the clergy the servants or representatives of the people; instead they assumed a mediatorial function as the channels through which divine grace was transmitted to the faithful. In this position, the clergy assumed a greater responsibility for church worship, forming and shaping the liturgy and the music involved.

Hellenistic Influences   At the Time of Christ, Hellenistic culture was the dominant influence throughout the Roman Empire. Greece had become a province of the Empire and as such was under political subjection to the Emperor, but the culture, philosophy, art, and language of the Greeks continued to be leading forces throughout the area under Roman rule. The Old Testament had been translated from Hebrew into Greek (this translation is known as the Septuagint), and the new Testament was written first in neither Latin nor Hebrew, but in Greek. It was the language of the culture and the language of the church and remained such for three hundred years, even in Rome. Athens was the university city of the Roman world. Greek poetic forms—the epic, the comedy, the epigram, and the ode—were taken over by Roman writers.

Clement of Alexandria (c. 170-c. 220), the author of "Shepherd of eager youth" and "Sunset to sunrise changes now" (90), has been called the father of Greek theology. As the head of the catechetical school at Alexandria, he was the first to approach Christian truth and teaching in the light of Greek thought and Gnostic speculation. His hymns reveal his efforts to combine the spirit of Greek poetry with Christian theology.

The Greek "Candlelighting Hymn" ("O gladsome light, O grace") (43), of unknown authorship, dates from the third century. This evening hymn from the pre-Constantinian period is still in use in the Greek church.

A strip of papyrus discovered at Oxyrhynchos in Egypt in 1918 is the only evidence now available concerning the character of the music to which the early Christian hymns were sung. This fragment reveals the closing part of a hymn to the Holy Trinity. It was first published by A.S. Hunt in the fifteenth volume of the Oxyrhynchos Papyri, 1922. The work of an anonymous poet of the Alexandrian School, this "Oxyrhynchos hymn" dates from the end of the third century. In spite of its Greek notation, Wellesz points out that this hymn is not of Greek origin, but in all probability was patterned after an older song of praise of the Primitive Church.[1]

The ten hymns of Synesius of Cyrene (c. 375-c. 414) reveal evidences of Semitic influence on classic Greek poetry. The tenth hymn, "Lord Jesus, think on me" (39), is an epilogue to the first nine hymns.

Throughout the first four centuries the influence of Greek culture upon the early church declined. Beginning in the fourth century, Latin began to replace Greek as the language of the Western church, and this change was almost universal by the close of the sixth century. The Greek Septuagint was replaced by the Latin Vulgate.

Because of the difficulties with the northern barbaric tribes, Emperor Constantine moved the seat of government of the Roman Empire to Byzantium in A.D. 330, making it the capital of the Empire and changing its name to Constantinople. A division of the Roman Empire into eastern and western areas resulted, and the departure of imperial power from Rome made possible the rise and spread of papal power. From the fifth century on, papal power gradually increased and imperial power decreased.

There was much activity in neighboring Syria as early Christians carried the Gospel beyond Palestine. In an effort to counteract the Arian heresy, the practice of antiphonal singing was introduced at Antioch early in the fourth century, and the chanting of the psalm verses became the responsibility of the congregation.

> Its members were divided into two semi-choruses, one of men, one of women and children, and the groups alternated with one another in the singing of the psalm-verses and combined in singing an Alleluia or, perhaps, some new refrain. The intercalating of passages of song between psalm-verses became, in the course of time, an organized practice and was destined to be imitated with telling effect in the West.[2]

In Syria, also, began the singing of hymns with texts in verse form. Ephraim (d. A.D. 373), the foremost Syrian hymn writer, employed the popular tunes of heretical groups and substituted orthodox texts for the people to sing.

Less than forty years after the founding of Constantinople, the Council of Laodicea, A.D. 367, prohibited the participation of the congregation and the use of instruments in the service. It further provided that only the Scriptures could be used for singing. With this restriction, hymn writers were limited to the canticles and the psalms, which accounts for the absence of hymns of personal experience during this period.

Byzantine Hymnody

The greatest contribution of the Eastern church to Christian song was Byzantine hymnody. Influenced by Jewish tradition and Syrian practice, these hymns developed in the worship of the Eastern church as unaccompanied monophonic chant, mainly diatonic, lacking in strict meter, and closely following the rhythm of the text.

The earliest Byzantine hymns, appearing in the fourth and fifth centuries, were *troparia*, short prayers sung between the reading of the psalms. In the sixth century there developed the *kontakion*, consisting of a short introduction followed by eighteen to thirty stanzas of uniform structure and ending with a refrain. The stanzas were connected either alphabetically or by an acrostic. If the connection was alphabetical, the initial letter of each stanza followed the alphabet in usual order. If an acrostic was used, the initial letters of each stanza made a sentence that gave the title of the hymn and the name of the author. The outstanding writer of *kontakion* was Romanus (c. 500), whose identification in the acrostic was usually given as "the humble Romanus."

In the eighth century there developed a longer, more complex form of Greek hymnody known as the canon (Greek *kanon*), which consisted of nine odes, each including from six to nine stanzas. The nine odes were based upon biblical canticles and were characteristically hymns of praise.[3] Within a single ode, the same rhythmic structure was used for each stanza. The early development of the canon occurred at the monastery of Mar Saba, located in the Judean wilderness between Jerusalem and the Dead Sea, where both of the principal writers of canons resided.

Andrew of Crete (660-732), also known as Andrew of Jerusalem, was the earliest writer to make significant contributions in this form. He was followed by John of Damascus (d. c. 780), who is generally considered to be the most significant of the Greek hymnists. The focus of John's writing is the Incarnation, the scope of which (in his writings) includes the entire earthly life of Jesus. "The day of resurrection" (58) is a translation of the first ode of the "Golden Canon" for Easter Day, often cited as the pinnacle of Greek sacred verse. "Come, ye faithful, raise the strain" (63) is a translation of the first ode of the canon for the first Sunday after Easter.

These three forms—*troparion*, *kontakion*, and canon—continued in use in the Eastern church. From the beginning of the ninth century the Studium monastery at Constantinople became the center of Byzantine hymnic activity. Among the monks associated with this monastery who wrote hymns were Anatolius and Theoctistus, the author of "Jesus, Name all names above."

The Development of Latin Hymnody

In the first three centuries, because of their persecution, Christians met in secret and therefore made limited use of singing. Following the Edict of Milan, A.D. 313, Christianity became the religion of the Empire, and the singing of Christians emerged as a joyful expression of their freedom. There was the singing of the psalms and the joyous *Alleluia* with its concluding *jubilus*, an extended musical phrase sung on the final *-a* of the *Alleluia*. Responsorial singing, which employed an ornate solo followed by a refrain sung by the people, was widely used.

The person significant in first transferring hymnody based upon Greek models to the West seems to have been Hilary, Bishop of Poitiers (c. 310-366). During a four-year exile in Asia Minor, he became familiar with the hymnody of the Greek church. Upon his return to Poitiers, his hymns were intended to present Trinitarian doctrines to combat the Arian heresy.[4]

Ambrosian Hymnody   The practice of antiphonal singing in the Western church was adopted in the fourth century at Milan by Ambrose, Bishop of Milan (340-397). From Milan this practice spread to Rome where it was officially adopted during the papacy of Celestine I, 422-432. As has been previously noted, antiphonal singing had been used in the Eastern church, and the term originally meant "octave," such as the singing of boys and men together in octaves. Later, the term came to mean one group answering another group of singers.

Ambrose, like Hilary, realized the value of hymns in combating Arianism. More than a dozen hymns have been attributed to him, but only four are accepted as being authentic: *Aeterna rerum Conditer* ("Framer of the earth and sky"); *Deus Creator omnium* ("Maker of all things God most high"); *Iam surgit hora tertia* ("Now appears the third hour"); and *Veni Redemptor gentium* ("Come, thou Saviour of our race").[5] Another hymn traditionally attributed to Ambrosian authorship is *Splendor paternae gloriae* ("O splendor of God's glory bright") (1). These hymns deal with fundamental Christian teachings. The language is dignified, yet simple, making use of the expressions of the people for whom they were written. In contrast with the irregular, asymmetrical prose form of the psalms, these hymns appeared in a new symmetrical form. Each hymn was made up of a number of stanzas, usually eight, and each stanza contained four lines of iambic dimeter, a popular folklike rhythm rather than a classical metrical form. Here is the foundation for the long meter hymn form, which became, centuries later, one of the three basic hymn forms. The melodies were constructed usually with one note to each syllable.

The result was a plain, easily remembered tune, quite similar to the popular tunes of later antiquity. In short, the hymn may be called a spiritual folk song and the Ambrosian hymn became, a thousand years later, the model for the chorale of the Protestant Church.[6]

Thus, by the end of the fourth century, the pattern of Christian song had developed along three basic lines: responsorial psalm singing, antiphonal psalm singing, and the metrical hymn.

Office Hymns   The adaptation of existing Latin hymns to daily worship in monasteries resulted in the office hymns. By the fifth century, the services of canonical hours were established. They consisted of the nocturnal cursus: Vespers, Compline, Matins, Lauds, and the diurnal cursus: Prime, Tierce, Sext, and Nones. Through the influence of Benedict, hymns were introduced into use for all canonical hours, whereas the Ambrosian hymns had previously been used only for Matins, Lauds, and Vespers. An early collection of these sixth-century office hymns, known as the Old Hymnal, contained thirty-four hymns.

Beginnings of the Roman Liturgy   During the early centuries the various parts of the Roman liturgy slowly began to take shape. By the time of Gregory, the Kyrie eleison, the Gloria in excelsis, and the Sanctus were sung by the congregation.[8] The Kyrie appeared in the Eastern church in the first century, and its Greek form was retained in the Latin Mass. The Gloria, known as the Greater Doxology, appeared in part in the second century in the Eastern church and in the sixth century was translated into Latin and adopted by the Western church. The Sanctus, which is of Hebrew origin, was used in Jewish worship before the Christian era.

The Gloria Patri, the Lesser Doxology, which was added to each psalm sung in the service, was known in its present form by the end of the fourth century in both Eastern and Western churches. The Te Deum laudamus, while similar in form to early Greek praises, seems to be wholly of Latin origin. The Credo (based on the Nicene Creed), first used in the Eastern church in the sixth century and later in the Western church, was introduced for congregational use to strengthen and confirm the faith of the people against the influence of Arianism. The Agnus Dei was adopted in the seventh century, and from this century the Ordinary of the Mass became gradually standardized. By the tenth century, Mass was sung by the choirs, congregational participation having been gradually abandoned. These early expressions of praise and worship remain to-day in the Roman Mass and also are found in the Anglican, Episcopal, and Lutheran liturgies.

Early Latin Hymnody   The influence of the hymns of Ambrose led to an increasing interest in the writing of hymns. The first significant successor to Ambrose was Aurelius Clemens Prudentius (348-413), a Spanish lawyer, judge, and poet. At the age of fifty-seven, Prudentius retired from a successful legal career to devote himself to the writing of sacred verse, which resulted in the creation of extended cycles of hymns, often written for the canonical hours or the festivals of the church year. The most familiar of his hymns still in use by English-speaking congregations is "Of the Father's love begotten" (3) (as translated by John Mason Neale), which presented the orthodox doctrine of the nature of Christ, in contrast with the heretical Arian view.

The last five hundred years of the first millenium A.D. are often called the Dark Ages. During this era of transition (in the aftermath of the demise of the Roman empire), hymnody became a vehicle both for promoting the spread of Christianity and for combatting the continuing presence of heresies within the church. In describing the hymns of this period, Albert E. Bailey wrote:

> The hymns express the fighting theology of the earlier classical period, they embody the fears and longing of men whose world was chaotic, they present Jesus as a King surrounded with the paraphernalia of the Old Testament and Apocalyptic imagery, and they are shaped to fit the requirements of the Christian year and of the daily Office as developed by the monks in their abbey churches.[9]

Some of the hymns from the Dark Ages have survived in use to the present day. Venantius Honorius Clementianus Fortunatus (c. 530-609), though born in Italy, settled in Gaul (France) in 565, where he remained for the rest of his life. He became Bishop of Poitiers around 600. Fortunatus is said to have written a cycle of *Hymns for All the Festivals of the Christian Year*, but the manuscripts have been lost. His lingering contribution to hymns in current use is "The royal banners forward go" (John Mason Neale's translation of *"Vexilla regis prodeunt"*), which was written to celebrate the arrival of a holy relic at the convent of St. Croix.

Theodulph of Orleans (c. 760-821) served as poet and counselor in the court of Charlemagne, for which he was rewarded with the title of Bishop of Orleans. In that role he became a pioneer for education, establishing schools not only in monasteries and cathedrals for the education of clergy, but also in towns and villages of his diocese for poor children. His hymn *"Gloria, laus et honor"* has become familiar as "All glory, laud and honor" (15), as translated by Dr. Neale. Written as a poetic version of the account of Jesus' triumphal entry into Jerusalem, as recorded in Mark 11:1-10 and John 12:12-19, it is widely used as a favorite hymn for Palm Sunday.

The anonymous ninth-century hymn, *"Veni, Creator Spiritus,"* has been attributed by some scholars to Rabanus Maurus (d. 856), who served as Bishop of Fulda and Archbishop of Mainz. In its translation by John Cosin, "Come, Holy Ghost, our souls inspire" (4), this hymn forms a prayer for the presence and ministry of the Holy Spirit.

Gregorian Chant   At the beginning of the seventh century, the melodies of the Roman chant were gathered together in a recognized repertoire. While this codification had, no doubt, begun earlier, it is generally attributed to Pope Gregory I (590-604) and, throughout the centuries that followed to the present day, these chants bear his name. With few additions they remain the body of Roman plainsong today. Gregory is also credited with adding the four plagal modes to the already existing authentic modes. These chants are characterized as monophonic, unaccompanied, mainly diatonic, having an absence of strict meter, and freedom of rhythm to fit the rhythm of the text. Examples of these melodies found in present-day hymnals are: DIVINUM MYSTERIUM (3), SPLENDOR PATERNAE (1), and VENI CREATOR (4). The version of VENI CREATOR given here is from the Mechlin *Vesperale Romanum*, 1848, a collection of plainsong melodies designed to restore the use of plainsong in the Roman Catholic churches of France at a time when the practice of this ancient church song had been forgotten.

So strong was the influence of the Gregorian plainsong that it soon became the accepted pattern for Western churches. Before the end of the seventh century, it had reached England and was taken from England to Germany early in the eighth century. During the reign of Charlemagne, the Roman church prospered, and its influence increased. Churches, schools, convents, and monasteries were established throughout Europe, and the practice of Christian song was an integral part of this expansion.

The Sequence   Mention has already been made of the *jubilus*, the extension of the final syllable of the *Alleluia*. Gradually the musical phrases of this extended melody were supplied with new text material. This new form, known as the *sequence*, first appeared in France, but its greatest development is attributed to Notker Balbulus (840-912) at the Benedictine monastery of St. Gall in Switzerland.

> In order to understand the extraordinary popularity and wide diffusion of the sequence it must be emphasized that it is not just another hymn, but an ornament to the mass, individually created for each and every festival with a particular theme in mind . . . The original Latin hymn was associated with daily secular worship and then with the canonical hours of the monastery. The sequence was associated with the celebration of the divine sacrifice.[10]

"*Victimae paschali laudes*" ("Christians, to the Paschal victim") (2), traditionally ascribed to Wipo of Burgundy (d. c. 1050), represents the development of the sequence in the eleventh century. The use of dialogue, as evidenced in this text, was a contributing factor in the development of the liturgical drama for Easter. Of further significance is the fact that the pre-Reformation chorale, "*Christ ist erstanden*," and Luther's "*Christ lag in Todesbanden*" are patterned after this sequence.

The unrhymed style of the Notkerian sequence was gradually replaced by the rhymed metrical sequence of Adam of St. Victor in Northern France in the late twelfth century. The two best-known examples of the rhymed metrical sequence may be found in the "*Dies irae*" ("Day of wrath! O day of mourning") and the "*Stabat mater*" ("At the cross her station keeping"). Both the "*Dies irae*," whose opening line is taken verbatim from the Vulgate translation of Zephaniah 1:15, and the plainsong sequence date from the thirteenth century. The "*Stabat mater*," originally a rhymed prayer intended for private devotions, is the work of an unknown Italian author of the thirteenth century. In the revised Roman Missal of 1570, made by the Council of Trent, all sequences were abolished except four: "*Victimae paschali*" for Easter; "*Veni Sancte Spiritus*" for Pentecost; "*Lauda Sion*

Salvatorem" for Corpus Christi; and "*Dies irae, dies illa*" for Masses for the Dead. A fifth, "*Stabat mater dolorosa*," was added in 1727 for Friday after Passion Sunday.

Latin Hymnody of the Middle Ages   The spread of hymn singing through the Dark Ages had been carried primarily by the activities of the monastic orders which also developed during those years. The Benedictine order, in particular, was influential because of its insistence upon the discipline of praise and prayer for the seven daily Offices (Canonical Hours). Hymns had regularly become incorporated into these services, leading to the compilation of large bodies of hymnody into manuscript collections in many of the important monasteries and cathedrals of Western Europe by the twelfth century. This voluminous body of hymnody served as a foundation for continuing developments in this form of faith expression.

Three hymnists from the twelfth century are still represented in many contemporary hymnals. From the writings of Peter Abelard (1079-1142), brilliant philosopher whose rationalistic approach to faith kept him in frequent trouble with church authorities, have come "Alone thou goest forth, O Lord" (44) translated by F. Bland Tucker, 1938), and "O what their joy and their glory must be" (translation by John Mason Neale, 1854).

"*Jesu, dulcis memoria*," an extended poem which represents the mystical element in medieval faith, has often been attributed to Bernard of Clairvaux (c. 1091-1153), one of the most influential churchmen of his day whose eloquent preaching is said to have launched the Second Crusade. Two hymns which continue in use in English owe their origins to "*Jesu, dulcis memoria*:" "Jesus, the very thought of thee" (28) (translated by Edward Caswell, 1849) and "Jesus, thou joy of loving hearts" (55) (a paraphrase of selected excerpts by the American clergyman, Ray Palmer, 1858).

It is ironic that these two leading medieval writers—Abelard, a teacher and advocate of a reasoned, intellectual approach to Christian faith, and Bernard of Clairvaux, who espoused personal piety and devotion—engaged in extended, bitter debates with each other.

The third twelfth-century writer who has contributed a hymn to current repertoire is another Bernard, Bernard of Cluny, whose lengthy poem (approximately three thousand lines), "*De contemptu mundi*" (a tirade against the evils of the time), is the source of a hymn which Dr. Neale translated as "Jerusalem, the golden" (60).

Significant to hymnic developments in the thirteenth century was the emergence of the mendicant orders, the Dominicans and the Franciscans, both established to provide reform within the Roman Church. The foremost Dominican hymn writer was Thomas Aquinas (c. 1227-1274), who was commissioned by the Church to write new hymns for the newly established Office of *Corpus Christi*. For this reason, his hymns focus upon the meaning of the Eucharist (communion).

The best-known hymnist from this era is St. Francis of Assisi (1182-1226), founder of the Franciscan Order. There is some ambiguity in placing St. Francis in a discussion of Latin hymnody, for his "Canticle of the Sun," from which his most familiar hymn is taken, was written in a language which is a hybrid of Latin mixed with colloquial distortions. In this respect, St. Francis became part of a literary movement which led to the standardization of the Italian language. From the "Canticle of the Sun" has come William H. Draper's translation/adaptation "All creatures of our God and King" (25).

Laudi Spirituali   In the thirteenth and fourteenth centuries a body of nonliturgical music developed in Italy outside of the auspices of the Roman church. These *laudi spirituali* were religious songs of devotion and praise sung to simple melodies. The texts were not in Latin, but in the vernacular of the people, and their popularity was widespread. One of these texts from a fourteenth-century collection is "*Discendi, amor santo*" ("Come down, O love divine") (82).

Perhaps the most important writer of *laude*, as these vernacular songs of praise were also called, was Jacopone da Todi (1230-1306), who left a successful career as a lawyer at the age of forty to embark on a life of asceticism and eventually entered the Franciscan Order.

Attempts at Reform   The wide variance in the Gregorian melodies used in different parts of Europe, the infiltration of secular melodies into the liturgy, and the use of vernacular texts prompted the Council of Trent, 1545-1563, to initiate reforms. Official books were published—the Missal, Gradual, Antiphonary, Breviary and others—containing approved plainsong melodies for all churches to use. This attempt to purify the music of the Roman church and to restore the ancient monophonic song faced severe obstacles in the rising tide of polyphony and strong opposition to anything medieval in nature. In manuscript collections that followed, many variations appeared as well as new original melodies. The restoration of ancient plainsong awaited the work of the monks of the Abbey of Solesmes in the nineteenth century, which, with authentic texts, is now authorized for use by papal decree.

Later Developments in Latin Hymnody   The stream of Latin hymnody did not cease with the end of the Middle Ages. Illustrative of a continuing interest in the writing of hymns in Latin in succeeding centuries are "*O filii et filiae*" ("O sons and daughters, let us sing") by Jean Tisserand in the late fifteenth century and "*Adeste Fideles*" ("O come, all ye faithful") (95), written by John Francis Wade in the mid-eighteenth century. Also significant to the development of Latin hymnody was the series of revisions of the Breviary that occurred from the sixteenth through the eighteenth centuries.

ENDNOTES

[1] Cf. Egon Wellesz, *A History of Byzantine Music and Hymnography*, 2d ed. (Oxford: Clarendon Press, 1961), pp. 152-156.

[2] Gustave Reese, *Music in the Middle Ages* (New York: W.W. Norton & Company, 1940), p. 68.

[3] Of the nine odes, most were based upon Old Testament canticles. The only New Testament canticle used as a source was the Magnificat.

[4] Arius (c. 250-336), an influential leader in the church at Alexandria, proposed the theological doctrine that the Son was not equal to the Father, but was secondary to the Father. Though his views were condemned as heretical by both the Council of Alexandria (321) and the Council of Nicaea (325), the Arian doctrine was widely spread and popularized through the use of song.

[5] Reese, p. 104.

[6] Hugo Leichtentritt, *Music, History, and Ideas* (Cambridge: Harvard University Press, 1944), p. 31.

[7] Ruth Ellis Messenger, *The Medieval Latin Hymn* (Washington: Capital Press, 1953), p. 10.

[8] Winfred Douglas, *Church Music in History and Practice*, rev. ed. (New York: Charles Scribner's Sons, 1962), p. 37.

[9] Albert Edward Bailey, *The Gospel in Hymns* (New York: Charles Scribner's Sons, 1950), p. 225.

[10] Messenger, p. 44.

Chapter Two

THE LUTHERAN CHORALE

The sixteenth century saw the Renaissance at its height, and vocal polyphonic technique developed to its highest degree in what is recognized as the "golden age of polyphony." The five-line music staff had been established, but bar lines were not in common usage. Modality predominated, but major-minor tonality was emerging. The development of music printing was a great advance over the circulation of most literature by oral tradition and by laboriously copied manuscripts.

The Significance of Martin Luther

At the time of Martin Luther (1483-1546), the practice of music in the Catholic church was dominated by the clergy, with the congregation as spectators and listeners rather than participants. The same conviction that motivated Luther's translation of the Bible into the vernacular of the people also produced the desire for congregational song in the language of the people, so that all Christians might join in singing praises to God.

Luther's Hymns It is extremely significant that Martin Luther, who led the Reformation, was also the first evangelical hymn writer. In addition to his interest in poetry, he was a musician and composed tunes to some of his own hymns. His hymn writing dates from 1523, shortly after he had completed his translation of the New Testament into the German language, and continued until two years before his death. Of his thirty-seven hymns, twenty-three were written during 1523-1524. Of these thirty-seven hymns, eleven were translations from Latin sources, four were revisions of pre-Reformation hymns, seven were versifications of psalms, six were paraphrases of other scripture selections, and nine are classed as original hymns. Luther possessed the ability to express profound scriptural teaching in a simple, straightforward manner. Yet in the simplicity of his hymns there is evidence of strength and courage.[1]

Luther has been called the Ambrose of German hymnody, and his *"Ein' feste Burg ist unser Gott"* ("A mighty fortress is our God"), has been called the Marseillaise Hymn of the Reformation.[2] His great hymn, a paraphrase of Psalm 46, apparently was written in 1529 for the Diet of Speyer, when the German princes made their formal protest against the revoking of their liberties, and thus received the name "protestants." An earlier hymn by Luther, a metrical paraphrase of Psalm 130, *"Aus tiefer Not schrei' ich zu dir"* ("Out of the depths I cry to you") (6), written in 1523, was first published the following year in *Etlich Christlich Lieder*. At the time of the Diet of Augsburg, 1530, Luther remained in the Castle of Coburg. During these days of anxiety he would gather the servants of the castle about him and say: "Come, let us defy the devil, and praise God by singing the hymn, 'Aus tiefer Not schrei' ich zu dir.' " In 1546, the people of Halle sang this hymn with tears in their eyes as they lined the streets when Luther's coffin passed through the city on its way from Eisleben to Wittenberg, its final resting place.

Early Lutheran Hymn Writers   In the early years of the Reformation, Luther wrote to Nicholaus Haussman, pastor at Zwickau:

> I also wish that we had as many songs as possible in the vernacular which the people could sing during mass, . . . But poets are wanting among us, or not yet known, who could compose evangelical and spiritual songs, . . . worthy to be used in the church of God.[3]

In response to that plea came hymn texts and melodies from numerous German poets and musicians. Koch, in his *Geschichte des Kirchenlieds und Kirchengesanges*, cites fifty-one hymn writers active during the years 1517-1560. A presumably exaggerated view of the extent of that response appears in the preface to a 1546 hymnal: "Throughout half of Germany there is scarcely a pastor or shoemaker who lacks the skill to make a little song or tune to sing at church with his neighbors."[4]

Among the most important early contributors to chorale literature were Justus Jonas (1493-1555), Hans Sachs (1494-1576), Paul Speratus (1484-1551), Nicolaus Decius (c. 1458-c.1546), Nicolaus Hermann (c. 1480-1561), and Paul Eber (1511-1569). Some of these, like Luther, were poet-composers; others made their primary contribution through either texts or melodies.

Sources of Early Texts and Tunes   Luther and his contemporaries drew upon four principal sources for their texts and tunes:[5] (1) the liturgy, both Mass and Office, of the Catholic Church, (2) pre-Reformation nonliturgical vernacular and macaronic hymns, (3) secular folk song, and (4) works of original creativity. The borrowed materials were treated in differing ways. In some instances, text and melody were used, with textual alterations or paraphrases made in translating the Latin liturgical text into the vernacular. In this manner, Decius transformed the *Gloria in excelsis* into *"Allein Gott in der Höh sei Ehr"* ("All glory be to God on high") (7). The most literal translations of this type took as their source the office hymns. For other adaptations, new texts were provided for appealing melodies, and vice versa.

Musical Characteristics   Johannes Riedel, in his excellent monograph on the Lutheran chorale, provides a concise description of the essential characteristics of the chorale melodies:

> The stately melodies of the chorale display economy of musical materials, and can often be reduced to a few primordial motives. Cadence formulae at the ends of the various phrases have a balance or relationship which stresses feeling for a certain key center or modal area. The rhythmic structure usually rests upon only one basic pattern.[6]

Structurally, the early chorale tunes displayed an indebtedness to the traditions of the German Meistersingers through the use of barform (AAB) and its variants. Melodic contour of original tunes often also reflected a relationship to the *lied* tradition through the use of a descending melodic passage spanning an octave.

One of Martin Luther's most significant musical contributions in the chorale was the use of the Ionian mode, by which he moved beyond the traditional church modes and anticipated the development of major tonality. Luther utilized the Ionian mode particularly in his original works, such as "A mighty fortress is our God" and "From Heaven above to earth I come."

Rhythmic vitality was a distinctive trait of the early chorale, which differed substantially from the isometric chorale, with its characteristic movement in equal note values. The latter rhythmic style did not become standardized until the mid-seventeenth century.

Early Lutheran Collections   In addition to his own writing, Luther secured the services of Johann Walther of Thuringia (1496-1570) and Conrad Rupff, both skillful musicians, whose services were invaluable in laying the foundations for Lutheran hymnody. Luther played a major role in selecting hymns and tunes and in guiding the publication of hymnal collections and their subsequent editions.

The first hymnals of Luther appeared in 1524. *Etlich Christliche Lieder*, known as the *Achtliederbuch*, contained eight hymns, four of them by Luther. Another collection was the *Erfurter Enchiridion*, which contained twenty-six hymns. The chorale melodies in these collections were unaccompanied. Both of them were for the congregation, to be used both at home and at church. In addition to his urging that these hymns be learned at home, Luther advocated the teaching of them to children in the parochial schools. Johann Walther's *Gesangbüchlein*, also published in 1524, was the first collection of polyphonic settings of chorale tunes for choir use.

The popularity of these three early hymnals necessitated subsequent editions. The appearance of other hymnals without Luther's approval caused him to publish, in 1529, Joseph Klug's *Geistliche Lieder auff neue gehessert*, which replaced the *Erfurter Enchiridion* as the basic hymnal for congregational usage. No copy of Klug's 1529 collection is known to exist today, but it was the first to include "*Ein' feste Burg ist unser Gott*." During the following sixteen years other hymnals appeared by Rauscher, 1531; Klug, 1535[7] and 1543; Schumann, 1539[8]; and Babst, 1545, but these were largely reprints of Klug's 1529 collection to which other hymns were added. Babst's collection of 1545, containing 120 hymns and 97 melodies, was the last publication Luther supervised.

Other Early Hymn Writers   The objective pattern of hymn writing set forth by Luther was carried on throughout the last half of the sixteenth century. Hymns of praise and adoration as well as hymns revealing an increased doctrinal emphasis came from other writers in the first century of the Reformation. Nicolaus Selnecker (1530-1592), Bartholomaeus Ringwaldt (1530-1598), Martin Moller (1567-1606), and Philipp Nicolai (1536-1608) carried on this early tradition. Some of these wrote melodies for their hymns, the most outstanding of which are Nicolai's "*Wachet auf! ruft uns die Stimme*" ("Wake, awake, for night is flying") (8,9) and "*Wie schon leuchtet der Morgenstern*" ("O morning star, how fair and bright") (10).

Increasing Popularity of Congregational Singing

In spite of the great concern that Luther had for congregational song and his efforts in writing and publishing hymns, congregational singing developed slowly. The tradition of congregational participation in the church service did not develop immediately, and it was not until the last of the sixteenth century that hymn singing gained great prominence. The congregation continued to sing unaccompanied unison melodies, while the choir sang elaborate polyphonic settings of the tunes with the melody in the tenor voice.

The Influence of Homophonic Style   At the close of the sixteenth century there were evidences of revolt against polyphonic writing throughout the musical world in the dawn of the baroque. Polyphony continued, but homophonic writing took on new importance. Contrapuntal techniques gave way to harmonic ideas, and vertical chord structure and progressions received greater attention. About the time of the appearance of the "Camerata" in Italy, and prior to the development of the recitative in the operatic efforts of this group, Lukas Osiander published an unusual hymnal in Nürnberg in 1586. The tunes in this hymnal, *Fünfzig geistliche Lieder und Psalmen* (Fifty Spiritual Songs and Psalms), were written in four parts with the melody in the soprano voice harmonized with simple chords. This type of hymn tune could be sung in parts by the congregation. All previous hymnal publications had been designed for either the congregation or the choir, but not for both. Osiander brought the two forces together, each reinforcing the other. Hymn singing in the churches took on added strength and vitality through this new device. The technique of this simple four-part harmonization of the tunes was followed in Johannes Eccard's *Geistliche Lieder auff den Choral*, 1597; Bartholomaeus Gesius' *Geistliche deutsche Lieder*, 1601; Hans Hassler's *Kirchengesänge*, 1608; and Melchior Vulpius' *Gesangbuch*, 1609.[9]

In addition to Eccard, Gesius, Vulpius, and Hassler, composer of PASSION CHORALE (12), other significant names in the development of the chorale during this period were Melchior Teschner, composer of ST. THEODULPH (15), and Michael Praetorius. The latter published *Musae Sioniae*, 1605-1610, containing 1,244 settings of chorale melodies, one of which is ES IST EIN' ROS' (16).

Seventeenth-Century Developments

The Thirty Years' War, 1618-1648, had a significant influence on German hymnody. Beginning first as a Catholic-Protestant conflict, it spread rapidly until it became a political and religious struggle engaging, at one time or another, the entire continent. Silesia and Saxony, provinces of Germany, became the battlefields on which nations fought for three decades.

> It was a time when men's hearts failed them for fear. State hurled itself at the head of state, army at the head of army, and those who fell not in battle perished before the still deadlier scourges of plague and famine. The very abomination of desolation seemed to be set up: raping and pillage, outrage and slaughter, reigned unchecked and unconfined. In vain, to all outward appearance, did the saints cry: How long? Yet of their cries and tears, and of the amazing tenacity of their faith, the hymns they have left us bear irrefragable witness.[10]

Influence on Hymn Writing   The hymns written in the seventeenth century, during and following the strife and conflict, revealed a changing emphasis from the previous objective characteristics to a more subjective emphasis. The experience of the war which tested and tried Christian faith and courage resulted in a greater sense of dependency of the Christian on God's providence and care. Reliance on an omnipotent God for comfort and consolation was written into the hymns of this period, producing expressions of Christian devotion and individual self-consciousness.

> A study of hymn texts written during this period reveals man's quest for an intimate relationship between himself and God. Confronted with the horrible killing and pillaging of the Thirty Years War, the individual sought enlightenment, self-understanding, comfort, and consolation in a personal subjective approach to God . . . These texts, which centered more and more upon the needs of the individual, were not intended for congregational use but for private devotionals in the home.[11]

The most significant hymn writer from this period, in terms of his continuing influence upon congregational singing, is Paul Gerhardt (1607-1676). Though not as prolific as some of his hymn-writing contemporaries, Gerhardt represents well the transition that occurred in the seventeenth century from the objective hymnic expressions of earlier chorale writers to the more personalized expressions that emerged from the Thirty Years' War and later culminated in the hymns of the Pietistic movement. He was strongly influenced by the literary reforms introduced by Martin Opitz (1597-1639) and his Silesian school of poets, whose efforts concentrated upon refinement of poetic writing through greater emphasis upon the purity and quality of the language. Through collaborations with Johann Crüger and later Johann Georg Ebeling, Gerhardt's hymn texts were given musical settings and incorporated into published collections that gave them wide circulation.

Gerhardt continues to be well-represented in contemporary German hymnals. Among American hymnals, his most frequently included hymns are "Jesus, thy boundless love to me," "Give to the winds your fears" (118) (illustrative of those hymns from this period which offered comfort and hope during that era of trauma and uncertainty), "All my heart this night rejoices," and his translation of "O sacred Head, now wounded" (12).

Other important writers of this period were: Martin Rinkart (1586-1649), author of "Now thank we all our God" (87) (perhaps the best-known hymn from this period in current use), Johannes Olearius (1611-1684), who wrote "Comfort, comfort ye my people" (40) (a paraphrase of Isaiah 40:1-8), Johann Franck (1618-1677), author of "Jesus, priceless treasure" (17), Georg Neumark (1621-1681), author of "If you will only let God guide you" (19) and composer of NEUMARK, Johann Heerman (1585-1647), author of "Ah, holy Jesus" (18), and Johannes Rist (1607-1667), one of the most prolific hymn writers of the period.

Johann Crüger's Collection   The outstanding hymnal of the seventeenth century was Johann Crüger's *Praxis Pietatis Melica (The Practice of Piety Through Music),* 1644. For forty years Crüger (1598-1662) served as cantor for St. Nicholas Church, Berlin, and his concern for congregational singing is evidenced by the great number of tunes he wrote and the five collections he published. Crüger was a skillful composer whose tunes are sturdy, simple, and syllabic, with firm metrical rhythm. They possess a distinctive lyric quality, which provides a fresh influence in chorale melody construction. Crüger's harmonic and rhythmic treatment of his melodies was influenced by the music of the French psalters, which he encountered through the influence of the Calvinistic movement in Berlin, where he was active as a composer and publisher.

Crüger provided new tunes for many of the hymns of Gerhardt, Franck, Heerman, Rinkart, and others. At the St. Nicholas Church, he worked closely with Gerhardt, whose texts appeared extensively in Crüger's publications.

His *Praxis Pietatis Melica* was the most influential and widely used collection of Lutheran tunes during the seventeenth century. By 1736, it had passed through forty-four editions. Two familiar tunes from this collection are: NUN DANKET ALLE GOTT and JESU, MEINE FREUDE (17).

Two seventeenth-century German tunes which originated outside the bounds of the Lutheran tradition are STABAT MATER (MAINZ) and LASST UNS

ERFREUEN (25). These appeared in Roman Catholic collections primarily prepared for use in a local diocese. The first tune is an adaptation of a melody that was found in the Mainz *Gesangbuch*, 1661, and the second tune is from the Cologne *Ausserlesene Catholische Geistliche Kirchengesänge*, 1623.

Pietism

The subjective religious thought that emerged during the Thirty Years' War developed during the seventeenth century and reached its culmination in Pietism in the latter part of the century. This Pietistic movement began with Jakob Spener, who founded the Collegium Pietatis in Halle in 1670 to encourage purer and more strict Christian living and personal devotion. Johann Jakob Schütz, author of "Sing praise to God who reigns above" (30), was an associate of Spener. Adam Drese, whose home in Jena was the meeting place for the Pietists, composed the tune SEELENBRÄUTIGAM (35). The outstanding Lutheran hymn writer in Denmark during this period was Thomas Hansen Kingo, 1634-1703, author of "Print thine image pure and holy" (46). Joachim Neander, author of "Praise to the Lord, the Almighty" (24) and composer of NEANDER, was a close friend of Spener and Schütz and actively supported the cause of Pietism. He was the foremost hymn writer of the German Reformed (Calvinist) Church, and has been called the "Paul Gerhardt of the Calvinists." Gerhard Tersteegen was the major hymn poet of the later years of the Pietistic movement.

The influence of Pietism produced hymns of greater subjectivity—more personal and passionate in character—than the earlier Lutheran hymns. Singular pronouns replaced the plural forms of the earlier hymns, and the intense personal quality of these hymns made them far more suitable for private devotion than for congregational use.

The subjective expression of these Pietistic hymns did not fit the virile Reformation melodies passed on by preceding generations. The new sentiment demanded new tunes or the adapting of old ones. The songlike lyric quality of Crüger's tunes soon reflected the melodic influence of the Italian operatic style. The grandeur and elaborate character of the baroque era, which began in Italy, spread throughout Europe, and the chorale melodies being written at this time did not escape its influence. The outstanding hymnal of this period and the first to challenge the prominence of Crüger's collection was Freylinghausen's *Gesangbuch*, 1704. Many of the melodies in Freylinghausen's collections appeared with a figured bass line, indicating the growing importance of *basso continuo* practices. The *Gesangbuch*, which was combined in 1741 with a second collection published in 1714, provided an extensive and comprehensive hymnal of 1,600 hymns and more than 600 melodies. One of these tunes was GOTT SEI DANK (29).

Benjamin Schmolck, a popular hymn writer of the early eighteenth century, was not of the Pietistic group. His hymns reveal the warmth of practical Christianity, but maintain a High Church spirit. He published more than a dozen collections, some of which ran into many editions and were widely used. Of his more than 900 hymns, two that remain in common usage are "My Jesus, as thou wilt," and "Open now thy gates of beauty" (26). Erdmann Neumeister, author of "Sinners Jesus will receive," followed the example of Schmolck in becoming an ardent champion of the older, conservative Lutheranism. He strongly opposed the influences of Halle and Herrnhut and used both pulpit and press to speak out against the "novelties" of the Pietists and the Moravians. Because of his publication of poetic paraphrases of Scripture appropriate for the various feasts of the church year, he is recognized as an originator of the church cantata.

Decline of Congregational Singing   Hymn singing by the congregation declined in the eighteenth century. Stalwart hymns of praise to God had given way to words of personal piety and individual expression. The organ became more and more prominent in the service as the facilities of the instrument and the skill of the organist increased. The use of ornamental interludes between stanzas and excessive alteration of the hymn tune, melodically and rhythmically, could only be detrimental to the singing of the congregation.

Johann Sebastian Bach

The influence of Johann Sebastian Bach upon the development of congregational song was the least of his impact upon church music as a whole. The forces of the Pietistic movement and rise of secular music had resulted in a general decline in church music. Spitta says that "Pietism had finished off good church music so that when Bach came he had little to work with."[12]

Apparently, Bach had only minor interest in chorale tunes as far as congregational singing was concerned, for his contribution primarily lies in his original songs and his chorale arrangements or harmonizations, neither of which were intended for the congregation.

Evidently, congregational singing in Bach's time had little importance, for the music of the service was largely provided by the choir and the organist. The immense output of organ and choral literature by Bach seems to bear this out.

> Not until the concert style of music was banished from the service, in the generation after Bach, and the town choirs that had been allotted to the churches ceased to exist did congregational singing become the characteristic and sole service music of the Protestant church.[13]

The Bach Chorales   In spite of his seeming disinterest in congregational song, Bach employed the chorale melodies extensively in his writing. They were used frequently in his choral and organ compositions. The so-called Bach Chorales are those existing melodies that he arranged or harmonized. These were collected and published in 1769 by C.P.E. Bach in the *Vierstimmige Choralegesänge*.

An interesting comparison may be made of the melodic, rhythmic, and harmonic characteristics of Nicolai's WACHET AUF (8) and Bach's adaptation of this tune (9). Here this sixteenth-century chorale melody is adorned with Bach's contrapuntal technique and structured within the confines of a steady rhythm of four beats to each measure. Bourgeois' PSALM 42 (40) received similar treatment from Bach (46). Here the flowing rhythm of this French psalm tune is reduced to Bach's four-square rhythm of equal quarter notes, and the rhythmic strength typical of Genevan style is lost. Criticism has been made of similar treatment these Genevan tunes received at the hands of English editors in adapting them to fit the meters of English psalmody. While the English adaptations and Bach's versions both show this reduction to notes of equal value, the distinguishing difference is Bach's great skill in contrapuntal writing.

The Decline of the Chorale In the last half of the eighteenth century, Pietism faded rapidly and was replaced by rationalism—the pursuit of truth for its own sake—which invaded religious thought. Excessive revising and editing of antiquated expressions in the older hymns resulted in the loss of much of their strength and virility. Alteration of the chorale melodies was confined to the removal of the melodic ornamentation, melodic innovations of Freylinghausen, and the changing of all notation to notes of equal value with a loss of the sturdy rhythmic movement so characteristic of early melodies.

Hymnody Outside the Lutheran Tradition

Mention should be made of an extraordinary collection of Protestant hymns and carols compiled by Theodoric Petri, a young Finnish student at the University of Rostock. *Piae Cantiones*, published in Nyland in 1582 is significant, not for the new tunes it contained, but for the old tunes, familiar throughout Sweden, which were "revised and corrected" by Petri. Three tunes familiar today are recorded in this collection: DIVINUM MYSTERIUM (3); PUER NOBIS (14); and TEMPUS ADEST FLORIDUM (13).

The Anabaptists The Anabaptist movement, an expression of the Reformation spirit that emerged at approximately the same time as the Luther-led movement in Germany, traces its origin to Ulrich Zwingli, a Catholic priest who resigned his priesthood, married, and became an evangelical pastor in Zurich, Switzerland. However, it was a group of young men who initially were among Zwingli's followers, but rejected his leadership over the issue of infant baptism, who became the early leaders of the Anabaptist movement. From its early development in Zurich in the early 1520's,

> the movement spread into South Germany, the Tyrol, Austria, and Moravia. Before 1527 Anabaptists were found in the regions of the Upper Danube and the Upper Rhine valleys, and by 1530 their missionaries had swept northward into the Netherlands and Northwestern Germany, where numerous congregations had developed in nearly all large cities.[14]

The term Anabaptist ("re-baptizer") was not used by the members of the movement, who called themselves Brethren, but was a term used derisively by their
enemies as a reference to Anabaptist insistence on baptism as a symbol of a
mature commitment to Christian discipleship. Hence, they were vigorously opposed to infant baptism and insisted upon the re-baptism of those who joined
the movement. Because many of the Anabaptist doctrines were considered
heretical by the established church, members of the sect were often subjected
to extreme persecution.

Like the Lutherans, the Anabaptists used vernacular hymns, generally sung
to familiar melodies. These hymns were used extensively for private and family
devotions, as well as for congregational singing. Because they were viewed with
suspicion and distrust by other religious groups, there was little acceptance of
Anabaptist hymnody outside of its own fellowship. Many of the early Anabaptist hymns circulated for several decades in manuscript before being published
in a hymnal.

The most significant collection of Anabaptist hymnody published in the sixteenth century was the *Ausbund*, which appeared c. 1565. The *Ausbund*, as it
was published by Swiss Anabaptists in 1583, was in two distinct parts, the first
including hymns written by and about several of the early martyrs of the group,
among whom were Felix Manz, sentenced to death by drowning in 1527; Jorg
Wagner and Michael Sattler, burned at the stake in 1527; Hans Schlaffer, beheaded
in 1528; and Balthasar Hubmaier, burned at the stake in 1528. The second part,
which had been published in 1564 under the title *Etlich Schöne Christliche Geseng*,
contained hymns written by Swiss Anabaptists imprisoned in the castle of Passau.
The two principal hymn writers of this group who have been identified were
Hans Betz and Michel Schneider. The "*Lob Lied*" (praise song), attributed to
Leonaerdt Clock, is still in use in the present day among the Old Order Amish.
Ernest A. Payne's translation is "Our Father God, thy name we praise" (121).

A predominant number of texts in both parts reflects the effect of constant
persecution upon early Anabaptist thought. Several recount in great detail specific
instances of martyrdom of both individuals and groups. Because of the persecution directed toward Anabaptists and their sympathizers, editions of the *Ausbund* published in the sixteenth and early seventeenth centuries contained neither
the name of the publisher nor the place of publication.

The first edition of the *Ausbund* contained only texts, but indicated underneath
the number of each hymn the melody to which that hymn might be sung. These
melodies were predominantly popular folk tunes, but Lutheran chorale melodies
were also employed.[15] The *Ausbund*, in one of its later editions, is still used by
the Old Order Amish in the United States, giving it the distinction of being
the oldest hymnal still in use today.

Around the middle of the sixteenth century, the Anabaptists became known
as Mennonites, the movement being named after Menno Simons. Simons, who
left Catholic priesthood to become an Anabaptist in 1536, became an influential leader in the development of the movement in the Netherlands and north
Germany until his death in 1561.

Moravian Hymnody   A facet of German hymnody that paralleled the

Lutheran tradition in the eighteenth century was the revival of Moravian activity. The Moravians, known earlier as the Hussite or Bohemian Brethren, had been the followers of John Hus of Bohemia, who was burned at the stake in 1415. In the congregations of the Bohemian Brethren, hymn singing seems to have been an accepted practice in the latter part of the fifteenth century, and their singing has continued to be characterized by great vitality and enthusiasm.

What seems to be the first collection of hymns published on the European continent, predating both Luther and Calvin, was brought out by this group in 1501. This hymnal, a copy of which is in the Bohemian Museum, Prague, contains eighty-seven texts. The most significant Moravian hymnist of the early sixteenth century was Michael Weisse, who was an acquaintance of Luther and whose texts were widely used in the Lutheran chorale tradition. MIT FREUDEN ZART (30) first appeared in the Bohemian Brethren's *Kirchengesänge*, published at Eibenschutz, Moravia, 1566.

Through more than three hundred years, this group, though small, had been frequently persecuted and ridiculed for its religious zeal and enthusiasm. The surge of evangelical revival, which affected its members in the eighteenth century, may be contributed to Count Zinzendorf, a man of noble birth possessing considerable wealth. Beginning in 1722, Moravian emigrants settled on his estate in Saxony, in the settlement called Herrnhut. Not the least of his significant contributions to this group were the hymns he wrote for their singing. His more than two thousand hymns reveal not only pietistic influence but also strong evangelical and missionary zeal. Many of them deal with the suffering and death of Christ and are lyric expressions of personal devotion.

The first hymnal published for the Herrnhut congregation was *Das Gesangbuch der Gemeine in Herrnhut*, 1735. Among the 208 hymns by Zinzendorf found in the 999 hymns of this collection were "Jesus, still lead on" (35) and "Christian hearts, in love united" (31), both of which had appeared in an earlier collection by Zinzendorf. No tunes were included in this collection; however, a manuscript tune book was kept at Herrnhut, and material appropriated from Lutheran chorale tunes and familiar German popular melodies was added to this growing body of Moravian tunes. Three that date from this time are: CASSELL (31), HAYN (32), and SEELENBRÄUTIGAM (35).

The first tune book published by the Moravians in Europe was the *Choralbuch der evangelischen Brüdergemeinen vom Jahr gehorige Melodien*, Leipzig, 1784. Christian Gregor, who compiled this collection for the 1778 hymnal, which he also supervised, was perhaps the outstanding leader among the Unitas Fratrum, or Moravian Brethren, during this period. His role of hymn writer, tune composer and arranger, and compiler was of extraordinary value in the development of Moravian hymnody during his lifetime.

Nineteenth Century Efforts at Reform

The Lutheran Confessional Revival in Germany, beginning early in the nineteenth century, sought to reestablish the traditions of sixteenth century Reformation. The rhythmic vitality of the chorale had declined by the practice of reducing the chorale melodies to notes of equal value. The manner of congregational singing had deteriorated in churches in Germany, and an account written in 1847 revealed:

> The hymns of Luther have had their wings clipped and have put on the straight-jacket of 4/4 time. And so it came about that the more inflexible the singing of the chorale was, the more solemn it was thought to be.[16]

Old hymns, long since lost, appeared in new collections. Altered and mutilated versions were dropped, and the originals were restored. Historical research by such scholars as Karl von Winterfeld (1786-1852), Philip Wackernagel (1800-1877), Friedrich Layriz (1808-1859), and Johannes Zahn (1817-1895) helped to reclaim the German hymnody of the Reformation. Collections which helped to accomplish this were the *Berliner Gesangbuch* (1829), *Sammlung Geistlicher Lieder* (1831), and the *Deutsches Evangelische Kirchen-Gesangbuch* (1852). The latter book was the result of the Eisenach Conference which selected a core of 150 chorales which could be used in the Lutheran churches in Germany.

Scholarly research produced valuable information, but it did not effect the reforms in actual practice as had been hoped. One of the results of the evangelical influence was the appearance of missionary hymns, such as "Spread, O spread thou mighty word" (29), written by Jonathan Friedrich Bahnmaier (1774-1841). Also originating from this period is the popular Christmas hymn "Silent night, holy night" by Joseph Mohr (1792-1849) and its familiar tune STILLE NACHT by Franz Gruber (1787-1863). It should be noted, however, that the origin of this hymn was in Austria rather than Germany.

Scandinavian Contributions

Recent hymnal compilations in the United States, especially the 1978 *Lutheran Book of Worship*, have called attention to important contributions to hymnody by Scandinavian Lutherans during the nineteenth century. "Built on the Rock, the church doth stand" (125) was written by Nicolai Frederik Severin Grundtvig (1783-1872), Danish pastor who was a contemporary and critic of philosopher/theologian Sören Kierkegaard. KIRKEN was composed by Ludwig Mathias Lindeman (1812-1887), Norwegian organist and educator, for Grundtvig's text.

Swedish writers have also made significant additions to the body of hymnody. Johan Olof Wallin (1779-1839), considered that country's leading hymnist, is represented by numerous contributions to Swedish hymnals, and his texts have recently appeared in English translations in this country. Caroline Vilhelmina Sandell-Berg (1832-1903) wrote "Children of the heavenly Father," which is usually associated with the appropriately gentle tune TRYGGARE KAN INGEN VARA, a Swedish melody of unknown authorship.

Among evangelicals in America the best-known Scandinavian hymn is "How great Thou art" by Carl Boberg (1859-1940), Swedish preacher, journalist, and statesman. O STORE GUD, the tune to which Boberg's hymn is sung, is also a Swedish melody whose origin is unknown.

ENDNOTES

[1] See Carl Schalk, "Martin Luther's Hymns Today," *The Hymn*, Vol. 34, No. 3 (July 1983), pp. 131-3.

[2] See Jaroslav Vajda, "Translations of 'Ein Feste Burg,'" *The Hymn*, Vol. 34, No. 3 (July 1983), pp. 134-140.

[3] Ulrich S. Leupold (ed.), *Liturgy and Hymns* (Vol. 53 of *Luther's Works*) (Philadelphia: Fortress Press, 1965), p. 36.

[4] Quoted in Edwin Liemohn, *The Chorale: Through Four Hundred Years of Musical Development as a Congregational Hymn* (Philadelphia: Muhlenberg Press, 1953), p. 12.

[5] For a more detailed study of this subject, see Johannes Riedel, *The Lutheran Chorale: Its Basic Traditions* (Minneapolis: Augsburg Publishing House, 1967), pp. 15-31, and Friedrich Blume, ed., *Protestant Church Music* (New York: W.W. Norton & Company, 1974), pp. 14-35.

[6] Riedel, pp. 9-10.

[7] Luther's hymn text *"Von Himmel hoch, da komm' ich her"* ("From heaven above to earth I come") first appeared in Klug's *Geistliche Lieder*, 1535.

[8] Schumann's *Geistliche Lieder*, Leipzig, 1539, marked the first appearance of the tune, VOM HIMMEL HOCH, sometimes attributed to Luther.

[9] Edwin Liemohn, *The Chorale* (Philadelphia: Muhlenberg Press, 1953), p. 40.

[10] Sydney H. Moore, *Sursum Corda* (London: Independent Press Ltd., 1956), p. 16.

[11] Riedel, p. 56.

[12] J.A. Spitta, *Johann Sebastian Bach* (London: Novello & Co., 1899), II, 115.

[13] Albert Schwietzer, *J.S. Bach* (New York: Macmillan Co., 1950), I, 39.

[14] Rosella Reimer Duerksen, "Anabaptist Hymnody of the Sixteenth Century" (unpublished S.M.D. dissertation, Union Theological Seminary, New York, 1956), p. 7.

[15] Duerksen, p. 18.

[16] Quoted in Johann Daniel von der Heydt, *Geschichte der Evangelischen Kirchenmusick in Deutschland* (Berlin: Trowitzsch and Son, 1926), p. 195.

Chapter Three

PSALMODY

Through the psalms of David and other writers the children of Israel found expression for religious experiences. Psalm singing was a vital part of the services of the Temple and the synagogue, and this practice was continued in the early Christian church. The psalms were sung in prose form, and the recitation melodies were known as psalm tones, one for each church mode.

Influence of John Calvin

In the sixteenth century, the practice of singing metrical forms of the psalms assumed an important role in the form of worship developed by John Calvin in Geneva. Calvin recognized early the value of Christian song to nourish church piety and worship. His services were dignified yet simple and consisted of praying, preaching, and singing. Calvinistic theology and philosophy focused upon the Bible and centered upon the sovereignty of God. Calvin's firm conviction that congregational singing should employ only the psalms in the vernacular of the people excluded any hymns such as those that developed in the Lutheran traditions.

Calvin's philosophy of church music hinged upon two basic factors: simplicity and modesty. Since music was to be used by the people, it needed to be simple, and because it was used to worship a sovereign God, it needed to be modest. In singing, according to Calvin's viewpoint, these qualities were best achieved by the unaccompanied voice.[1]

Origins of Metrical Forms   The metrical structure of the psalms sung at Geneva followed the pattern of the popular songs of the day, many of which were inherited from the trouvères and troubadours of previous centuries. Several stanzas of four or more lines were sung to the same melody, and the singing was in unison without accompaniment.

Literary Work of Marot and Beza   Clement Marot (c. 1497-1544) began making metrical versions of the psalms a number of years before his first contact with Calvin. For at least fifteen years following about 1523, he was a favorite in the court of Francis I at Paris, and, following the same style of his translation of Latin and Greek poems, he turned his attention to the book of Psalms.

> History is full of strange ironies, but none more strange than the chain of circumstances which led to Metrical Psalmody beginning as the favourite recreation of a gay Catholic court and ending as the exclusive 'hall-mark' of the severest form of Protestantism.[2]

Marot's publication of thirty metrical psalm translations in 1542 brought forth such opposition, including an indictment for heresy from church authorities, that he sought sanctuary in Geneva. Here he met Calvin, who enlisted his poetic ability for the preparation of additional metrical psalm versions. Apparently, Calvin had been acquainted with Marot's work before that time, for included among the nineteen psalm versions appearing in a psalter issued in 1539 under Calvin's leadership during his brief sojourn in Strasbourg were thirteen by Marot. The Marot texts which were used in *Aulcuns pseaulmes et cantiques mys en chant* (generally known as the *Strasbourg Psalter*) differed from his original version, which had been completed in manuscript earlier in the same year.[3]

For about a year, Marot labored under Calvin's careful supervision and completed nineteen more psalm versifications. He left Geneva after that year of collaboration with Calvin and died soon afterward, in 1544. Following Marot's departure, Calvin unsuccessfully sought a successor to continue the work until the arrival in Geneva of Theodore de Bèze, or Beza (1519-1605), in 1548. By 1551 Beza had completed thirty-four psalms, and seven more were added by 1554. In succeeding years, Beza continued to produce psalm versifications until 1562, when the entire one hundred and fifty psalms were prepared for publication.

Musical Works of Bourgeois   About the same time that Calvin settled in Geneva, 1541, Louis Bourgeois (c. 1510-c. 1561), a noted composer, arrived in the same city. Calvin enlisted his assistance and, for more than a decade, he served as music editor for Calvin's psalters. His scrupulous setting of the tunes to fit the poetry of the text was done in a most skillful manner. The tunes, many of which were based at least in part upon secular chansons, were carefully designed for ease of singing by the congregation.

As cantor of St. Peter's Church in Geneva, 1545-1557, Bourgeois occupied a position of great influence, but it was his work as a composer and editor of psalm tunes that brought to him, more than to any other individual, recognition as the father of the modern hymn tune. Five of these tunes are: OLD 100TH (36), OLD 134TH[4], PSALM 42 (40), LES COMMANDEMENS DE DIEU (33), and DONNE SECOURS.

The Genevan Psalter   The writing and publishing of metrical psalms in Geneva culminated in the *Genevan Psalter*, 1562. This monumental publication was made up of previously published psalters: the 1542 edition, having thirty psalms by Marot; the 1551 edition including nineteen more by Marot and thirty-four by Beza; and the 1554 edition, including seven additional psalms by Beza. With these psalms were included metrical versions of the Ten Commandments and the Nunc Dimittis, with tunes provided for each.[5] The use of the Decalogue in this psalter and the inclusion of the Nunc Dimittis can be accounted for by the recurring use of these texts and their importance in Calvin's Genevan liturgy.

In this completed psalter of 1562, there were 125 tunes in 110 different meters. These tunes, almost entirely syllabic, had emerged under the careful editing of Bourgeois. Repetition of phrases, only one point of climax in each tune, and the frequent use of a four-note motive, that is, the descending four-note pattern in the first phrase of OLD 100TH, are basic characteristics of these tunes. The presence of harmonic implications in the melodic lines for these tunes indicates a breaking away from modality.[6]

During the formative years of the French psalter, 1542-1562, more than thirty publications of words alone or words and tunes appeared. In 1562, the year in which the completed psalter appeared, more than twenty-five editions were published, and during 1600-1685, at least ninety more editions appeared. From Geneva the *Genevan Psalter* spread through France and on throughout Christendom. Perhaps no other publication has so influenced Christian song. Within a few decades after its appearance, it was translated into more than twenty languages. Among these translations, the most widely used were the Dutch version by Peter Datheen published in 1566 and the translation into German by Ambrosius Lobwasser in 1573. A complete English translation with tunes appeared in 1592, but, because of the popularity of the work of Sternhold and Hopkins, it had little influence in England.

Polyphonic Settings   In addition to his editing of unison psalm tunes for Calvin's psalters, Louis Bourgeois also composed polyphonic settings of the same tunes. Twenty-four harmonizations were published in 1547 at Lyons. In 1561, settings for four, five, and six voices of eighty-three of the Marot and Beza psalm versions were printed in Paris.

Two of France's finest musicians of the sixteenth century were fond of applying their skill at harmonization to the Genevan psalm tunes. Claude Goudimel (c. 1505-1572) published polyphonic settings of these tunes prior to his conversion to the Huguenot faith, for he published Catholic masses as late as 1558. He had written motet-like settings of some of the Genevan tunes as early as 1551. In 1565, Goudimel's harmonization of the entire psalter appeared, with a preface which indicated that it was intended to be used in the home rather than in the church service. Sometime after 1558, while living at Metz, Goudimel became a Huguenot. In 1572, as a victim of the St. Bartholomew's Day massacres, which spread throughout France in the wave of Roman Catholic persecution, he paid the supreme price for his faith.

Claude LeJeune (1528-1600) wrote settings of Genevan psalm tunes for three to seven voices. A collection for four and five voices was published posthumously in 1613 and widely used throughout France and Holland. The compositions of both Goudimel and LeJeune were published in Germany with translations of the psalms into German.

Among other significant composers to make polyphonic settings of the Genevan psalm tunes were Orlandus Lassus and Jan Sweelinck.

Sternhold and Hopkins

It is quite possible that the early work of Marot had reached England and had come to the attention of Thomas Sternhold, Groom of the Royal Wardrobe of Henry VIII and later of Edward VI. Sternhold experimented in making metrical psalm versions, at first without any thought of publication, in the hope that they might replace the currently popular bawdy, obscene songs of his fellow courtiers. Written primarily in ballad meter (forty-one of Sternhold's forty-four versifications were in this form), originally two lines of fourteen syllables, Sternhold's psalm versions were designed to be sung to familiar ballad tunes of his day. The first edition containing nineteen psalms, undated, appeared about 1547, with the title: *Certayne Psalmes chose out of the Psalter of David and drawe into English metre, by Thomas Sternhold, Grome of ye Kynges Maiesties roobes. Excudebat Londini Edvardus Whitchurche.*

A second edition, published posthumously in 1549, added eighteen more psalms by Sternhold. In 1557, a third edition appeared adding seven psalms by John Hopkins, a Suffolk clergyman and schoolteacher. From this point, two important psalters became intertwined as they developed—the *Anglo-Genevan Psalter* (1561) and the *English Psalter* (1562).

The Anglo-Genevan Psalter   The persecution of Protestants by Queen Mary, 1553-1558, caused many to leave England and settle temporarily on the Continent. A large group settled at Frankfurt. However, dissension arose, and one group moved to Geneva where a church was established in 1555 with John Knox as its pastor.

A partial psalter for those displaced English Protestants appeared in 1556 in Geneva. Of the fifty-one psalms it contained, forty-four were by Sternhold and Hopkins, and seven by William Whittingham. Of the tunes included, two were from the French psalter, and the rest were of English origin. In 1558 another edition appeared containing sixty-two psalms, including nine new versions by Whittingham and two by John Pullain. The final edition of the *Anglo-Genevan Psalter* was published in 1561, and, in addition to the texts previously included, it contained twenty-five psalm versions by William Kethe. One of these, his version of Psalm 100, "All people that on earth do dwell" (36), is the earliest example of the metrical psalm still in common usage. Tunes for eighteen of Kethe's twenty-five psalms were borrowed from the *Genevan Psalter* tradition.

By 1560, after the death of Queen Mary, the refugees returned home to England, taking with them the influence of Genevan psalm singing. Kethe remained in Geneva to complete the 1561 edition of the psalter.

The English Psalter, 1562   Beginning in 1560, a series of publications were issued under the editorship of John Day, culminating in 1562 in *The Whole Book of Psalms*, later to become known as the "Old Version" and also popularly called "Sternhold and Hopkins." A majority of the psalm versions in this completed *English Psalter* were by Thomas Sternhold and John Hopkins. However, the influence of the Anglo-Genevan developments is illustrated by the inclusion of fourteen psalms by Whittingham and seven by Kethe. Additionally, there appear a substantial number by Thomas Norton. Most of the texts in the *English Psalter* were in Common meter, in contrast to the metrical diversity of the *Genevan Psalter*, published in the same year.

In 1563, Day published an edition of the *English Psalter* with sixty-five tunes set in four-part harmony, with melody in the treble. The tunes were largely of English origin, but some of the texts were altered to fit the longer meters of the French melodies, and, in other instances, French melodies were altered to fit the shorter meters of the English texts. Each succeeding edition of the English psalter revealed an increasing influence of the French psalm tunes.

The Whole Book of Psalms became the accepted psalm book for English worship for almost a century and a half, until challenged by the "New Version" of Tate and Brady in 1696.

Other English Psalters

The popularity of the texts of the *English Psalter* ("Sternhold and Hopkins") led to the publication of a number of psalters which retained its psalm versions but provided different musical editions.

Damon's Psalter   The first harmonized collection following John Day's 1563 edition was the psalter published by William Damon in 1579 under the title *The Psalmes of David*. This psalter, intended for the private use of John Bull and published without Damon's permission, provided the most extensive collection of common meter tunes available at that time. Damon's *Psalmes* also introduced the short meter tune SOUTHWELL (39).

Este's Psalter   The early psalters with harmonized tunes were published in separate part books. Thomas Este's collection (*The Whole Booke of Psalmes*, 1592) was the first to provide four-part harmony for the tunes on opposite pages in one book. The tunes were harmonized by ten different composers, the most significant being John Dowland, John Farmer, Giles Farnaby, and George Kirbye. Of unusual significance is the fact that in this collection tunes were designated by specific names for the first time. This practice illustrated the emerging use of the "common tune," a tune that may be used with any psalm of appropriate metrical structure, in contrast to a "proper tune," which is identified with one particular psalm. The early tune names often designated the supposed place of the tune's origin. One of the tunes from Este's *Psalter* is WINCHESTER

OLD (11), the harmonization of which is credited by Este to George Kirbye.

Ravenscroft's Psalter   The psalter published by Thomas Ravenscroft in 1621 under the title *The Whole Book of Psalmes* provided an extensive compilation of many of the psalm tunes in use at that time. According to Ravenscroft's title page, the tunes contained were "usually sung in England, Scotland, Wales, Germany, Italy, France, and the Netherlands." Of the ninety-seven different tunes included, almost two-thirds had been used in the Este psalter. However, the Ravenscroft collection also reflects his familiarity with the Scottish psalters (several tunes from the 1615 *Scottish Psalter* were included) and gives evidence of the lingering influence of the tunes of the 1562 *English Psalter*.

The tunes of the *Ravenscroft Psalter* appeared in four-part harmonizations. As had been the case with earlier psalters in England, the melody consistently is found in the tenor voice. The practice of naming tunes after places had originated with Este, but it was Ravenscroft who systematically applied this procedure and established it in England. Ravenscroft's collection was widely used and became a basic source for tunes by subsequent compilers.

Archbishop Parker's Psalter with Tallis' Tunes   The psalters discussed above have been related to each other by their connection with the *English Psalter*. Matthew Parker's *The Whole Psalter Translated into English Metre* contains the metrical version of all one hundred and fifty psalms prepared by that English clergyman, who became Archbishop of Canterbury in 1559. Its publication date has been debated by scholars, but the concensus view suggests 1567.[7] The significance of this psalter rests not with Parker's psalm versification, but with the nine tunes by Thomas Tallis which were appended to it. These tunes by one of England's most outstanding Renaissance composers included TALLIS' ORDINAL (42) and TALLIS' CANON (41).

Sandys' Psalms   In 1637 George Sandys' *A Paraphrase upon the Divine Poems* was published. The psalms in this collection exhibited greater variety in metrical structure than those in the *English Psalter*. Tunes for twenty-four of Sandys' psalm versions were composed by Henry Lawes.

Scottish Psalters

Psalmody developed along parallel lines in Scotland.[8] The *English Psalter* had been introduced by 1550, and later the *Anglo-Genevan Psalter* of 1558, with its tunes. John Knox had returned from Geneva in 1559 and provided leadership in the compilation of a psalter for Scotland. The texts of the resulting *Scottish Psalter*, 1564, were drawn primarily from the *Anglo-Genevan Psalter* of 1561 and the *English Psalter* of 1562, including psalm versions by Sternhold, Hopkins, Kethe, Whittingham, Norton, Pullain, and John Marckand. The remaining psalm versions were the contributions of Scottish writers John Craig and John Pont, who probably collaborated with Knox in the publication of the *Scottish Psalter*. One hundred and five tunes were included from both the English and the French psalters. Musically, the Scottish psalter was superior to the English psalter because of its greater reliance on the French psalm tunes.

In addition to a group of proper tunes, the 1615 *Scottish Psalter* included twelve "common tunes," tunes not attached to any specific psalm, two of which were DUNDEE (20) and CAITHNESS (27). The *Scottish Psalter* of 1635, edited by Edward Millar, provided a harmonized version of the tunes, with the settings provided principally by Scottish musicians. LONDON NEW, one of the common tunes added to the 1635 edition, was used by John Playford in his *Psalms and Hymns in Solemn Music*, London, 1671, and came into English usage through this inclusion. Other tune-book compilers recognized the strength of these Scottish tunes and used them frequently in their collections.

It is interesting to note that in spite of the established tradition of a century of including the music in each psalter, the authorized 1650 *Scottish Psalter* contained no tunes at all. This 1650 edition marks the first appearance of the well-known version of Psalm 23, "The Lord's my shepherd, I'll not want" (67).

Tate and Brady's "New Version"

In 1696 Nahum Tate and Nicholas Brady published *A New Version of the Psalms of David, Fitted to the Tunes Used in Churches*, London. Tate had been appointed poet laureate of England by William III, and this "New Version," as it came to be known as opposed to the "Old Version" of Sternhold and Hopkins, was faithfully dedicated to the king. This version was considered to be authorized or official to the extent that it was "allowed" by the king and the council and was "permitted to be used in all churches, as shall think fit to receive them."

There were no tunes in the 1696 edition, but a *Supplement* was published in 1708 which provided tunes. Among the new ones included were several by William Croft: HANOVER (21), and the familiar ST. ANNE usually ascribed to him.

As in every instance when an effort is made to change long-established church habits, the introduction of the New Version met strong opposition. Although the New Version was in use in the days of William and Mary, the Old Version was still being used when Queen Victoria was a girl. In all probability, the Old Version did not completely disappear from usage until the competition of these two versions had lasted for almost a century and a half, by which time the New Version itself was in rapid decline.

Other Tune Books

The publication of other tune books—Henry Playford's *Divine Companion*, London, 1701, and J. Bishop's *A Set of New Psalm-Tunes in Four Parts*, London,

1711—added to the tunes available for both new and old versions in the early eighteenth century. *Lyra Davidica*, London, 1708, the work of an unknown compiler, was largely a collection of translations of German and Latin hymns. The only surviving tune from this collection is EASTER HYMN (48).

William Tans'ur's *A Compleat Harmony of Syon*, London, 1734, described by Tans'ur on its publication as "the curiousest book ever published," included Tans'ur's tune BANGOR (44). The Scottish poet, Robert Burns, mentions this tune in his poem, "The Ordination," indicating its popularity in the late eighteenth century.

> Mak' haste an' turn King Dave owre
> An' list wi' holy clangour;
> O' double verse come gie us four,
> An' skirl up the BANGOR.

Musical Development in Psalm Tunes

Both in England and in Scotland, psalm tunes had been syllabic, and while this made for ease of singing by the people, it greatly restricted musical interest. To tune composers and editors of collections, there were at least three possible ways to overcome this musical restriction: harmonic enrichment, rhythmic variation, and melodic embellishment. Bach's harmonizations of chorale melodies is the ultimate example for the first method. Variety in rhythm of the tune was most skillfully achieved by Bourgeois, but the English adapters of his tunes greatly weakened the strength of these melodies by reducing them to notes of equal value. OLD 100TH, as only one example, suffered in this respect.

Efforts at melodic embellishment began cautiously with the addition of an extra note—two notes per syllable—in a few places. Jeremiah Clark's KING'S NORTON, in Playford's *Divine Companion*, is one of the early attempts at breaking down the restriction that tunes should be written only in whole notes and half notes. This tune, made up of whole, half, quarter, and eighth notes, was, no doubt, most striking in its day, for it makes use of forty-four notes, with a range of an octave and a half, for a common meter stanza of twenty-eight syllables. Clark's tunes "are always perfectly regular in rhythm, and often have a very free and captivating melody."[9] Clark, "one of the supreme melodists, and a fervent disciple of Purcell,"[10] reveals clearly Purcell's influence in his KING'S NORTON (28). Many composers, imitating this melodic embellishment, overly indulged in this device, and ridiculous excesses resulted. Patrick describes the profuse introduction of

> roulades, runs, repeats, which made the tunes they were intended to adorn much more attractive to the singer than the steady-going syllabic tunes which had palled by incessant repetition and by the slow long-drawn-out dullness of the manner which was thought appropriate in singing them. Their spirited melodic style was at the other extreme from the dreary drawl to which generations had been accustomed.[11]

The Decline of the Metrical Psalm

Following the work of Tate and Brady, other psalters appeared, but none of any significance. While the writing, publishing, and use of metrical psalm versions had been extremely popular throughout England, these poetic ventures were not immune to the scathing ridicule of critics and scholars who considered them largely sheer doggerel. The tunes did not escape scorn in this respect, for Queen Elizabeth was strongly opposed to these "Geneva jigs," and another critic wrote that "two hammerers on a smith's anvil would have made better music." On one occasion, the psalm singing in a certain church prompted the Earl of Rochester to pen these now famous lines:

> Sternhold and Hopkins had great qualms
> When they translated David's Psalms,
>   To make the heart right glad;
> But had it been King David's fate
> To hear thee sing and them translate
>   By God! 'twould set him mad!

Throughout the eighteenth and nineteenth centuries, the metrical psalm gradually gave way to the hymn. At times it is difficult to separate their activity and development, for much mutual influence is evidenced, one on the other. Many tunes were used by both psalm and hymn singers. Here was common ground which proved to be distinctly advantageous to both. Existing psalm tunes were appropriated for the singing of the early hymns of Keach, Watts, and others, and they served adequately as a vehicle for hymn singing until the expansion of hymn meters by Charles Wesley. The fervor of the Evangelicals and the Wesleys, which resulted in a more vigorous tune for hymn singing, greatly encouraged those who desired similar tunes for psalm singing.

Psalmody and Music Education

Beginning with Day's *Psalter*, 1562, and continuing into the nineteenth century, most of the psalters or tune books contained long introductions explaining the fundamentals of music. Only the imagination and initiative of the compiler limited the rules and studies designed to "enable most people to sing the psalm tunes correctly by notes according to the music, without the help of a master." An examination of these compilations reveals some of the interesting devices used to foster music reading. Motivation of the musically illiterate was sometime attempted by such doggerel as:

> Therefore unless
> Notes, Tunes and Rests
> Are perfect learn'd by Heart
> None ever can
> With Pleasure scan
> True Tune in Music's Art.

In their efforts to improve psalm singing by teaching music reading, these compilers frequently produced elaborate "instructions" which, no doubt, often left the learner more confused than enlightened. Nonetheless, these ardent musicians—Thomas Este, Thomas Ravenscroft, John and Henry Playford, Christopher Simpson, William Tans'ur, Aaron Williams, and others of the seventeenth and eighteenth centuries—brought musical enlightenment through psalmody to the towns and villages of England. Of no little significance was their influence on New England psalmody in colonial America as their tunes were borrowed, their books reprinted, and their style of tune composition imitated by the early American compilers and composers.

ENDNOTES

[1] Erik Routley, *The Church and Music* (London: Gerald Duckworth & Co., Ltd., 1950), p. 125.

[2] Richard R. Terry, *Calvin's First Psalter, 1539* (London: Ernest Benn Limited, 1932), p. 111.

[3] For an informative study of textual changes in Marot's psalm versions, see Cecil Mizelle Roper, "The Strasbourg French Psalters, 1539-1553" (unpublished D.M.A. dissertation, University of Southern California, 1972), pp. 151-168.

[4] This is the anglicized version of the original tune.

[5] The tune provided for the Nunc Dimittis is found today as NUNC DIMITTIS (43).

[6] For a comprehensive treatment of the music of this psalter, see Waldo Seldon Pratt, *The Music of the French Psalter of 1562* (New York: Columbia University Press, 1939).

[7] An excellent source of concise information about the Parker psalter, as well as several others from this period, is the dissertation by Ronald Eugene Anderson, "Richard Alison's Psalter (1599) and Devotional Music in England to 1640" (unpublished Ph.D. dissertation, University of Iowa, 1974).

[8] A comprehensive study of Scottish psalmody may be found in Millar Patrick, *Four Centuries of Scottish Psalmody* (London: Oxford University Press, 1949).

[9] Erik Routley, *The Music of Christian Hymnody* (London: Independent Press Limited, 1957), p. 87.

[10] Erik Routley, *The Music of Christian Hymns* (Chicago: G.I.A. Publications, Inc., 1981), p. 55.

[11] Patrick, p. 185.

Chapter Four

ENGLISH HYMNODY, I

The evolution of the English hymn as an expression of Christian song has its roots in the carol. This folk song, with stanza and refrain, was brought over from the Continent at an early date. By the thirteenth century, imported tunes began to give way to English alterations, which explains the English stanzas frequently followed by French or Latin refrains.[1]

The emergence of congregational song on the Continent predates both Luther and Calvin and seems to stem from the followers of John Hus in Bohemia, who produced their first hymn book in 1501.

The first English hymnal was Myles Coverdale's *Goostly Psalmes and Spirituall Songes drawen out of the holy Scripture*. This collection, issued about 1539, was the first attempt to introduce the use of the German chorale in England. Of the forty-one hymns, thirty-six were translations from German sources, one of which was the first English version of *"Ein' feste Burg."* Five hymns were originals, the last of which was a bitter tirade against Rome, entitled, "Let go the whore of Babilon." Coverdale's efforts to reproduce in England the chorale singing which had so impressed him on his visit to Germany were stymied by Henry VIII when this hymnal appeared on a list of prohibited works. An interval of almost two hundred years elapsed without any significant influence of the German chorale in English usage.

As the reformation spread from the Continent to England and Scotland, psalm singing became a vibrant part of the movement. Protestant forces in England in the sixteenth century chose to disregard Lutheran ideals and practices of hymnody and adopted Calvin's concept of congregational worship and praise, and psalm singing became the accepted practice.

The evolution of the hymn from the metrical psalm occurred, as Benson points out, along three lines: by way of an effort to improve the literary character of the authorized psalters; by accommodating the scriptural text to contemporary circumstances; and by the extension of the principle of scriptural paraphrase to cover the evangelical hymns and other parts of the Bible.[2]

Metrical Hymns Added to the Psalters

In spite of the dominating influence of psalmody, a small section of hymns appeared in English and Scottish psalters, a practice not found in any of the French psalters. Day's *Psalter*, 1562, contained a selection of nineteen hymns, eleven before the psalms and eight immediately following. Shortly afterward four other hymns were added in succeeding editions. Bassadine's edition of the Scottish psalter, *The CL Psalmes of David*, 1575, appended four hymns—metrical versions of the Lord's Prayer (Coxe), Whittingham's Ten Commandments with a responsory prayer, the first Lamentation, and the *"Veni Creator"* from the English Book of Common Prayer. This practice continued in other editions until by the 1635 edition thirteen hymns were included—eleven from the *English Psalter* and two by Scottish authors. The 1700 *Supplement* to Tate and Brady's New Version contained sixteen hymns, including Nahum Tate's "While shepherds watched their flocks by night" (11).

Devotional Lyric Poetry

Unfortunately, there was no Marot in England or Scotland to produce metrical versions of high quality, and the insistence of Puritan influence on pure, literal translations produced versions that were awkward and difficult to sing. During the reign of Queen Elizabeth, an abundance of lyric poetry was written. In this atmosphere of literary excellence, religious verse flourished. While these verses were often called hymns, they were intended neither to be sung nor to be used in the church services. In the latter part of the sixteenth century and the first half of the seventeenth, Robert Southwell, John Davies, John Donne, Thomas Campion, George Wither, Francis Quarles, Robert Herrick, and George Herbert contributed to this body of devotional lyric poetry. "Jerusalem, my happy home", a sacred ballad written in ballad meter consisting of twenty-six four-line stanzas, is the work of an anonymous English poet known only by the initials "F.B.P." and dates from the latter part of the sixteenth century.

George Wither published *The Hymnes and Songs of the Church*, 1623. While no hymn from this collection is in common usage today, this was a most extraordinary book for its day and time. Of greater significance than Wither's hymns were the tunes Orlando Gibbons prepared to accompany this collection of hymns. Fifteen tunes were provided for those hymns of Wither that did not fit existing psalm tunes. One of these tunes is SONG 1 (45).

By the latter part of the seventeenth century, psalmody was on the wane. The popularity of the hymn was slowly gaining ground. Isaac Watts had not yet appeared, but those immediately preceding him laid some groundwork of significance. Some of the compilations of hymnic writing that appeared during this time were Samuel Crossman's *The Young Man's Monitor,* and *The Young Man's Meditation,*[3] 1664; John Austin's *Devotions in the Ancient Way of Offices Containing Exercises for every day of the week,* 1668; Thomas Ken's *A Manual of Prayers for the Use of the Scholars of Winchester College,*[4] 1674; Richard Baxter's *Poetical Fragments: Heart Imployment with God and Itself; the Concordant Discord of a Broken-healed Heart,* 1681; and John Mason's *Spiritual Songs; or, Songs of Praise to Almighty God upon several occasions,* 1683.

Here the evolution of the hymn from the metrical psalm was under way, moving from a

> close translation of canonical Scripture, to a free paraphrase first of Psalms then of other Scriptural songs, and up to the point where the purpose of turning Scriptural materials into metre met the impulse to give hymnic form to devotional poetry, and coincided in the production of hymns, freely composed and yet more or less based upon Scripture.[5]

In this evolution the major change was in subject matter, for the metrical form remained much the same. Since this was true, the same tunes could be used for both psalms and hymns alike. The writing and publishing of these seventeenth-century hymns was one thing, but introducing the singing of hymns in the churches was quite another.

Initial Efforts Among Anglicans and Presbyterians

Because of the decadence of psalm singing in the Anglican churches, John Playford, a London music publisher, sought to improve congregational singing by introducing some of the new hymns. To aid in the singing of the tunes, he published *Introduction to the Skill of Musick,* 1654, appending in the seventh and later editions instructions for "The Order of Performing the Cathedral Service." His *Psalms and Hymns in solemn musick of foure parts on the common tunes to the Psalms in metre,* 1671, interspersed the hymns between the psalms, placing them on an equal basis with psalms. This was followed in 1677 by *The Whole Book of Psalms: with the usual Hymns and Spiritual Songs.*

Playford's son, Henry, published *The Divine Companion; or, David's Harp new tun'd,* 1701. The second edition of this collection, 1707, contained Jeremiah Clark's ST. MAGNUS (23) and KING'S NORTON (28). The partial success of these collections was due to the psalms they contained and the new tunes they included, but new hymns were not used. Playford's efforts to introduce them into the Anglican church services were unsuccessful.

The Presbyterian churches in England had great zeal for psalm singing and generally used the *Scottish Psalter,* 1650. However, Richard Baxter's *Paraphrase* on *Psalms of David in Metre with other hymns*, London, 1692; Joseph Boyse's *Sacramental Hymns*, Dublin, 1693; and Matthew Henry's *Family Hymns*, London, 1695, reveal the favor with which these eminent Presbyterian divines looked upon the "freely composed" hymn and their hopes for its use by their congregations.

Baptists Initiate Congregational Hymn Singing

While the aforementioned activity was in progress in the Church of England and among the Presbyterians, controversy was stirring among the smaller dissenting groups. The problem among the General, or Armenian, Baptists was not whether to sing hymns or psalms, but whether there should be any congregational singing at all. In spite of the predominantly negative view among the General Baptists toward it, there are indications that some churches did employ congregational singing in their services in the mid-1680's.[6]

It was in the Particular, or Calvinistic, Baptist churches that congregational singing of hymns was used more extensively. Records of the Broadmead Church of Bristol indicate that congregational singing was regularly carried on from 1671 to 1685.

Benjamin Keach   The recognition for leading the movement for hymn singing must go to Benjamin Keach,[7] who became pastor of the Particular Baptist Church in Southwark in 1668. With the consent of his congregation, he began, about 1673, the practice of singing a hymn at the close of the Lord's Supper. About six years later, the church agreed to sing hymns on "public Thanksgiving days," and about 1691, hymn singing became a weekly practice of the congregation. Most of the hymns used at Southwark were written by Keach.

Controversy at Southwark   The opposition of a small minority of Keach's congregation, led by Isaac Marlow, produced bitter controversy in which both sides issued pamphlets representing their beliefs. The most significant of these writings was Keach's *The Breach Repaired in God's Worship; or, Singing of Psalms, Hymns and Spiritual Songs, proved to be an Holy Ordinance of Jesus Christ*, 1691. The issues in this controversy were: (1) whether or not the only vocal singing in the Apostolic Church was the exercise of an extraordinary gift of the Spirit; (2) whether the use of a set form of words in artificial rhyme was allowable; and (3) whether the minister sang alone, or together with a promiscuous assembly made up of the sanctified and profane, of men and of women (even though the latter were enjoined to keep silent in the churches). The advocates of hymn singing ultimately prevailed, and the practice became generally established among Particular Baptists by the end of the century. Keach had published some hymns as early as 1674 for use in his church and, in 1691, he published *Spiritual Melody*, a collection of about three hundred original hymns.

Hymn Singing and the Lord's Supper It is of particular interest that the introduction of hymn singing into church service occurred in connection with the Lord's Supper. There is indisputable scriptural precedent, for in the New Testament account it is stated, "And when they had sung an hymn, they went out into the Mount of Olives," Matthew 16:30. Another Baptist preacher, Joseph Stennett, pastor of the Seventh-Day Baptist Church, Devonshire Square, London, began, after 1690, to write hymns for use by his own congregation at the service called the Lord's Supper. A collection of thirty-seven hymns was published in 1697 as *Hymns in Commemoration of the Sufferings of Our Blessed Saviour Jesus Christ, compos'd for the celebration of his Holy Supper*. Stennett's collection went through three editions and was included as an appendix to a 1720 edition of Tate and Brady's "New Version," along with seventeen hymns by Isaac Watts.

John Bunyan During the years when Keach and others were trying to persuade Baptist congregations to sing hymns, the pastor of the Baptist church in Bedford, John Bunyan, was having difficulties of his own. The powerful effect of Bunyan's sermons resulted in severe persecution and, for the crime of preaching, he was imprisoned for more than twelve years. Much of his time in jail was devoted to the writing of books, one of which was *Pilgrim's Progress*. His "He who would valiant be" (83) from the second part of *Pilgrim's Progress*, 1684, was added to hymnic compilations by nineteenth-century editors.

Isaac Watts

At the turn of the eighteenth century, the early rays of the dawn of English hymnody were already evident, but the first sunburst came with Isaac Watts (1674-1748), and a new epoch of Christian song began. Watts's basic philosophy was founded on the conviction that the song of the New Testament church should express the gospel of the New Testament, whether in psalm versions or in freely composed hymns. He was further persuaded that Christian song should not be forced to maintain the Calvinistic standards of strict adherence to literal Scripture, and he freely composed expressions of praise and devotion. Also, he held that Christian song should express the thoughts and feelings of those who sang, rather than merely relate the experiences and circumstances of the psalm writers of the Old Testament.

Early Writings Watts was significantly influenced in his early hymn writing by his familiarity with the work of the seventeenth-century devotional poets and seems particularly indebted to the writings of John Milton. Apparently, his first efforts at hymn writing were encouraged by both his father and his brother. The first published collection of Watts's verse was *Horae Lyricae*, which appeared in 1705, containing an interesting assortment of Latin poems, poems on Divine Love (which carried an implied reference to the Songs of Solomon), four psalm versions, and twenty-two devotional poems which may be considered initial experiments in hymn writing. The purpose of this collection, as indicated in the author's preface, was twofold: to provide concise poetic expressions suitable for meditation and worship and to sample the readiness of its readers (and the church) to incorporate hymnody into worship more extensively.[8] Indeed, Watts suggested in his preface that, should public opinion warrant, there were other similar poems ready for publication:

> These are but a small part of two hundred Hymns of the same kind which are ready for Public Use if the World receive favourably what I now present.

Hymns and Spiritual Songs   Acceptance of Watts's religious verse was sufficiently favorable to prompt the publication in 1707 of *Hymns and Spiritual Songs*, in which his first significant contributions to hymnody were made. The hymns in this book were in three divisions: (1) hymns based on scripture; (2) hymns composed "on divine subjects"; and (3) hymns written for the Lord's Supper. There were 210 hymns, with an appended group of doxologies and fourteen psalm imitations. All were written in common, short, or long meter. Response to *Hymns and Spiritual Songs* was so favorable that a new edition was published in 1709 which added 135 new hymns, made minor revisions in some of the texts from the earlier edition, and deleted the psalm versifications. From this collection have come several hymns which remain favorites among congregations today:

"Alas, and did my Savior bleed"
"Am I a soldier of the cross"
"Come, we that love the Lord"
"When I can read my title clear" (107)
"When I survey the wondrous cross" (101)

Included in the 1707 edition of *Hymns and Spiritual Songs* (but deleted from the later version) was an intriguing statement of Watts's views concerning psalmody and hymnody under the title "A Short Esay Toward the Improvement of Psalmody." This essay was significant because it both addressed the deficiencies in the psalmody of the time (as he perceived them) and presented a rationale for the use of hymnody (or songs of "human composure").

The Psalms of David Imitated   Underlying the experiments in which Watts engaged in writing texts for congregational song was his concern for the quality of psalm singing among the Congregationalist churches. In his preface to the 1707 edition of *Hymns and Spiritual Songs* he had written:

> Perhaps the Modes of Preaching in the best Churches still want some Degrees of Reformation, nor are the Methods of Prayer so perfect as to stand in need of no Correction or Improvement: But of all our Religious Solemnities Psalmodie is the most unhappily manag'd.

The inclusion of psalm versions in both of his earlier collections has already been mentioned. But it was with the publication of *The Psalms of David imitated in the language of the New Testament, and apply'd to the Christian state and worship* in 1719 that his ideals were expressed most vividly, both in an introductory essay and in the psalm versions themselves. This collection included metrical versions of 138 psalms, excluding twelve which Watts thought to be unsuitable for Christian usage.

At the heart of Watts's reforms in writing psalm versions was his concern that the psalms be "Christianized" for use in Christian worship. By this process the content of a psalm was interpreted in light of the life, death, and teachings of Jesus. Thus, Watts's version of Psalm 72 begins "Jesus shall reign where'er the sun does his successive journeys run."

Another Watts concern was for the "naturalizing" of the Psalms, by which they were made directly relevant to the persons singing them. Illustrating this principle is this opening stanza from his version of Psalm 100:

> Sing to the Lord with Joyful Voice;
> Let every Land his Name adore;
> The British Isles shall send the noise
> Across the Ocean to the Shore.

The psalm versions in *The Psalms of David Imitated* were cast predominantly in the familiar metric patterns of his earlier collections and of his predecessors in psalm versification—long, short, and common meters. However, in this collection Watts included four other meters, providing greater variety in the possibilities of metrical construction.

As was the case with *Hymns and Spiritual Songs*, Watts's psalm versions have provided texts which continue to be sung by worshiping congregations today, including the following:

> "From all that dwell below the skies" (Psalm 117)
> "I'll praise my Maker while I've breath" (Psalm 146)
> "Jesus shall reign where'er the sun" (Psalm 72) (38)
> "Joy to the world! the Lord is come" (Psalm 98) (94)
> "O God, our help in ages past" (Psalm 90)

Though its contents have not had significant impact on modern hymnals, Watts's *Divine Songs Attempted in Easy Language for the Use of Children*, published in 1715, was extremely popular in his own day. As the title suggests, the collection was intended for use in the religious instruction of children and was utilized extensively for that purpose.

Tunes for Watts's Hymns   Since Watts wrote his hymns in the meters used for psalm versions, they could be sung to the psalm tunes the people knew. In addition to this body of tunes, there appeared early in the eighteenth century several tune books that provided additional tunes for hymn singing as well as psalm singing. The most important of these tune books are three already mentioned: Playford's *Divine Companion*, 1701; the 1708 *Supplement* to Tate and Brady's *New Version*; and Bishop's *A Set of New Psalm-Tunes in Four Parts*, 1711.

The Significance of Watts   Watts is called the father of English hymnody not because he vastly improved or reformed the hymns that were already being written in his day, nor because of any radical change in form of structure. It is because he produced a "new song" based on the experiences, thoughts, feelings, and aspirations common to all Christians, expressed in what might be called classic objectivity.

STYLE Regarding the practical requirements of congregational song in the hymns of Watts, Benson points out his skill in

> the adaptation of the opening line to make a quick appeal, the singleness of theme that holds the attention undivided, the brevity and compactness of structure and the progression of thought toward a climax, that gives the hymn a unity.[9]

APPROPRIATENESS TO THE SERMON One further aspect of Watts's writing should be noted here. Being of the dissenting tradition and outside the realm of the Church of England, the emphasis of his hymns was related to the sermon of the day rather than to the season of the year. This aspect of appropriateness led him to write hymns that would illustrate, reenforce, and climax the sermon from the pulpit. Perhaps one of the reasons for the enduring quality of so many of these hymns is the fact that they were written during the week in the quiet of his study as the sermon for the coming Lord's Day was taking shape in his mind. Sermon and hymn emerged together, but the hymn remains long after the sermon has been forgotten.[10]

INFLUENCE UPON HIS CONTEMPORARIES The influence of Watts upon his contemporaries can be noted in the hymns of Joseph Addison,[11] Philip Doddridge, Thomas Gibbons, Joseph Hart, and others. Some of these, though lacking Watts's genius and literary skill, were inspired by his work to write hymns. Doddridge, like Watts, was a Congregational minister and carried on the tradition of Watts in the Independent Church. While he wrote in the meters and style of Watts, he did not possess his poetic gift. His hymns are impersonal, yet have a greater awareness of the social message of the gospel than Watts's. His writings reveal the first missionary zeal in hymnic development, anticipating by more than half a century the missionary movement of the early nineteenth century. He wrote about 370 hymns which were published posthumously in 1755 by his devoted friend, Job Orton.

Wesleyan Hymnody

While Charles Wesley was the poet of Wesleyan hymnody, his older brother John must be given recognition as the founder of Methodist hymnody. As the driving force of the Wesleyan movement, he guided skillfully the planning, publishing, and promotion of this new stream of Christian song. He despised the prevalent manner in which the psalms were sung, and he ridiculed the psalmody of the Old Version. He felt keenly the need for revitalization and reform in the practice of congregational singing. As leaders in the Holy Club at Oxford, the Wesleys encouraged psalm and hymn singing. Benson suggests that both the New Version of Tate and Brady as well as the psalms and hymns of Watts were used there.[12]

Visit to America   In 1735, John Wesley sailed for America to visit the British colony in Georgia. He was one of a group of thirteen members of the Oxford "Methodists," which also included his brother Charles. Among the several hymnals he took with him were the New Version and Watts's psalms and hymns. Of strange coincidence was the presence on board ship of twenty-six Moravians who were going to establish a colony in America. In the daily religious services during the voyage, Wesley's group became deeply interested in the enthusiastic singing of these Moravians, and, by the third day at sea, John Wesley had begun serious study of the German language. Soon he was reading and studying the Moravian *Gesangbuch*, and shortly he began to make translations of these German hymns for his use.

The Charlestown Collection   It is unique that the first Wesleyan hymnal was published on American soil, and the hymns written by Wesley for this collection seem to be the first hymns in English to be written in America. During this brief visit to Georgia, John Wesley published *A Collection of Psalms and Hymns* at Charlestown, 1737.[13] Seventy hymns taken from the hymnals and manuscripts that Wesley brought from England, plus the translations he had made from the Moravian hymnal, made up the contents of this collection. The hymns were arranged as a "Christian Week" rather than a Christian Year. They are divided into three sections: for Sunday, for Wednesday and Friday, and for Saturday. Wesley returned to England the following year and there produced his second hymnal, *A Collection of Psalms and Hymns*, London, 1738, which contained seventy-six hymns. As in the Charlestown Collection, about half of the hymns were from Watts, some of which were altered by Wesley.

Other Wesleyan Collections   The year 1739 marked the beginning of intense activity by both Wesleys, but particularly on the part of Charles. The use of hymn singing as an ally to their preaching became very much a trademark of the Wesleyan movement in this year. The third Wesleyan collection, *Hymns and Sacred Poems*, by John Wesley,[14] appeared in this year. It was the first collection to bear the name of either brother. Editions of previous collections and other small pamphlets of hymns followed, and these were largely designed for use in revival services and in the small "societies" that gathered in village and town.

The first major hymnal designed for Sunday and weekday services was *A Collection of Psalms and Hymns*, London, 1741, containing 152 hymns. The concern of the Wesleys for hymn singing and the need for hymns is evidenced by the fact that they published fifty-six collections within a period of fifty-three years. The most comprehensive compilation of Wesley hymns was *A Collection of Hymns for the Use of the People called Methodists*, published in 1780.

Wesleyan Hymn Tunes   The wise judgment of John Wesley was evident in the tunes of the Wesleyan movement as well as in the hymns. While his technical knowledge of music was limited, his genius lay in practical sense and discernment. His basic concern was for tunes which all the people could sing, yet remain within the bounds of sobriety and reverence.

THE FOUNDERY COLLECTION   The first Wesleyan collection to contain tunes was *A Collection of Tunes, set to Music, as they are commonly sung at the Foundery*, 1742. The "Foundery" was the Wesleyan headquarters, located near Moorfields, a suburb of London. For a number of years it had been used by the government for the casting of cannon. However, in 1716 it was almost demolished, and several workmen were killed by an explosion that occurred during the recasting of the guns captured by the Duke of Marlborough in his French wars. The site was abandoned, and it remained in ruins until 1739, when Wesley purchased it and turned it into the first Methodist meetinghouse in London.

The *Foundery Collection* contained forty-two tunes. Because of his dislike for the old psalm tunes, Wesley included only three: OLD 81ST, because of its popularity; OLD 112TH, a German chorale that he especially liked; and OLD 113TH, a favorite tune of his. Wesley was much more considerate of the newer psalm tunes that had appeared in the various editions and supplements of the "New Version," and included among these BURFORD, HANOVER (21) and ST. MATTHEW. There were eleven new tunes, perhaps the finest of which was ISLINGTON.

The influence of Handel is found here in JERICHO TUNE[15], an adaptation from the march of *Riccardo Primo*, an opera that Handel had written fifteen years earlier. Among the fourteen tunes of German origin were the first anglicized versions of WINCHESTER NEW, and AMSTERDAM (47).

> The *Foundery Tune-Book* was one of the worst printed books ever issued from the press; not only is the printing itself bad, but the work is full of the most extraordinary mistakes, such as wrong bars and notes and impossible musical phrases, while in the tune from Handel's opera the editor has simply transcribed the first violin part from the score.[16]

OTHER TUNE COLLECTIONS   One of the two non-Wesleyan tune books used by the Methodists was J.F. Lampe's *Hymns on the Great Festivals, and Other Occasions*, 1746. Lampe, a bassoonist at Covent Garden where Handel's operas were performed, met John Wesley in 1745 and the year following published this collection of twenty-four hymn tunes at his own expense. Perhaps the outstanding collection of this era was *Harmonia Sacra*, 1753, compiled by Thomas Butts, a close friend and companion of the Wesleys. It contained all the Methodist tunes in use at that time and became the source book for subsequent compilations.

In time, John Wesley became dissatisfied with Butts's collection, and, in 1761, published his second tune book under the title, *Select Hymns with Tunes Annext*. The "tunes annext" had a separate title page, *Sacred Melody*, by which title this collection of tunes is known. It contained melodies only. A harmonized version of the 1761 tune book appeared in 1781, entitled *Sacred Harmony*. Here the tunes were arranged for two and three voices, and the hymns for each tune were provided. Wesley's *Pocket Hymn-book for the use of Christians of all Denominations*, 1785, marked the first hymnal inclusion of Thomas Oliver's "The God of Abraham praise" (49).

The character and quality of the Methodist tunes of the late eighteenth century declined. Trivial tunes became widely used, and the overly florid style that became so popular greatly weakened the strength of Methodist hymn singing as the nineteenth century approached.

Significant Contributions of the Wesleys Christian song was never the same after the impact of the Wesleys. Charles, the poet, added some 6,500 hymns to the growing treasure of hymnody. Among the nine hymns given here are some of the finest examples of his writing.

"Blow ye the trumpet, blow" (86)
"Christ the Lord is risen today" (48)
"Christ, whose glory filled the skies"
"Forth in thy name, O Lord, I go"
"Hark, the herald angels sing" (61)
"Jesus, lover of my soul" (70)
"Love divine, all loves excelling"
"O for a thousand tongues to sing" (108)
"Ye servants of God, your Master proclaim" (21)

John Wesley contributed only about twenty-seven hymns and translations,[17] but his role of leader, administrator, teacher, publisher, admonisher, and counselor far exceeded his own literary efforts.

Even more than any quantitative measure of significance is the consideration of what the Wesleyan movement did to the hymn itself. It changed it, both in a literary and in a spiritual sense.

EVANGELICAL EMPHASIS Here was a new evangelical element being sung. The unlimited atonement of Christ which they preached was sung from the pages of the hymnals. The scriptural teaching that Christ died for all mankind and that all mankind must give an account unto God was a basic tenet of their faith. The word "all" must have had a special place in Charles Wesley's vocabulary, for it appears so frequently in his hymnic writing. These were strange sayings in a day when the Calvinistic belief in a limited atonement—that Christ died to save only the "elect"—was widely held.

HYMNS OF CHRISTIAN EXPERIENCE In addition to these hymns of the free gospel—free to all people—were hymns of Christian experience. Charles Wesley's writings ran the gamut of Christian experiences—in public worship as well as in private devotion. For a comparison of the objective writings of Watts with the subjective character of Charles Wesley, it is interesting to contrast "Jesus shall reign where'er the sun" (38) with "O for a thousand tongues to sing" (108). Both hymns follow the same theme—the praise and adoration of Christ. Watts writes impersonally, viewing the worldwide sweep of Christian praise, as

People and realms of every tongue
Dwell on His love with sweetest song.

Wesley, on the other hand, writes of his own personal experience of salvation and the joy that overflows from his conversion.

His blood can make the foulest clean,
His blood availed for me.

Both the Wesleys had great reverence for the Lord's Supper, and constantly admonished their followers regarding the importance of its regular observance. The one hundred and sixty-six hymns included in *Hymns for the Lord's Supper*, published by the Wesleys in 1745, reveal their concern for this ordinance of the church.

LITERARY IMPROVEMENTS   Not only were spiritual changes made, but literary improvements also are evident. The Wesleys contended for lyric quality and poetical beauty in their hymns. Great care was exercised to create hymnic literature of the highest and noblest quality.

METRICAL EXPANSION   Watts confined his hymn writing largely to three meters, but Charles Wesley experimented freely, using thirty different metrical forms. Possibly because the old psalm versions employed iambic meters extensively, he seemed to prefer trochaic meters, for he used them with greater frequency than iambic.

Concern for the Manner of Singing   In addition to the evidence of critical judgment in the writing, publishing, and selection of tunes for their hymns, there was great concern about the manner in which they were sung. In the preface to *Sacred Melody*, 1761, John Wesley gave the following instructions for congregational singing.

I. Learn these *tunes* before you learn any others; afterwards learn as many as you please.

II. Sing them exactly as they are printed here, without altering or mending them at all; and if you have learned to sing them otherwise, unlearn it as soon as you can.

III. Sing *All*. See that you join with the congregation as frequently as you can. Let not a slight degree of weakness or weariness hinder you. If it is a cross to you, take it up, and you will find it a blessing.

IV. Sing *lustily* and with a good courage. Beware of singing as if you were half dead, or half asleep, but lift up your voice with strength. Be no more afraid of your voice now, nor more ashamed of its being heard, than when you sung the songs of Satan.

V. Sing *modestly*. Do not bawl, so as to be heard above or distinct from the rest of the congregation, that you may not destroy the harmony, but strive to unite your voices together, so as to make one clear melodious sound.

VI. Sing *in time*. Whatever time is sung be sure to keep with it. Do not run before nor stay behind it; but attend close to the leading voices, and move therewith as exactly as you can; and take care not to sing *too slow*. This drawling way naturally steals on all who are lazy; and it is high time to drive it out from among us, and sing all our tunes just as quick as we did at first.

VII. Above all sing *spiritually*. Have an eye to God in every word you sing. Aim at pleasing *Him* more than yourself, or any other creature. In order to do this attend strictly to the sense of what you sing, and see that your *Heart* is not carried away with the sound, but offered to God continually; so shall your singing be such as the Lord will approve of here, and reward you when He cometh in the clouds of heaven.[18]

Accompaniment for Hymn Singing   Almost all Wesleyan hymn singing was without any instrumental accompaniment. In the great services they conducted out of doors, any accompanying instrument would have been completely drowned out by the sound of the singing, and very few of the small chapels had sufficient funds to provide for organ installations. During Wesley's lifetime, not more than three chapels introduced organs into the services.[19]

Excerpts from Conference Minutes   Several rather interesting comments have been found by Curwen[20] in the Minutes of the Conferences, which shed additional light upon eighteenth-century Wesleyan hymnody.

From the Minutes of 1763:

> What can be done to make the people sing true? 1. Learn to sing true yourselves. 2. Recommend the tunes everywhere. 3. If a preacher cannot sing himself, let him choose two or three persons in every place to pitch the tunes for him.

From the Minutes of 1765:

> Teach them to sing by note, and to sing our tunes first; take care they do not sing too slow. Exhort all that can in every congregation to sing. Set them right that sing wrong. Be patient herein.

From the Minutes of 1768:

> Beware of formality in singing, or it will creep upon us unawares. "Is it not creeping in already," said they, "by these complex tunes which it is scarcely possible to sing with devotion?" Such is "Praise the Lord, ye blessed ones;" such the long quavering hallelujah annexed to the morning song tune, which I defy any man living to sing devoutly. The repeating the same word so often, as it shocks all common sense, so it necessarily brings in dead formality, and has no more religion in it than a Lancashire hornpipe. Besides that, it is a flat contradiction to our Lord's command, "Use not vain repetitions." For what is vain repetition, if this is not? What end of devotion does it serve? Again, do not suffer the people to sing too slow. This naturally tends to formality, and is brought in by those who have very strong or very weak voices. Is it not possible that all the Methodists in the nation should sing equally quick?

Hymnody of the Evangelical Revival

Before proceeding to the nineteenth century, it is necessary to return to 1741 and pick up the stream of the Evangelical Revival which, at the time, may have been of greater influence in the spread and popularizing of hymn singing than the Methodist or Wesleyan movement.

George Whitefield   George Whitefield had been a co-laborer with the Wesleys, but broke away in 1741 because of doctrinal differences. An immensely popular person and a preacher of rare talent, Whitefield had a large following

of faithful believers. His popularity brought him both fame and strong opposition. Complaints about his preaching were taken to King George II, who replied
that the best way to silence him would be to make him a bishop.

Whitefield attempted no organizational structure of his forces paralleling the
Wesleyan "methods" from which they received their name. From his association with the Wesleys, Whitefield knew the value of hymn singing and continued
it in all of his services. Great crowds thronged to hear him, and wherever he
preached, there was vigorous hymn singing. Gadsby states that "nearly twenty
thousand" made up his audiences in the mining area of Bristol, and the respon-
siveness of these miners to Whitefield's preaching was evidenced by the "white
gutters made by their tears, which plentifully fell down their black cheeks, as
they came out of their coal-pits."[21]

In spite of their fervent hymn singing, the Evangelicals lacked the leadership
of John Wesley and the poetic genius of Charles Wesley in the development of
their hymnody. Nevertheless, some of Whitefield's associates successfully engaged in the writing and publishing of hymns.

Evangelical Collections John Cennick, who was associated with the
Wesleys but separated from them with Whitefield after John Wesley's sermon
was published against the Calvinistic doctrine of election, published *Sacred Hymns
for the Children of God*, London, 1741-1744, and *Sacred Hymns for the Use of
Religious Societies*, Bristol, 1743.

Another associate, Robert Seagrave, published *Hymns for Christian Worship:
partly composed and partly collected from various authors*, London, 1742, in which
appeared "Rise, my soul, and stretch thy wings" (47). Designed for use by his
congregation at Loriner's Hall, London, this latter collection was quite widely used.

When Whitefield opened his new Tabernacle at Moorfields in 1753, he published
his own *Hymns for social worship, collected from various authors, and more particularly design'd for the use of the Tabernacle Congregation in London*. The following year he published a companion tune book, *The Divine Musical Miscellany*.
In this collection Whitefield endeavored to combine the doctrinal and stately
style of Watts with the evangelical fervor of Charles Wesley, Cennick, and
Seagrave. The liberties he took in making textual changes in the Wesleyan hymns
were bitterly resented by the Wesleys. Immensely popular and widely used,
Whitefield's *Hymns* ran through thirty-six editions between 1753 and 1796.

Lady Huntingdon A striking and extraordinary person associated with the
Evangelical Revival was the Countess of Huntingdon. She had a close association with Whitefield, whom she appointed as her chaplain, and at the same
time she was an intimate friend of the Wesleys. In addition to the group of
Evangelical hymn writers, she was a friend of Watts and Doddridge and of Toplady,
who remained in the Established Church, and also of William Williams, the
great Welsh hymnist. Her wide circle of acquaintances included many outstanding musicians, such as Handel and Giardini. While she wrote no hymns, she
was a constant source of encouragement to her many hymn-writing friends and
was directly or indirectly responsible for the publication of at least a dozen
collections.

Edward Perronet, the author of "All hail the power of Jesus' name" (50), which appeared in 1779, had left the Wesleys eight years before the writing of this hymn and had become associated with Lady Huntingdon. MILES LANE, the tune which was published with Perronet's hymn, was written by William Shrubsole. Because of Shrubsole's sympathetic attitude toward the Evangelical and Methodist movements, he was relieved of his post as organist of the Bangor Cathedral in 1784. He spent the remaining twenty-two years of his life as organist of Spa Fields Chapel, one of the chapels established by Lady Huntingdon.

Because of her great wealth and position, Lady Huntingdon was of invaluable assistance to both Evangelicals and Methodists. She was able, through her political influence, to intervene in times of persecution and opposition. After a long and fruitful Christian life, she died in 1791, at the age of eighty-four. Gadsby, writing seventy years later, says:

> I do not know that she ever wrote any hymns, but she compiled a selection which was once or twice enlarged, for the use of her connexion. Her "collegians" have discarded her book, as well as her doctrines, though they stick tenaciously to her endowment.[22]

Independents, Presbyterians, and Baptists

Congregational singing among the nonconformist groups in the eighteenth century shows the dominating influence of the psalms and hymns of Watts. As the popularity of Watts spread, numerous collections were published using either the entire Watts or a large selection from Watts, to which were appended a selection of hymns from other sources—the Wesleys, Toplady, Whitefield, and others. Not infrequently such a publication was motivated by the compiler's desire to attach his own original hymns to the popular hymns of Watts. Simon Browne, Thomas Gibbons, William Jay, and George Burder provided collections designed as an "appendix to Dr. Watts" for use in the Independent churches.

Michaijah Towgood, Michael Pope, and William Enfield were among those who published Presbyterian collections of this type. In the latter part of the eighteenth century, Presbyterianism experienced the influence of Unitarian thought and a concern for liturgical worship, both of which came from the Church of England. These factors are reflected in Presbyterian hymnody in the altering of existing texts to conform to Arian theology, and in the appending of these altered hymns and psalms to a liturgical "form of prayer." Several collections of this type were published for local use. The most widely accepted was Kippis' collection of 1795, which largely left the impression of cold and external piety. "The avoidance of personal Christian experience," says Benson, "seems to leave the worshipper a spectator at Bethlehem and Calvary rather than a participant in redemption."[23]

Those Baptist congregations which overcame the lingering opposition to congregational singing welcomed the psalms and hymns of Watts. By far the most popular collection among the Baptist churches was John Rippon's *A Selection of Hymns from the best authors, intended to be an appendix to Dr. Watts's Psalms and Hymns*, 1787, which marked the first appearance of "How firm a foundation, ye saints of the Lord" (104). Rippon's editorial judgment in appending to Watts the finest hymns of the Wesleyan and Evangelical writers made this collection and its subsequent editions of real significance, and it became the standard of Baptist hymnody well into the nineteenth century. It was used in Spurgeon's Tabernacle, London, until 1866, when it was replaced by Spurgeon's *Our Own Hymnbook*. Rippon's *Selection of Psalm and Hymn Tunes*, published in 1791, provided an important collection of more than two hundred fifty tunes which had far-reaching significance. The influence of Watts and Rippon touched other collections as it became a source book for many compilers both in England and in America.

Moravian Hymnody in England

The Moravian hymnody, which so impressed the Wesleys on their voyage to America, was brought from Herrnhut to England by Moravian missionaries about 1735. Following his return from Georgia, John Wesley associated himself for a while with this small group of Moravians in London and became more closely acquainted with their hymns and tunes. A small collection of English translations of the Herrnhut hymns was published in London in 1742. The lack of literary skill on the part of the Moravian translators and their insistence upon fitting the English versions to the unusual meters of the Herrnhut melodies often resulted in literary awkwardness. Later retranslations and alterations greatly improved the earlier translations.

Together with original Moravian hymns in English, these translations have remained the property of Moravian congregations both in England and America and are seldom found in the broad stream of English hymnody. Two hymns of this eighteenth-century activity in England are: "Christian hearts, in love united," (31) and "Jesus makes my heart rejoice" (32).

Hymn Singing in the Church of England

Throughout the eighteenth century, hymn singing was unauthorized in the Church of England. While this was the official rule, there were many exceptions. Watts's psalm versions were introduced into the service and, in some instances, gradually replaced the New Version, as the literal psalter versions gave way to Watts's versions in the "language of the New Testament." Furthermore, there was the impact of the Wesleyan movement, for most of the leaders of this movement remained ordained ministers of the Established Church. Finally, religious services outside the realm of the regular stated worship services became increasingly popular. It was in such meetings as these—prayer and devotional services—that evangelical power grew within the Church of England, and for these meetings many hymnal collections were compiled and used.

Publications of Madan, Conyers, and Toplady In 1760, Martin Madan published *A Collection of Psalms and Hymns*, London, which contained 170 hymns. While he borrowed many of Whitefield's textual alterations, Madan extensively tampered with many hymn texts, the results of which have been widely copied by subsequent compilers. In 1769, Madan published a tune book for his hymnal, *A Collection of Psalms and Hymn Tunes, never published before*.

Richard Conyer's *A Collection of Psalms and Hymns from various authors: for the use of serious and devout Christians of every denomination*, London, 1767, and Augustus M. Toplady's *Psalms and Hymns for public and private worship*, London, 1776, are collections of somewhat greater significance. Conyers relied heavily on Madan, appropriating approximately two-thirds of his 1760 hymnal. This collection was widely used, especially in northern England, and, as the title indicates, was designed to appeal beyond the limitations of any specific denominational group. Toplady's collection, which included his "Rock of ages, cleft for me," was predominantly Calvinistic. Because of this fact, and Toplady's violent doctrinal disagreement with John Wesley, it is surprising to find several of the Wesleyan hymns included.

All of the aforementioned "unofficial" hymnals of the Church of England have much in common. There was a common urgency to promote and encourage hymn singing and to provide suitable hymns to be sung. They all drew their material from the same sources. Most predominant were the hymns of Watts, plus those of Wesley, Hart, Doddridge, and others. The first works of Newton and Cowper are found here. While most of the titles of these collections included the words "psalms and hymns," there is little evidence of concern for the metrical psalms. Of the group, only Madan, who provided a book of tunes, indicated any interest in the musical aspect of hymn singing.

During the last half of the eighteenth century, the tunes that were used in this transitional period from psalmody to hymnody appeared in numerous collections. In addition to those collections already mentioned, other significant items seem to be: Caleb Ashworth's *A Collection of Tunes*, Manchester, 1760; William Riley's *Parochial Harmony*, London, 1762; Aaron Williams' *The Universal Psalmodist*, London, 1763; Isaac Smith's *A Collection of Psalm Tunes in Three parts*, London, c. 1770; Stephen Addington's *A Collection of Psalm Tunes*, London, 1780; Ralph Harrison's *Sacred Harmony*, London, 1784; James Leach's *A New Sett of Hymn and Psalm-Tunes*, London, 1784; Henry Boyd's *Select Collection of Psalm and Hymn Tunes*, Glasgow, 1793.

The Olney Hymns By far the most important and influential Evangelical hymnal was John Newton and William Cowper's *Olney Hymns*, published in 1779. This collection, containing 280 hymns by Newton and 68 by Cowper, was prepared for the use of the congregation at Olney, where Newton served as curate, 1764-1780.

The people of Olney were lacemakers, working by hand in their damp, ill-lit hovels; they were poor and they were ignorant, and suffered a great deal of hardship. Newton loved them and looked after them, even at the expense of the few wealthy members of his congregation who were by no means pleased to see their church filled up with noisy, uncouth villagers.[24]

A large empty mansion, which stood near the church, was used by Newton for special services, classes for children, prayer meetings, and weekday preaching services. Because of the popularity of these meetings, "The Great House" became the social center of the village in a day when

> there were no traveling facilities for the poor, few schools, no free libraries, and no village forums; to say nothing of popular newspapers, theaters, or broadcasting.[25]

It was in this atmosphere of an attempt at religious education that the hymns of Olney collection were published and used. Five hymns from this collection found in most present-day hymnals are Cowper's "O for a closer walk with God" (27), and "God moves in a mysterious way" (20); and Newton's "How sweet the name of Jesus sounds," "Glorious things of thee are spoken" (85), and "Amazing grace! how sweet the sound" (76).[26]

The Olney Hymns marked a point of transition in the introduction of hymnody in the Church of England. It was the last of a group of hymnals which sought to bring Evangelical hymnody within the Church of England without any effort at accommodation to the Book of Common Prayer.

Official Approval of Cotterill's Collection   Other evangelical books followed, and in their persistence to gain acceptance for hymn singing, efforts were made to adjust and adapt the hymns and hymnals to fit the traditional customs and practices of the Church. After much controversy, Thomas Cotterill's A Selection of Psalms and Hymns for Public Worship, ninth edition, London, 1820, received the approval of Archbishop Harcourt, Archbishop of York. With this long awaited acceptance of hymn singing into the liturgical services of the Anglican Church, the development of hymn writing and the publication of hymnals increased greatly to meet the opportunities thus afforded. Julian lists forty-two hymnals which were published during the first two decades of the nineteenth century for use in the Church of England.[27]

Transitional Writers: Montgomery and Kelly

In the controversy over his hymnal, Cotterill had the stalwart support of James Montgomery, editor of the Sheffield Iris, a radical political publication. Montgomery's hymn, "Angels from the realms of glory," first appeared in an issue of this paper. The Cotterill controversy turned Montgomery's literary talents to hymn writing, and he published two collections: Songs of Zion, 1822, and

Christian Psalmist, 1825. This latter collection contained an introduction which was the first English work on hymnology.

The fervent evangelical preaching of Thomas Kelly, the son of an Irish judge, brought him into disfavor with the archbishop, who restrained him from preaching in Dublin. He withdrew from the Church and established places of worship throughout Ireland. He published *A Collection of Psalms and Hymns*, Dublin, 1802, and *Hymns on Various Passages of Scripture*, Dublin, 1804. In these two collections and their subsequent editions appeared his 765 hymns.

Montgomery and Kelly stand between the eighteenth and nineteenth centuries. These two represent the transitional period between the Wesleyan and the Evangelical hymnody of the eighteenth century and the rising tide of Anglican hymnody of the nineteenth century. Routley[28] refers to Montgomery as "the typical English hymn writer," and to Kelly's hymn, "The head that once was crowned with thorns" (23), as "the greatest English hymn."

ENDNOTES

[1] One example in current usage is the French carol, "Angels we have heard on high," with its Latin refrain, "*Gloria in excelsis Deo.*"

[2] Louis F. Benson, *The English Hymn* (New York: George H. Doran Company, 1915), p. 461.

[3] This included Crossman's "My song is love unknown." (100).

[4] This contained Ken's morning and evening hymns, "Awake, my soul, and with the sun" and "All praise to thee, my God, this night" (41), to each of which was appended his four-line doxology, "Praise God from whom all blessings flow."

[5] Benson, p. 73.

[6] For an informative study of early developments concerning congregational singing in Baptist churches in England, see Robert H. Young, "The History of Baptist Hymnody in England from 1612 to 1800" (unpublished D.M.A. dissertation, University of Southern California, 1959).

[7] See David W. Music, "The Hymns of Benjamin Keach: An Introductory Study," *The Hymn*, Vol. 34, No. 3 (July 1983), pp. 147-154.

[8] For more detailed commentary on this matter, see Harry Escott, *Isaac Watts, Hymnographer* (London: Independent Press, 1962), pp. 37-40.

[9] Benson, p. 208.

[10] "Am I a solider of the cross?" appeared in Watts's *Sermons*, 1721-1724, to conclude a sermon based on I Corinthians 16:13.

[11] See Addison's hymn, "When all thy mercies, O my God" (42).

[12] Benson, p. 223.

[13] For a detailed account of this Charlestown collection, see Robert M. Stevenson, *Patterns of Protestant Church Music* (Durham, N.C.: Duke University Press, 1953), pp. 112-30. Also, see the facsimile reprint of the Charlestown Collection published in 1966 by the Methodist Publishing House, Nashville, Tenn.

[14] In this collection appeared Charles Wesley's "Christ the Lord is risen today" (48), "Hark, the herald angels sing" (61), and "O for a thousand tongues to sing" (108).

[15] See John Wilson, "Handel and the Hymn Tune: I, Handel's Tunes for Charles Wesley's Hymns," *The Hymn* (Vol. 36, No. 4), October 1985, pp. 18-23.

[16] James Lightwood, *Hymn-Tunes and Their Story* (London: The Epworth Press, 1923), p. 122.

[17] See John Wesley's translation, "Jesus, thy boundless love to me."

[18] Cited in Lightwood, pp. xix-xx.

[19] W. J. Townsend (ed.), *A New History of Methodism* (London: Hodder and Stoughton, 1909), I, 515.

[20] John Spencer Curwen, *Studies in Worship-Music* (London: J. Curwen & Sons, 1880), p. 12.

[21] John Gadsby, *Memoirs of the Principal Hymn-Writers and Compilers of the 17th, 18th and 19th Centuries* (London: John Gadsby, 1861), p. 144.

[22] Gadsby, p. 81.

[23] Benson, p. 135.

[24] John Henry Johansen, "The Olney Hymns," *The Papers of The Hymn Society*, XX (New York: The Hymn Society of America, 1956), p. 7.

[25] Johansen, p. 7.

[26] Cf. Hugh Martin, *They Wrote our Hymns* (Naperville, Ill.: Alec R. Allenson, Inc., 1961), pp. 57-80.

[27] John Julian, *A Dictionary of Hymnology.* (London: John Murray, 1915), p. 333.

[28] Erik Routley, *Hymns and Human Life* (New York: Philosophical Library, 1952), pp. 125, 146.

Chapter Five

ENGLISH HYMNODY, II

The Nineteenth Century

The rise of the romantic movement during the last of the eighteenth century reached its full flowering in the nineteenth century. This romantic spirit was a revolt against classical restriction. It was a triumph of subjectivity over objectivity, of emotion and imagination over the intellect and judgment. Literature, art, music, and philosophy were all affected by this change in intellectual life. Creative writing immediately took on an emotional and imaginative quality.

Literary Emphasis in Hymnic Writing The poetic ideals and literary style of the time were reflected in the appearance of hymnic literature which revealed a higher poetical quality than had been evident before. Hymns of didactic design and utilitarian purpose gave way to hymns of poetic feeling and literary art. Reginald Heber is apparent as the most significant hymnist of this period.

In a letter to a friend, John Thornton, dated February 15, 1809, Heber refers to the singing in his church at Hodnet.

> My psalm-singing continues bad. Can you tell me where I can purchase Cowper's *Olney Hymns*, with the music, and in a smaller size, without the music to put in the seats? Some of them I admire much, and any novelty is likely to become a favorite, and draw more people to join in the singing.[1]

From this interest in using *Olney Hymns* to increase the attendance in his services, Heber began to write hymns and proposed to compile a hymnal, which he referred to as a collection of religious poetry. For this collection he solicited hymns from his literary friends, among whom were Scott, Southey, and Milman. Only Milman submitted any hymnic writings.

In 1823, Heber sailed for India, where he served for three short years as Bishop of Calcutta until his death in 1826. The posthumous publication of his collection appeared the following year, entitled *Hymns, written and adapted to the weekly church service of the year*. It contained fifty-seven hymns by Heber, one of which was the familiar "Holy, holy, holy! Lord God Almighty!"

The significance of Heber's *Hymns* lay not only in its literary expression and lyric quality but in the accommodation of these hymns to the liturgical church year. Each Sunday and most Holy Days of the Anglican Church were provided with appropriate hymns, based generally on the teaching of the day as given by the Epistle or Gospel. The inclusion of several earlier translations of Latin hymns was a prelude to the emphasis of the forthcoming Tractarian Movement.

Other hymn writers of the early nineteenth century, whose hymns reflect the romantic spirit in hymnody, with one of their more familiar hymns, are: John Bowring, "In the cross of Christ I glory"; Charlotte Elliot, "Just as I am, without one plea"; Robert Grant, "O worship the King"; Henry Francis Lyte, "Abide with me"; and Hugh Stowell, "From every stormy wind that blows."

Musical Developments New trends in the music of Christian hymnody emerged in the nineteenth century. Tune books were published with greater ease and facility than earlier compilers had experienced. The surge of interest in the teaching of sight singing and the conflict of the "fixed do" method of Wilhem, imported from France, as against the "movable do" method, or tonic sol-fa system developed by Curwen, resulted in the widespread popularity of singing classes. Professional music teachers, such as Joseph Mainzer and John Hullah, became the urban counterpart of the itinerant singing-school teachers of the previous century.

The desire for hymn tunes in the romantic idiom reflected the romantic movement in secular music. Tunes with harmonic enrichment in this style became more in demand than the classical style of the previous period. Both the psalm tunes and the evangelical hymn tunes continued into the nineteenth century, but during the century the characteristics of each became less distinctive. The evangelical tunes lost some of their fervor and became more restrained, while the tunes of the Anglican service revealed more freedom in style.

Samuel Stanley's *Twenty-Four Tunes in four parts*, Birmingham, and Edward Miller's *Sacred Music*, London, both published in 1802, were tune collections of some significance. Miller's collection marked the first English use of AUSTRIAN HYMN (51). The two volumes of William Gardiner's *Sacred Melodies*, London, were published in 1812 and 1815. The latter volume included GERMANY (66) and LYONS. Gardiner's collections introduced the use of adaptations of melodies lifted from the classic works of Haydn, Mozart, Beethoven, and others. The appropriating of these melodies with the necessary alterations to hymn-tune requirements became a fashionable enterprise, and, no doubt, the compilers who indulged in this practice felt that the appearance of the names of outstanding musicians in their collections added greatly to their prestige.

Vincent Novello's *The Psalmist*, published in four volumes, 1833-1843; John Hullah's *Psalter*, 1843, and Henry J. Gauntlett's *Comprehensive Tune Book*, 1846, and *Hallelujah*, 1849, all had as a common objective the improvement of the musical quality of the tunes and the elevation of public taste in this regard. Here was an attempt at renaissance—to restore ancient psalm tunes and popularize the chorale melodies of the Lutheran tradition. Since the emphasis was on the tunes, usually no texts were included. Novello's four volumes, each containing one hundred tunes, were by far the most comprehensive and were very popular. However, few of the tunes which he introduced found a permanent place in English usage.

Tunes of the Methodist tradition from the previous period continued in the early nineteenth century and were used by the Independents and Baptists, as well as the Methodists. More popular than the early Wesleyan tunes, these were more restrained than the florid tunes of the late eighteenth century. Many of these new tunes were written by village musicians, and some were published for local use, while others, such as DIADEM (52), were not published until many years after they had become well known in many towns and villages. William Matthews, composer of MADRID, was a stocking maker by trade, who became a popular village choirmaster and music teacher. These two tunes, DIADEM and MADRID, both having wide melodic range, are typical of this period, and are now known as the "old Methodist tunes."

The Oxford Movement

The third decade of the nineteenth century witnessed the beginning of the Oxford, or Tractarian, Movement which had widespread influence on nineteenth-century English hymnody. This movement was originally known as the Tractarian Movement because of the pamphlets, *Tracts for the Times*, 1833-1841, written by John Henry Newman, John Keble, and E.B. Pusey. Keble, who had published *The Christian Year* in 1827, is credited with initiating this movement by his "Assize Sermon," preached on July 14, 1833, which dealt with the subject of national apostasy. Printed and widely distributed, this sermon marked the beginning of this movement, and the pamphlets of Newman, Keble, and Pusey, covering the fields of church history and doctrine, fanned the flame of Tractarianism throughout England.

Dedicated to this new cause, these men looked with alarm upon the influence of the sweeping evangelical revivals of the previous generations and the increasing strength of evangelicals within the Church of England. They were further concerned with Anglican apostasy and were bold in their efforts at reform. In their attempt to revitalize the Anglican Church through a purification of its service, great interest was aroused in the revival of the practices and ideals of the pre-Reformation Catholic Church.

Influence of the Oxford Movement The influence of the Oxford Movement affected the clergy, the sacraments, and the liturgy. A renewal of conventual life emerged in the concern for personal piety and asceticism on the part of the clergy. Colorful clerical garb, the practice of auricular confession, and the use of the name "Father" reflected the clergy's changing role. Greater respect and importance was placed upon the sacraments of the Church. Re-appraisal of the *Book of Common Prayer* in the light of Tractarian ideals resulted in changes in the Anglican liturgy reflecting the influence of the Roman Breviary.

The great emphasis placed upon the Roman Breviary resulted in the liturgical hymn in the Anglican service. As the liturgy was modeled after the worship of medieval Catholic practice, the content of the hymn was affected, and it was accorded a new place and purpose in the service. In contrasting this new liturgical aspect with the evangelical hymn, Benson states:

> The Evangelical Hymn is inevitably the voice of the believer; the Liturgical Hymn is the voice of the worshipping church. The Evangelical Hymn deals primarily with inward experience; the Liturgical Hymn, even though expressive of common experience, relates it objectively to the hour of worship, the church season or occasion, the ordinance and sacrament. The Evangelical Hymn is free; the Liturgical Hymn, closely articulated liturgical order, having its fixed place which determines its content.[2]

Translations of Greek, Latin, and German Hymns   The awakened interest in the piety and practice of the early church resulted in the appearance of translations of early Greek and Latin hymns, as well as those from German sources. The early Oxford leaders wrote few original hymns, and many of the translations they made were simply literary adventures not intended for hymnic use. Of the many translations made during this period, the following are found among those in common usage today:

Edward Caswall:
> "At the cross her station keeping"
> "Jesus, the very thought of thee" (28)

Frances E. Cox:
> "Sing praise to God who reigns above" (30)

John Ellerton:
> " 'Welcome, happy morning!' age to age shall say" (56)

John Mason Neale:
> "All glory, laud, and honor" (15)
> "Come, ye faithful, raise the strain" (63)
> "Jerusalem, the golden" (60)
> "O come, O come, Emmanuel" (57)
> "Of the Father's love begotten" (3)
> "The day of resurrection" (58)

Philip Pusey:
> "Lord of our life, and God of our salvation" (73)

Catherine Winkworth:
> "All glory be to God on high" (7)
> "Comfort, comfort ye my people" (40)
> "From heaven above to earth I come" (64)
> "If you will only let God guide you" (19)
> "Jesus, priceless treasure" (17)
> "Now thank we all our God" (87)

"O Morning Star, how fair and bright" (10)
"Open now thy gates of beauty" (26)
"Out of the depths I cry to you" (6)
"Praise to the Lord, the almighty" (24)
"Spread, O spread, thou mighty word" (29)
"Wake, awake, for night is flying" (8)

Many of these English versions first appeared in volumes of translations by individual writers. A large number of John Mason Neale's translations appeared in his *Translations of Medieval Hymns and Sequences* and became known to Anglican churches through their inclusion in *The Hymnal Noted*, which first was issued in 1851. Edward Caswall published his translations in *Lyra Catholica* (1849), and those of Catherine Winkworth appeared in *Lyra Germanica* (1855).

Of this group of translators, perhaps the most significant is John Mason Neale, a devout Anglican clergyman who spent most of his ministry as the warden of Sackville College, East Grinstead, a home for the indigent.[3] His strong attachment to the old Breviary hymns caused him to urge the omission of the Protestant hymns from the Anglican service in favor of the translations of medieval hymns. The work of the translators restored to the stream of hymnody a rich heritage long forgotten and provided an enrichment of lasting value in the spirit of medieval thought couched in nineteenth-century vocabulary.

Original Hymnody from the Oxford Movement Although the principal contribution to hymnody of the men associated with the Oxford movement was the rediscovery of the rich treasury of hymn materials from Greek, Latin, and German sources and the consequent translation of a large number of these hymns into English, some important contributions were also made through original text writing. Before the beginning of the Oxford Movement, John Keble had published a collection of hymns for the liturgical year under the title *Christian Year*. Included in this hymnal was "Sun of my soul, thou Saviour dear." Also prior to the movement, John Henry Newman wrote the autobiographical "Lead, kindly Light" (84).

Other lasting hymn contributions from the Tractarians are Frederick William Faber's "Faith of our fathers, living still" and Matthew Bridges's "Crown Him with many crowns."

Hymns Ancient and Modern

In respect to English hymnody, the surging sweep of the Oxford Movement and its resultant influences culminated in *Hymns Ancient and Modern*. The title was in itself a confession of faith in the new movement. Of the 273 hymns in this collection, 131 were of English origin, 132 were Latin translations, and 10 were German translations. Only 12 of the English hymns were new, 119 having been already in use. Provision was made for appropriate hymns for days of the week, feasts, fasts, and services of the *Book of Common Prayer*, occasions and saints' days, including the Annunciation and Purification of The Blessed Virgin Mary.

Forces at work for several decades had prepared the way for this significant compilation. New concepts of worship called for new hymns. Those hymns produced by the Tractarian writers—both originals and translations—were already being used. In the atmosphere of reforming Tractarian influence, this hymnal of High Church spirit appeared and is recognized as a monumental bench mark in the unfolding story of English hymnody.

Francis H. Murray, rector at Chislehurst, Kent, only one of many compilers of Anglican hymnals, was one of the first to express a willingness to discontinue his own publication, if others would do likewise, in order that a new representative collection might be compiled and published. In September, 1858, the initial meeting was held in London, and the October 20, 1858, issue of the Church of England *Guardian* carried an advertisement soliciting contributions for this proposed new hymnal. More than two hundred suggestions were received by Henry Williams Baker, secretary of the committee. After a trial pamphlet of thirty-six pages, containing fifty hymns, was circulated in May, 1859, and a larger trial edition of 108 pages in November, the first edition was published by Novello late in 1860.

The first music edition, with W.H. Monk as musical editor, was published in 1861. Adaptations of German chorales and plainsong melodies to English meters had appeared in W.H. Havergal's *Old Church Psalmody*, 1847, and Thomas Helmore's *Hymnal Noted*, 1852. Monk and those who assisted him drew upon these resources, carefully avoiding those tunes of eighteenth-century evangelical origin. Of the new tunes, Monk contributed seventeen, John B. Dykes, seven, and F.A.G. Ouseley, five.

Hymns Ancient and Modern became a national institution in England and exerted extraordinary influence throughout the English-speaking world. Sales figures of all editions have reached astronomical proportions.

> The total sales since 1860 cannot be ascertained, for the publishers' records were destroyed in the war of 1939-1945, but the hundred million mark was passed many years ago. If we say 150,000,000, we shall not be far wrong.[4]

In spite of its popularity, this hymnal did not become the official hymnal of the Church of England, for no hymnal has ever received such recognition. However, since its appearance one hundred years ago, its imprint is evident in the development of Christian hymnody. All subsequent hymnal compilers are debtors to this hymnal, for they have reprinted its liturgical hymns, copied its format, and maintained the marriages of many texts and tunes which appeared here for the first time together.[5]

Victorian Hymns and Tunes

As the nineteenth century progressed, new hymns reflected new concepts of liturgical emphasis, devotional piety, and humanitarian interests, as well as hymns of personal Christian experience. Never had hymnic writing encompassed such a wide range of Christian expression. In addition to the translations already mentioned, such original hymns as William W. How's "For all the saints" (75), Claudia Hernaman's "Lord, who throughout these forty days," John Ellerton's "The day thou gavest, Lord, is ended" (33), Edward H. Plumptre's "Thine arm, O Lord, in days of old," William Chatterton Dix's "As with gladness men of old," Henry Alford's "Come, ye thankful people, come" (62), Samuel John Stone's "The church's one foundation" (59), and Frances Ridley Havergal's "Take my life and let it be" illustrate the scope of hymnic material produced in England during these years.

New hymns demanded new tunes, and these new tunes played a large role in the acceptance of this new hymnic material. Reflecting secular music influences, these tunes followed the patterns of contemporary part songs. Their appeal often relied more on rich-sounding harmonies than on sturdy melodic lines. As in previous periods, many inferior tunes appeared, but the composers of Victorian hymn tunes gave a new impetus to congregational song as they spoke in the musical language of the day in which they lived. Dyke's NICAEA and ST. AGNES, Smart's REGENT SQUARE (37) and LANCASHIRE (58), Sullivan's ST. KEVIN (63) and FORTUNATUS (56), Elvey's ST. GEORGE'S WINDSOR (62), Wesley's AURELIA (59), Smith's MARYTON, Monk's EVENTIDE, and Baker's QUEBEC (55), rank among the most familiar of these Victorian hymn tunes now in common usage.

Among the collections that added to the repertoire of hymn tunes were the 1868, 1875, and 1889 editions of *Hymns Ancient and Modern*; Henry Smart's *Psalms and Hymns for Divine Worship*, 1867; Arthur S. Sullivan's *The Hymnary*, 1872; Samuel S. Wesley's *The European Psalmist*, 1872; and John Stainer's *The Church Hymnary*, 1898.

Non-Anglican Hymnody

With few exceptions, little significance is found in the hymnals and tune books published by the dissenting church groups—Congregationalists, Baptists, and Methodists—during the last half of the nineteenth century. A great many collections appeared that reprinted hymns in current use, but added little of value beyond that previously mentioned of the Anglican hymnody. A great furor arose among the Congregationalists over a small collection of hymns, *The Rivulet*, published by Thomas T. Lynch in 1855. Known as the "Rivulet Controversy," this difficulty centered around the hymns of Lynch, which dealt with the goodness of God as seen in nature. Strong opposition within the church denounced Lynch's *Rivulet* as an "unspiritual publication," and, as Routley comments, "it was over a handful of hymns that the Congregational Union very nearly floundered."

Hymn singing gained new vitality because of the evangelical revival spirit that appeared about 1858. The fires of evanglism burned brightly through England, Northern Ireland, Wales, and Scotland. While activity was greatest among the Methodists, Baptists, Congregationalists, and Presbyterians, the Anglican Church, in spite of strong opposition by High Church leaders, did not completely escape the influence of this evangelical fervor. First beginning in the larger cities, this movement spread to every village and hamlet. One of the many outgrowths was the establishment of the Salvation Army. Vigorous hymn singing accompanied these revivals, and the hymns of the eighteenth-century Evangelical writers enjoyed a fresh popularity. Hymns of Watts, Wesley, Newton, and others were sung with a new meaning by Christians, who had discovered a new joy in their Christian life, and new converts in their conversion experience.

By the 1870's this evangelistic zeal had prepared the way for Dwight L. Moody, the American evangelist, and his musical associate, Ira D. Sankey, who were outstanding personalities in English evangelical activity for more than two decades. The story of Sankey and the gospel hymn will be dealt with in the development of hymnody in America. It is sufficient to say that the use of "Sankey's songs" among evangelical congregations in England today bespeaks the influence of the "gospel hymn" imported from America.

Hymnic interest awakened late among the psalm-singing Presbyterians in Scotland. The writing of devotional hymns reveals the influence of the Evangelical Awakening that first began in Wales and also a breaking away from the metrical psalms. George Matheson's "O love that wilt not let me go," Elizabeth Clephane's "Beneath the cross of Jesus," and Horatius Bonar's "No, not despairingly" are illustrative of this era. These hymns supplemented the use of the *Scottish Psalter*, and other psalters, with some new tunes, appeared. *The Northern Psalter*, Aberdeen, 1872, marked the first appearance of CRIMOND. In the last half of the century, the influence of Anglican hymnody in Scotland increased, and these efforts culminated in the Scottish *Church Hymnary*, 1898, with John Stainer serving as musical editor.

The hymnody of the Wesleyan and Evangelical Movements had found fertile soil in Wales in the eighteenth century, and the Second Evangelical Awakening in the middle nineteenth century added an increased vigor to Welsh hymn singing. Many tunes from a folk-like tradition emerged, and the melodic strength of these Welsh tunes, together with the virile manner in which they were sung, produced a hymn tune of unusual, distinctive flavor. Early in the twentieth century some of these tunes came into usage in England and America and have added greatly to the repertoire of hymn tunes. LLANGLOFFAN (71), LLEDRED, and Joseph Parry's ABERYSTWYTH (70) illustrate the sturdy vitality so characteristic of these Welsh tunes. John Hughes' CWM RHONDDA (72), written shortly after the turn of the twentieth century, has become widely known.

Near the close of the nineteenth century, John Julian, England's greatest hymnological scholar, produced his *Dictionary of Hymnology*, London, 1892. It is most appropriate that this monumental work should climax a century of almost unbelievable development in congregational song. Between Edward Miller's *Sacred Music*, 1802, and Robert Bridges' *Yattendon Hymnal*, 1899, hymnody had undergone tremendous change, and strangely enough, both of these collections were efforts at reform. Both were produced by men who were greatly dissatisfied—

Miller, with the dullness of psalmody, and Bridges, with the trite conventionality of the Victorian hymnody. The prolific output of hymns and the expansive development of hymnal publications throughout the century produced kaleidoscopic changes in congregational song. Bridges stood at the threshold of a new century and with his *Yattendon Hymnal* opened the door for those who were bold enough to follow. Among the excellent translations of his own which Bridges included in the *Yattendon Hymnal* was "Ah, holy Jesus" (18), his translation of Nicholaus Heerman's "Herzliebster Jesu."

The Twentieth Century

The emphasis of hymn singing in the chapel services of the public schools in England resulted in an unusual development in English hymnody that should be noted here. Beginning in the middle of the nineteenth century, hymnals were published for specific use in these schools—Rugby, Harrow, Marlborough, Repton, Willington, Clifton, Sherburne, and others. Latin translations and hymns of literary excellence found in these collections reveal the strong influence of the Oxford Movement. Tunes in the earlier collections were borrowed from those in common usage. However, toward the end of the century there began to emerge a distinctive "public-school hymn tune" that featured a broad melodic line for unison singing, supported by warm, rich harmonies in the organ accompaniment. Hearing these tunes sung by several hundred boys in a school chapel can be an impressive experience. However, the extremely wide compass of these melodies greatly restricts their usage with the ordinary church congregation. An example of the development of twentieth-century public-school tunes may be seen in W.H. Ferguson's LADYWELL, which appeared in the *Public School Hymn Book*, London, 1919. P.H.B. Lyon's "Lift up your voice, ye Christian folk" (74) was written for the *Rugby School Hymn Book*, 1932.

The hymns and tunes of the early twentieth century indicated a new awakening in English hymnody. Such hymns as G.K. Chesterton's "O God of earth and altar" (71) and John Oxenham's "In Christ there is no east or west" (109) and "Peace in our time, O Lord" gave evidence of growing social consciousness and the revolt against the hymnic ideals of the previous period. A new musical vocabulary appeared through the efforts of Parry, Stanford, Davies, and Vaughan Williams in the growing dissatisfaction with the Victorian tunes of Dykes, Barnby, Wesley, and Stainer. The extreme efforts—both literary and musical—of the compilers of the 1904 edition of *Hymns Ancient and Modern*[6] produced strong opposition and resulted in its failure.

Major Twentieth-Century Hymnals   *Worship Song*, 1905, *The English Hymnal*, 1906, and *Songs of Praise*, 1925, are three outstanding hymnals of the early part of the century. The first of these, the work of Garrett Horder, reveals the fullest expression of the literary hymn since the efforts of Heber.

The English Hymnal, because of its wide variety of material, is one of the most catholic of English hymnals. Under the literary editorship of Percy Dearmer, new hymns and new translations of ancient hymns were added, with a strong emphasis upon high scholarly standards. The refusal of the proprietors of *Hymns Ancient and Modern* to grant permission for the use of forty-four copyrighted tunes (the proprietors were exceedingly wary regarding possible rivals of their hymnal), caused Ralph Vaughan Williams, music editor of *The English Hymnal*, to seek other tunes. Fortunately, he turned to folk melodies, and perhaps the outstanding contribution of this hymnal was the popularizing of the use of folk material for hymn tunes. Two of Vaughan William's folk-tune arrangements are KINGSFOLD (79) and MONKS GATE (83). Among his original tunes appearing in this hymnal are SINE NOMINE (75) and DOWN AMPNEY (82). Also included are a number of French church melodies, such as ISTE CONFESSOR (73). These measured tunes came into use in the cathedrals at Chartres, Rouen, Angers, and other centers of church music in France, replacing the older unmeasured plainsong melodies. Some of these were based on older plainsong melodies, but they were set in major or minor modes and were to be sung in unison and in free rhythm. These tunes have their origin in the French Diocesan Service Books that appeared toward the end of the seventeenth century, through the eighteenth century, and continued into the nineteenth century. A strong nationalistic trend in the Roman Catholic Church in France resulted in a recasting or replacement of the Latin Office Hymns. The musical vocabulary of Christian song was greatly enlarged by *The English Hymnal*, and it has exerted a profound influence upon later hymnals, both in England and America.

Percy Dearmer's *Songs of Praise* (1925) followed the pattern of *The English Hymnal*, yet was more liberal in thought and more daring and adventurous musically. Two brothers, Martin and Geoffrey Shaw, exerted great influence in this collection and made it the most advanced hymnal of its time with regard to its tunes. W.H. Harris's ALBERTA (84), is from the *Enlarged Songs of Praise*, 1932.

The third complete revision of *Hymns Ancient and Modern*, begun in 1939, was published in 1950. One of the new tunes that appeared here in Cyril V. Taylor's ABBOT'S LEIGH (85). The following year the Congregational Union published *Congregational Praise*, replacing the 1916 *Hymnary*. Eric H. Thiman served as chairman of the Musical Advisory Committee and contributed a number of fine tunes. The *BBC Hymnal*, 1951, was prepared as a source book for the hymns used in the religious broadcasts of the British Broadcasting Corporation. The compilers sought to prepare a "popular" hymnal of highest quality without any evidence of denominational restriction. The tunes combine the traditions of the cathedral, the parish church, and the public school.

The Baptist Hymn Book was published late in 1961 and released to the churches in the spring of 1962. Hugh Martin served as chairman of the Editorial Committee, E.P. Sharpe as chairman of the Music Advisory Committee. Maintaining the high quality of other contemporary English hymnals, this publication offers to the English Baptist churches an excellent collection of hymns for congregational singing. The influence of Sankey is evident in the number of gospel songs found in this hymnal. Perhaps this also can be attributed to the evangelistic crusades conducted in England by Billy Graham.

The Anglican Hymn Book, edited by Arthur Pollard (literary editor) and Robin

Sheldon (musical editor), was published in 1965 and was intended to be "a completely new hymn book . . . for use in the Church of England," as indicated in its preface. Among the tunes commissioned for this hymnal is David Willcocks' CONQUERING LOVE, given as an alternate setting for the Ascension hymn, "Let all the multitudes of light" by Frederick B. Macnutt.

The *New Catholic Hymnal* published in 1971 contains both a representative collection of texts and tunes covering a broad historical development and a good selection of tunes and texts published for the first time. Edited by Anthony Petti and Geoffrey Laycock, the hymnal provides interesting new materials both textually and musically. The greatest number of new texts (fourteen) was contributed by Brian Foley. Among the composers whose tunes are included are Lennox Berkeley, Edmund Rubbra, Jean Langlais, and Benjamin Britten, who provided realizations of two melodies from Schemelli's *Gesangbuch*, 1736. One of the more attractive new tunes is Laycock's VERBUM DEI (91), written to be used with Fred Kaan's "God who spoke in the beginning." Another successful combination is Hamish Swanston's "In Babylon Town" (92), which was given a hauntingly beautiful melodic setting in Ian Copley's tune of the same name, which was commissioned for this hymnal and which illustrates the continuing influence of the English carol tradition.

English Hymnal Companions   The "historical edition" of *Hymns Ancient and Modern* (1909) was so designated because of its inclusion of an extended essay by W.H. Frere treating the historical development of hymnody. *The Historical Companion to Hymns Ancient and Modern* (1962), edited by Maurice Frost, retained much of Frere's historical introduction and added detailed notes on the texts and tunes of the 1950 edition, with brief notes on material contained in other editions.

As a source of reference to be used with his *Songs of Praise*, Percy Dearmer produced *Songs of Praise Discussed* (1933). *Companion to Congregational Praise*, published in 1953, was edited by K.L. Parry, with notes on the music by Erik Routley. *The Baptist Hymn Book Companion* appeared in the same year as its hymnal namesake, 1962.

New Developments   New sounds in church music emerged in England in the mid-fifties, and such terms as "light," "pop," and "folk" became labels applied to some new music composed for the churches. An Anglican priest, Geoffrey Beaumont (1903-1970), together with some friends, formed the Twentieth-Century Church Light Music Group. In October, 1956, on a BBC Sunday evening hymn sing, Beaumont introduced his tune CHESTERTON, a new setting for Henry W. Baker's traditional hymn, "Lord, thy word abideth." Two years later, Beaumont introduced his *Twentieth-Century Folk Mass* which caused quite a stir. GRACIAS (87), one of the tunes from Beaumont's "Jazz Mass," is strongly reminiscent of American Tin Pan Alley tunes of the twenties and thirties, which were considered out of date by the forties. Malcolm Williamson (b. 1931) became the first serious musician to write hymn tunes in a popular style. These "pop" tunes, beginning in the early sixties, were usually composed for traditional hymns by eighteenth- and nineteenth-century writers. In the milieu of the sixties, no one was more controversial than Sydney Carter (b. 1915). Frequently satirical in nature, his biting texts were often set to adapted folk or folklike melodies. His most popular hymn is "Lord of the dance," set to the Shaker tune SIMPLE GIFTS. Carter's hymn "It was on a Friday morning" became the subject of considerable controversy when it was included in the *Book of Worship for United States Forces*, 1974.

George W. Briggs (1875-1956), an evangelical Anglican minister, was an early pioneer. His hymns, beginning in the 1920's, expressed new ideas in simple vocabulary and pointed the way for others. One of his later hymns, "God has spoken by his prophets" (140), was written for the Hymn Society of America commemorating the publication of the Revised Standard Edition of the Bible in 1952. Albert Bayly (1901-1984), a Congregational minister, who gave himself to a succession of small churches, mostly in the rural area, began his writing in the mid-1940's. The freshness of his hymns, among which was "What does the Lord require" (149), helped prepare for the rising tide in hymn writing that swelled in the 1960's.

Great changes occurred among the English people and the English churches in the years that followed World War II. An ecumenical spirit, an openness to changes in traditional practices, and a concern for a greater participation on the part of the congregation in worship were evident. With the openness for hymn singing came a need for new hymns to sing, a need that five articulate ministers began to address. In the early 1960's, Timothy Dudley-Smith (b. 1926) wrote his first hymns. By the mid-1960's, the names of Erik Routley (1917-1982) and Brian Wren (b. 1936) appeared on newly written hymns. In the late 1960's, Fred Pratt Green (b. 1901), and Fred Kaan (b. 1926) joined the circle of creative hymn writers in England.

Of these five ministers, Dudley-Smith was Anglican, Fred Pratt Green was Methodist, and Routley, Wren, and Kaan were of the Congregational branch of what became, in 1972, the United Reformed Church of England. Timothy Dudley-Smith, bishop of Thetford, Norwich, since 1981, has produced more than 125 hymns.[7] A skillful practitioner of hymnic writing, he fully understands the craft of poetic writing as related to congregational song. His "Tell out, my soul" (123), a new version of the "Magnificat," written in 1961, reflects the language of the *New English Bible* published earlier the same year. "Sing a new song to the Lord" (124) is a joyful song of praise and worship. Erik Routley's first efforts at hymn writing occurred long after he was well-known in England and America as a distinguished author, lecturer, hymnologist, and church musician. "All who love and serve your city" (128), with Peter Cutts's hymn tune BIRABUS, is a song for city folk, reminding them that God is there. Abounding praise for God's greatness and goodness is the theme of Routley's "New songs of celebration render" (127). From his student days there, in the 1930's, Routley was a familiar presence at Mansfield College, Oxford, and his influence on and encouragement of other hymn writers were most significant.[8]

In the 1960's comfortable and complacent churchgoers were jarred by the hymns of Fred Pratt Green that forced them to confront the realities of the world. In 1968, he wrote "When the church of Jesus" (139) and "Christ is the world's light" (133). Perhaps his best-known hymn is "When in our music God is glorified" (135), written in 1972, to be sung to Charles V. Stanford's hymn tune ENGEL-

BERG. Fred Kaan, born in the Netherlands, has spent his ministerial life in England.[9] More adventuresome in language, and devoid of traditional cliches, his hymns reveal his deep concern for social conscience and the problems of today's world. His hymns include "We meet you, O Christ" (142), "Let us talents and tongues employ" (129), and "God who spoke in the beginning" (91).

Brian Wren received his theological education at Mansfield College, Oxford, and his hymns boldly reflect his theological study, understandings, and his imagination. Two of his earliest hymns were written at Mansfield College: "Lord Christ, the Father's mighty son" (112), to John Wilson's EAST MEADS, and "Christ upon the mountain peak" (134), to Peter Cutts's fascinating tune SHILL-INGFORD. The spontaneity and freshness of Wren's hymns may also be seen in his "I come with joy" (141) and "Thank you, God, for water, soil, and air" (143).

Hymnal Supplements   As an indication of the continuing search for fresh materials, from both historical sources and contemporary writers, for use in the churches of England, several supplements to major hymnals have been published. In the summer of 1969, British Methodists issued *Hymns and Songs* as a supplement to *The Methodist Hymn Book* (1933). This collection included hymns and tunes of the "traditional" type and a sizable number of songs reflecting the folk influence on contemporary hymnody. In the same year, the proprietors of *Hymns Ancient and Modern* published *100 Hymns for Today*. Both of these 1969 supplements included materials from both English and American sources.

Praise for Today, a supplement to *The Baptist Hymn Book* of 1962, not only reflects the influence of contemporary developments in England and the United States, but includes hymns from a variety of other national origins. Published in 1974, it is one of several hymnals from this decade to carry a number of hymns by Fred Kaan (eleven in this compilation).

Two important supplements appeared in 1975. The title of *English Praise: a Supplement to the English Hymnal* is self-explanatory. Though this collection contains fewer "new" texts than the others, it is significant because of its emphasis upon tunes that bear the characteristics of the carol and folk song. Serving a dual function, *New Church Praise* is intended as a supplement for both *The Church Hymnary* (third edition, 1973) and *Congregational Praise* (1951). A substantial percentage of the texts was produced by four contemporary writers: Green, Kaan, T.C. Micklem, and Wren. Principal contributors of new tunes were Micklem, Cutts, and Routley.

Hymns for Today's Church, a large and impressive hymnal, was published in 1982, with Michael Baughen, Bishop of Chester, serving as chairman of the editorial group. The preface points out that

> In many churches the most old-fashioned part of worship is the hymnody with its unrevised language. Yet hymnody is an essential part of 'addressing one another' and of worshipping God.[10]

For this reason, the compilers undertook the task of revising hymns to match today's Bible and liturgy translations by replacing "thee-thou-thy" words with "you-your." This same group is responsible for *Carols for Today*, 1986, presenting

184 carols, old and new, following the basic guidelines of the earlier work.

Recent hymnals and hymnal supplements have provided an opportunity for making known the products of creative writing by contemporary English authors and composers for congregational singing. Future generations in the English-speaking world will sing the hymns and hymn tunes that survive the test of time and usage and be grateful to those who were a part of the exciting movement that brought forth new songs in the last half of the twentieth century.

ENDNOTES

[1] Amelia Shipley Heber, *Memoirs of Reginald Heber, D.D. Bishop of Calcutta* (Boston: John P. Jewett and Company, 1856), p. 50.

[2] Louis F. Benson, *The English Hymn* (New York: George H. Doran Company, 1915), p. 498.

[3] See the account of Neale given in Robert M. Stevenson, *Patterns of Protestant Church Music* (Durham, N.C.: Duke University Press, 1953), pp. 139-50. Also see J. Vincent Higginson, "John Mason Neale and 19th-Century Hymnody: His Work and Influence," *The Hymn*, Vol. 16, No. 4 (October, 1965), pp. 101-17.

[4] W.K. Lowther Clarke, *A Hundred Years of "Hymns Ancient and Modern"* (London: William Clowes & Sons, Ltd., 1960), p. 88.

[5] Cf. Erik Routley, *The Music of Christian Hymnody* (London: Independent Press Limited, 1957), pp. 119-21.

[6] One of the new tunes included here was Parry's INTERCESSOR (81).

[7] Timothy Dudley-Smith, *Lift Every Heart* (Carol Stream, IL: Hope Publishing Company, 1985), pp. 272-284. In this work, an introductory section entitled "Hymns and Poetry—a Personal Reflection" should be studied.

[8] The listing of Routley's 34 hymns and 98 hymn tunes may be found in Carlton R. Young (ed.), *Duty and Delight: Routley Remembered* (Carol Stream, IL: Hope Publishing Company, 1985), pp. 272-284.

[9] For an interesting autobiographical insight into the purposes and methods of Mr. Kaan's hymn writing, see Fred Kaan, "Saturday Night and Sunday Morning," *The Hymn*, Vol. 27, No. 4 (October, 1976), pp. 100-108.

[10] Michael Baughen (ed.), *Hymns for Today's Church* (London: Hodder and Stoughton, 1982).

Chapter Six

AMERICAN HYMNODY, I

Huguenot immigrants to the coast of South Carolina and Florida in 1562-1565 were the first to bring French metrical psalms and psalm tunes to American soil. It is said that native Indians, friendly to these settlers, picked up the French tunes and sang them long after the French settlements were wiped out by the Spaniards. Baird mentions that later visitors to this area would be greeted "with some snatch of a French Psalm uncouthly rendered by Indian voices, in strains caught from the Calvinists."[1]

English psalm tunes first reached America through the visit of Sir Francis Drake to the coast of northern California in June 1579. During the five weeks he and his men camped ashore while ship repairs were being made, friendly Indians visited their camp. Drake's chaplain, Francis Fletcher, tells of the impression that psalm singing made on the Indians during their frequent visits.

> In the time of which prayers, singing of Psalmes, and reading of certaine Chapters in the Bible, they sate very attentively: and observing the end at every pause, with one voice still cried, Oh, as greatly rejoycing in our exercises. Yea they tooke such pleasure in our singing of Psalmes, that whensoever they resorted to us, their first request was commonly this, *Gnaah*, by which they intreated that we would sing.[2]

Psalmody in Colonial America

The Jamestown settlers who arrived in 1607 brought with them from England the Old Version sung to the tunes in Este's *Psalter*, 1592.

The Pilgrims   The Pilgrims who settled at Plymouth, Massachusetts, in 1620, were part of an English Separatist group, led by Robert Browne, who moved to Amsterdam, and later to Leyden, before they ventured to the New World. Because of the beginning of the Thirty Years' War in Germany and the hostility of Cardinal Richelieu in France, the Pilgrim fathers turned to the New World for freedom to exercise their religious and spiritual ideals.

By the time the Pilgrims arrived in Holland, the *Dutch Psalter*, Peter Datheen's 1566 translation of the *Genevan Psalter*, was known and used widely. This was the point of immediate contact through which the French psalm tunes from Geneva came to be known by the Pilgrims, who in turn brought them to America. Henry Ainsworth, a Hebrew scholar and teacher and one of the "Brownists," prepared for this group a new psalter which they felt adhered more closely to the meaning of the original than had the Sternhold and Hopkins psalm versions. The *Ainsworth Psalter*, published in Amsterdam in 1612, contained a new prose translation of each psalm placed adjacent to its metrical versification. Thirty-nine different tunes, borrowed from the traditions of both the Sternhold and Hopkins and Genevan psalters, were provided with Ainsworth's publication. Longfellow refers to this psalter in *The Courtship of Miles Standish*, as he describes Priscilla sitting at home singing.

> Open wide in her lap lay the well-worn psalmbook of Ainsworth
> Printed in Amsterdam, the words and music together,
> Rough-hewn, angular notes, like stones in the wall of a churchyard,
> Darkened and over hung by the running vine of the verses.

Although Ainsworth's *Psalter* was used at Plymouth until the end of the seventeenth century, it did not exert great influence in the further development of psalmody in America.

When the French and the Dutch settled New Amsterdam in 1628, they sang the metrical versions in their respective languages, using the *Genevan Psalter* and the *Dutch Psalter*, but they sang the same tunes. The melodies that Bourgeois had prepared for Calvin's psalters in Geneva were well known to the Dutch.

The Bay Psalm Book   A decade after the landing of the Pilgrims at Plymouth, a larger and more aristocratic group of settlers from England arrived north of Boston. Within ten years of their arrival, these Puritans had produced their own psalter and printed it on their own press at Cambridge. This book, *The Whole Booke of Psalmes Faithfully Translated in English metre*, 1640, commonly known as the *Bay Psalm Book*, was the first book of any kind published in the American Colonies. New translations were made by prominent New England divines who considered Sternhold and Hopkins crude, unscholarly, and much too free. Concerning the origin of this book, Cotton Mather related:

> Resolving then upon a New Translation, the chief Divines in the Country, took each of them a Portion to be Translated: Among whom were Mr. Welde and Mr. Eliot of Roxbury, and Mr. Mather of Dorchester. These, like the rest, were of so different a Genius for their Poetry, that Mr. Shephard of Cambridge, on the Occasion addressed them to this Purpose.

You Roxb'ry Poets, keep clear of the Crime,
Of missing to give us very good Rhime.
And you of Dorchester, your Verses lengthen,
But with the Texts own Words, you will them strengthen.[3]

The ministers who provided the psalm versions for the *Bay Psalm Book*[4] employed only six metrical forms. No tunes were included in this first edition, but the compilers recommended the tunes contained in the *Ravenscroft Psalter* and, for a few psalms, tunes from "our English psalme books," presumably musical editions of Sternhold and Hopkins. The final paragraph of John Cotton's preface to the new psalter sets forth the sincere conviction of those men who contributed to America's first book for Christian song.

> If therefore the verses are not alwayes so smooth and elegant as some may desire or expect; let them consider that Gods Altar needs not our pollishings: Ex. 20. for wee have respected rather a plaine translation, than to smooth our verses with the sweetnes of any paraphrase, and soe have attended Conscience rather than Elegance, fidelity rather than poetry, in translating the hebrew words into english language, and Davids poetry into english meetre; that soe we may sing in Sion the Lords songs of prayse according to his owne will; until hee take us from hence, and wipe away all our teares, and bid us enter into our masters ioye to sing eternall Halleluiahs.

In the decade following the publication of the *Bay Psalm Book* there apparently developed dissatisfaction with many of the versifications which, because of various imperfections in poetic structure, were unsuitable for congregational singing. As Cotton Mather later wrote:

> It was thought that a little more of Art was to be employ'd upon them: And for that Cause, they were commited to Mr. Dunster, who Revised and Refined this Translation; and (with some Assistance from one Mr. Richard Lyon...) he brought it into the Condition wherein our Churches have ever since used it.[5]

The collaboration of Henry Dunster, president of Harvard, and Lyon resulted in the publication in 1651 of the third edition of the *Bay Psalm Book* under a new title, *The Psalms Hymns and Spiritual Songs of the Old and New Testament, faithfully translated into English metre*. It was in this revised form, which became known as the *New England Psalm Book*, that the psalter continued in use for more than a century.

The ninth edition of the *Bay Psalm Book*, 1698, was the first to include music. The thirteen tunes, which appeared in the back of the book, were mostly in common meter and were printed in two parts—soprano and bass—with the sol-fa names printed under the notation on the staff.[6] As a source for these tunes, the editors had used Playford's *Introduction to the Skill of Musick*, the eleventh edition of which had appeared in London in 1687. In addition to these thirteen tunes, the editors reprinted Playford's "instructions for singing the psalms." This seems to be the earliest publication in America using the old English method of solmization, sometimes referred to as "Lancashire Solfa." The syllable names for the notes of the scale, fa, sol, la, fa, sol, la, mi, fa, are identical to those associated with "fasola" singing of the Southern Harmony and Sacred Harp, oblong tune books found in the southern region of the United States in the nineteenth and twentieth centuries.

The *Bay Psalm Book* enjoyed widespread popularity, which extended throughout New England and as far south as Pennsylvania. It replaced Ainsworth's *Psalter* in the Salem church in 1667, and in the Plymouth church in 1692. Twenty-seven editions were published in New England by 1762, and seven years after the first edition appeared, it was reprinted in England, where at least twenty editions followed, the latest being that of 1754. In January 1947, the *Bay Psalm Book* became a matter of public interest when one of the eleven extant first edition copies was sold at public auction in New York for $151,000, at that time the highest price ever paid for a book in the English language.

Psalterium Americanum Cotton Mather, whose writings have provided several helpful bits of information concerning early American psalmody, himself produced a unique, though unsuccessful psalter. His *Psalterium Americanum*, published in 1718, provided psalm versions in blank verse (so that the meaning of the original Hebrew would not be distorted "for the sake of preserving the Clink of the Rhime," as he said in his preface). The psalm versions were written in common meter, but several were adapted to the use of long meter tunes by the addition of two extra syllables, placed in brackets, with each six-syllable line. Thus, the first two lines of Mather's version of Psalm 23 reads:

My Shepherd is th' Eternal God.
I shall not be in [any] want;

Psalm Translations for the Indians John Eliot, "Apostle to the Indians," published at Cambridge in 1661 a versification of the psalms in the language of the Algonquin Indians entitled *Wame Ketoohomae Uketoohomaongash David*. These metrical psalms, bound with the translation of the Bible that Eliot had made earlier, represented some of the first efforts at presenting the gospel to the Indians.

Attempts to Improve Psalm Singing

During the latter part of the seventeenth century, the repertoire of psalm tunes used by the colonists gradually dwindled, and their manner of singing the tunes that were retained became freer, more improvisatory, rather than precisely according to the notes and rhythms in which the tunes had been originally written.[7] Thomas Symmes, in his pamphlet, *The Reasonableness of Regular Singing, or Singing by Note*, explains this trend by saying:

The declining from, and getting beside the rule, was gradual and insensible. Singing Schools and Singing books being laid aside, there was no way to learn; but only by hearing of tunes sung, or by taking the run of the tune, as it is phrased.

The rules of singing not being taught or learnt, every one sang as best pleased himself, and every leading singer, would take the liberty of raising any note of the tune, or lowering of it, as best pleased his ear; and add such turns and flourishes as were grateful to him; . . .

The lack of tune books necessitated the singing of the few tunes familiar to everyone in any given gathering of people. Had there been sufficient tune books, the inability of most people to read by note would have still required the use of only those tunes that were familiar.

The traditional practice of "lining out" the psalm became symptomatic of the conditions of the time. Because of the absence of psalters from which the congregation could sing, a deacon was appointed to "line out" the psalm. He would read aloud a line or two, and then the congregation would join in singing the text that had just been read. In many churches a precentor would lead the singing through the strength of his own voice.[8] As indicated by Symmes's comment cited above, the congregational singing of the psalm tune was characterized by a general lack of uniformity in both melody and rhythm. Tunes were distorted until they became almost unrecognizable, and the breakdown of rhythmic structure reduced the tempo to the slowest possible movement.

The Reformers   In an effort to restore the former practice of psalm singing and to improve the manner in which the people sang, a group of young ministers initiated needed reforms. They desired to teach the people to read music from notes, enabling them to sing from the printed page rather than from memory only. This movement became known as the "new way," "regular singing," and "singing by note," as opposed to the "old way" of singing, sometimes called the "common way" or "singing by rote." The leaders of the "regular singing" movement were John Tufts, Thomas Symmes, and Thomas Walter.

Tufts published a small collection, *An Introduction to the Singing of Psalm-Tunes*, c. 1721. No copies of the first four editions of this first American reprint exclusively devoted to music are known to exist today.[9] An examination of a facsimile reprint of the fifth edition, 1726, reveals thirty-seven tunes arranged for three-part singing.[10] Initial letters, F, S, L, M, of the syllable names, fa, sol, la, mi, were used instead of notes on the staff, and the rhythm was indicated by a system of dot punctuation. For example, "F" was a quarter note; "F." was a half note; and "F:" was a whole note.

> These letters will serve also to measure the *Length* of the Notes, or to show how long each Note is to be sounded. For instance in Common Time, A Letter with two Points on the right side of it thus (F:) is to be sounded as long as you would be distinctly telling, *One, Two, Three, Four.* A Letter with but One Point thus, (F.) is to be sounded while you are telling *One, Two.* A Letter without any Point thus (F) only half so long.[11]

The tunes for the 1726 edition were drawn primarily from John Playford's *Whole Book of Psalms* and Thomas Walter's *Grounds and Rules of Music Explained* (1721 and 1723). Tufts's instructions for singing indicated his familiarity with similar writings by Ravenscroft, Playford (in his *Introduction to the Skill of Musick*) and

Christopher Simpson (*Compendium of Practical Music*). Tufts's *Introduction* evidently filled genuine need, for it went through eleven editions and was frequently bound with copies of the *Bay Psalm Book.*

Thomas Symmes made two important literary contributions to the "regular singing" cause. *The Reasonableness of Regular Singing, or Singing by Note,* printed anonymously in 1720, proposed that the "new way" of singing by note was actually not new, but was the oldest way of psalm singing and needed to be revived. In *Utile Dulci or a Joco-Serious Dialogue, concerning Regular Singing,* a pamphlet published in 1723, Symmes presented a humorous refutation of the principal arguments against the "new way."

Thomas Walter's *The Grounds and Rules of Musick Explained,* 1721, was the other primary literary vehicle for the propagation of the ideas of the reformers.

Early American Singing Schools

The persuasiveness of the advocates of "regular singing" generated a renewed interest in expanding the repertoire of congregational singing and in developing music-reading abilities, especially in urban areas. From this interest emerged the singing school, which became institutionalized in colonial America after the midpoint of the eighteenth century as a means of providing instruction in music reading and in singing psalm tunes and anthems.[12] New and larger tune books were needed as these singing schools increased in popularity.

Urania   The first of the larger tune books was published in 1761 by James Lyon. *Urania,* as Lyon's compilation was entitled, contained psalm tunes, hymn tunes, and anthems from both British and American sources. Among other distinctives, *Urania* was the first American publication to contain a considerable number of settings for four voices, rather than two or three, and it was the first to include fuguing tunes, a type of hymn tune that was to become extremely popular in the late eighteenth century.

The American fuguing tune, like its British counterpart, featured contrasts between homophonic and polyphonic textures. The opening section was customarily homophonic and ended with a cadence, usually on the tonic. There follows a section in which the various voice parts enter imitatively, after which the homophonic texture returns for the final cadence.

Urania was followed by other collections, including Josiah Flagg's *Collection of the Best Psalm Tunes* (1764), Daniel Bayley's *American Harmony* (1769), and Simeon Jocelyn's *Chorister's Companion* (1782). The latter publication included Lewis Edson's LENOX (86), which became one of the most popular fuguing tunes of the period.

William Billings and His Contemporaries   The best-known among the singing-school teachers of the Revolutionary War period was William Billings (1746-1800), who was only twenty-four when he published his first tune book, *The New England Psalm Singer,* in 1770. Billings used this and subsequent collections as he organized and conducted singing schools throughout the area surrounding Boston. The collections, *The Singing Master's Assistant* (1778), *Music in Miniature* (1779), *The Psalm Singer's Amusement* (1781), *Suffolk Harmony* (1786), and *Continental Harmony* (1794), enjoyed widespread usage. While Billings did not originate the fuguing tune,[13] he was successful in composing and popularizing the form. None of Billings' tunes, however, have been retained in present-day hymnals. The texts for which Billings wrote his tunes were drawn from a wide variety of sources, the favorite being the psalm versions and hymns of Isaac Watts.

Billings was not alone in his significance as compiler or composer during the Revolutionary War era. The more significant among his contemporaries were Daniel Read, Samuel Holyoke, and Oliver Holden, whose hymn tune CORONATION is the earliest American tune still in common usage. It was first published in Holden's *Union Harmony*, 1793.

Immigrants and Influences

Immigration in the seventeenth and early eighteenth centuries resulted in numerous settlements of Europeans. Dutch settlers in New York in the 1620s became the first permanent Lutheran settlement. Swedish Lutherans settled a decade later on the Delaware River, southwest of Philadelphia. Mennonites settled in Germantown, Pennsylvania, in 1683. The Dunkards (German Baptists) arrived at Germantown in 1719, and the Moravians, Schwenkfelders, and others established their own settlements in colonial America. All these groups exercised great diligence in maintaining their distinctive characteristics, as well as their native language. Along with their customs, manners, and religious beliefs, they brought their hymns and tunes.

The hymnal the Mennonites brought to America was *Ausbund, Das ist: Etliche schöne Christliche Lieder*. The first American edition was published in Germantown in 1742 and was followed by more than a dozen reprints. It is still used in the present day by the Old Order Amish in Pennsylvania and has the distinction of being the oldest hymn book officially in use by any church in America.[14] *Die Kleine Geistliche Harfe der Kinder Zions*, Germantown, 1803, was the first American Mennonite hymnal.

In 1735 a small group of Moravians landed at Savannah, Georgia. These were followed a few months later by a larger group whose fellow passengers on the voyage were the Wesleys and Governor James Oglethorpe. The missionary work in Georgia was abandoned in 1740, after which these Moravians settled in Philadelphia. The following year a settlement was established at Bethlehem, Pennsylvania. Some of the group moved to North Carolina a few years later, where the chief settlement was established at the site of today's Winston-Salem. In their hymn singing, the Moravians used their Herrnhut hymnal, *Das Gesangbuch der Gemeine in Herrnhut*, 1735, and after their settlement in Pennsylvania, their first American hymnal, *Hirten Lieder von Bethlehem*, was printed at Germantown in 1742. The reluctance of this group to abandon their native tongue for the language of their adopted country is evidenced by the fact that their first hymnal in English, a reprint of the *British Province Hymnal* of 1801, did not appear until 1813.[15]

The first Lutheran hymnal published in the colonies was *Psalmodia Germanica* (1756), a reprint first published in England in 1732. The first English language Lutheran hymnal was *A Hymn and Prayer-Book* (1795), compiled by John Christopher Kunze. In the eighteenth century, other collections of hymns were published by various Lutheran groups reflecting their cultural and language backgrounds—German, Norwegian, Danish, Swedish, and Finnish. Slowly these congregations accepted the English language of the New World for their hymn singing and services.

American Printings of Watts and Wesley   The transition from psalms to hymns in the American colonies, as in England, was a very gradual process which hinged on the psalm versions of Isaac Watts. The poor manner of singing and the controversy of "regular singing" as opposed to "common singing" did not provide fertile soil for the immediate transplanting of Watts's psalms and hymns. A decade after its first appearance in England, Watts's *Psalms* was reprinted in Philadelphia in 1729 by Benjamin Franklin. Appararently Franklin's publication of this work was motivated by his admiration for Watts rather than public demand for the work, for he complained two years later that the copies remained unsold in his shop. The first American edition of Watts's *Hymns and Spiritual Songs* was published in 1739.

John Wesley's *Charlestown Collection*, 1737, published on his visit to Georgia, had no influence on hymnic development in the American colonies at that time. The translations of German hymns which Wesley made on this visit cannot be acknowledged as belonging to American hymnody, yet it is true that they are the earliest English hymns written in America.

It is interesting to reflect that both the beginning of Wesleyan hymnody and the opening to the English-speaking world of the treasury of German worship-song took place in Georgia in the fourth decade of the eighteenth century, when that colony was still only an outpost in the wilderness.[16]

Hymn Singing of the Great Awakening

A revival of religion, known as the Great Awakening, occurred in the American colonies and was accompanied by fervent singing. Launched by Jonathan Edwards, pastor of the Congregational church in Northampton, Massachusetts, this movement endeavored to rescue deteriorating Congregationalism, the established denomination in Massachusetts. Edwards' efforts were greatly aided by the English preacher, George Whitefield, who visited the colonies in 1739-1740. Whitefield preached to great throngs on his tour through the middle and southern colonies, and news of his successes reached New England before his arrival there in 1740.

Emphasizing individual conversion, the preaching of Edwards, Whitefield, and others of the Great Awakening aroused evangelical enthusiasm and opened the way for the Calvinistic hymns of Isaac Watts. Whitefield's admiration for Watts and his high regard for the singing in his services were major factors in the transition from psalmody to hymnody. The spread of Watts's hymns by this movement created a demand for their publication, and the first reprintings were made in Boston, 1739; in Philadelphia, 1742 (by Benjamin Franklin); and in New York, 1752. These opened the way for a flood of publications of Watts's *Psalms and Hymns*, and from Benjamin Franklin's 1729 edition until 1778, almost fifty editions appeared. Many of these contained, in addition to the psalms and hymns of Watts, hymns added by the compilers in an effort to provide a collection acceptable to a particular denominational group. This resulted in the publication of collections known as *Barlow's Watts*, *Dwight's Watts*, *Winchell's Watts*, *Worcester's Watts* and *Worcester's Watts and Select*.

Denominational Activity

With the growth of denominational groups following the Revolutionary War, the hymns they sang and the collections they used became more significant. Opposition to the introduction of new psalm versions among the Presbyterians brought about the "Great Psalmody Controversy." Presbyterian churches split into the "Old Side" and the "New Side" in 1741, and the controversy continued for almost a century. The "Old Side," representing largely the Scottish and Irish influence, clung tenaciously to the psalters of Rous and Barton, while the "New Side" adopted the New Version of Tate and Brady, or Watts's *Psalms*. The Synod of 1787 gave cautious approval to *Barlow's Watts* and left the decision on whether it should replace Rous to the local parishes. In 1802, the General Assembly gave formal authorization to *Dwight's Watts*, and the first official Presbyterian hymnal appeared in 1831.

The Church of England congregations among the colonies used the metrical psalms of the Old Version or the New Version which were bound in at the end of the *Book of Common Prayer*. The forming of these congregations into the Protestant Episcopal Church began in Philadelphia in 1784, and an American edition of the *Prayer Book* was published and officially adopted in 1790, which predated by thirty years the official acceptance of hymn singing by the Church of England. Twenty-seven hymns were added to the metrical psalms, and the inclusion of these hymns marked the first official acceptance of hymnody into Episcopal usage. While it was not achieved without opposition, this transition did not result in the bitter controversy and harmful division experienced by other groups.

Because of controversies concerning it, the practice of congregational singing among the Baptist churches developed slowly. That the *Bay Psalm Book* should have been found in Baptist hands in New England seems highly improbable—at least until many decades had erased from Baptist minds the memories of the persecution they had suffered at the hands of Boston divines, some of whom were responsible for this psalter. John Cotton, who assisted in preparing it and wrote its preface, opposed the Baptists and engaged in extended controversy with Roger Williams. In 1644 a law was passed in Massachusetts primarily designed to stop the preaching of the Baptists. Imprisonment, harsh fines, and public whippings meted out to faithful Baptist preachers are matters of record. The settlement of Baptist Welsh immigrants in Delaware in the early eighteenth century introduced hymn singing to Baptist churches in the middle and southern colonies. While singing had been introduced in the First Baptist Church of Boston by 1728, it was not accepted in the First Baptist Church of Providence, Rhode Island, until 1771, and even then it was accomplished "by allowing the women to vote for it, and caused a division."[17]

Those Baptist churches that felt the impact of the Great Awakening became receptive to the hymns of Isaac Watts. Several collections, intended to be supplementary to Watts, were published that included hymns emphasizing the believer's baptism.

Camp-Meeting Songs

Following the Revolutionary War, pioneer settlements sprang up west of the Alleghenies. Wilderness life in these primitive societies was culturally and spiritually destitute. Moral standards were lax in the dull, isolated existence of the frontier.

> Hard-working Methodist circuit riders, poverty-stricken Baptist farmer-preachers, and self-sacrificing Presbyterian teacher-preachers fought the continuing battle for the Christian faith in that remote border region.[18]

The sudden outbreak of the Great Revival of 1800 occurred in Logan County, Kentucky, under the leadership of James McGready, a Presbyterian preacher. The outdoor revival, or camp meeting, became immensely popular as Presbyterians, Methodists, and Baptists joined forces in meetings that attracted thousands. From Kentucky, the camp-meeting movement spread through Tennessee and the Carolinas into Ohio, Georgia, Virginia, Maryland, Delaware, Pennsylvania, New York, Massachusetts, Connecticut, Vermont, and New Hampshire.[19]

This evangelistic movement on the American frontier produced the camp-meeting hymn. The words were in ballad style, couched in the simplest language, mainly concerned with the salvation of the sinner. The tunes were simple and folklike in character. The refrain, which was most important, was sometimes appended to an existing hymn and tune. Collections of these camp-meeting hymns were not plentiful in the early camp meetings, and those available usually contained words without any tunes. The teaching of these hymns by rote demanded that the tunes be easy, singable, and instantly contagious. Under these circumstances, a popular "catchy," repetitious refrain was of invaluable assistance.

Among the collections prepared for these camp meetings were: David Mintz's *Spiritual Song Book*, North Carolina, 1805; Solomon Wiatt's *Impartial Selection* of *Hymns and Spiritual Songs*, Philadelphia, 1809; John C. Totten's *A Collection of the Most Admired Hymns and Spiritual Songs, with the choruses affixed as usually sung at camp-meetings*, New York, 1809; Thomas S. Hinde's *The Pilgrim Songster*, Cincinnati, 1810; Peggy Dow's *A Collection of Camp-Meeting Hymns*, Philadelphia, 1816; John J. Harrod's *Social and Camp Meeting Songs for the Pious*, Baltimore, 1817; and J. Clarke's *The Camp Meeting Chorister*, Philadelphia, 1827.

After 1805, Presbyterian activity in camp meetings rapidly declined, and by 1825, the outdoor camp meeting was almost exclusively a Methodist institution. Baptists had moved in the direction of the "protracted meeting" held in their churches. Methodist camp-meeting activity continued, particularly among the Pentecostal Holiness branch of Methodism, into the beginning of the twentieth century.

Folk Hymnody

Along with metrical psalms and hymns that were sung in the late eighteenth century, a folk hymnody emerged. These simple folk hymns were found among the Baptists in New England. Uncultured and unlearned, these Baptist folk expressed their strong and uncomplicated faith with these sturdy songs.

> They craved highly emotional preaching and songs of the same type in free rhythms that could be sung to popular melodies with choruses.[20]

Joshua Smith, a Baptist layman of New Hampshire, published *Divine Hymns or Spiritual Songs* (Norwich, 1784). The term "spiritual songs" became synonymous with folk hymnody, and some subsequent collections included a section under this heading. One of the most popular of these folk hymns was the anonymous "Christ the Appletree," which begins

> The Tree of life, my soul hath seen,
> Laden with fruit, and always green:
> The trees of nature fruitless be,
> Compar'd with Christ the Appletree.
>
> This beauty doth all things excell,
> By faith I know, but ne'er tell
> The glory which I now can see
> In Jesus Christ the Appletree.

Other collections of folk materials were Samuel Holyoke's *The Christian Harmonist* (1804) and Jeremiah Ingalls' *Christian Harmony* (1805). The anonymous "I love thee, I love thee" (93) is from Ingalls' collection. In these early collections, texts from Watts, Wesley, Newton, and other familiar hymn writers were used, along with anonymous folk texts. The major emphases of these folk hymns dealt with the repentance of the sinner, the anticipation of death, and the certainty of final judgment. Many of the texts were in the form of religious ballads.

Though these earliest collections of folk hymns originated in New England, the major developments in the history of American folk hymnody occurred in the South.

> The transit of folk-hymnody from the North to the South seems to have taken place during the second decade of the 19th century, roughly coinciding with the retreat of the quasi-folk composed American music of the singing-schools from urban to rural surroundings. During the crucial decade, these two related types of music joined hands, so to speak, and ever since then the Yankee fuguing tune and psalm-tune are found side by side with the folk-hymn. In this form they become a prominent feature of Southern musico-religious life throughout the 19th century.[21]

From this point forward, the history of folk hymnody is closely liked with the development and use of shaped notation.

Shaped Notation

The "fasola" solmization, introduced in America by the English colonists in the seventeenth century and continued by Tufts and Walter, remained in use throughout the eighteenth century. Each subsequent compiler of singing school tune books included prefatory instructions designed to simplify the "rudiments" in order to make music reading easier. Most of these tune books, following European style, use diamond-headed half notes and square whole notes.

The beginning of the nineteenth century saw the introduction of shaped-note heads—a different shaped-note head representing each of the four syllables, *fa, sol, la, mi*. These first appeared in William Smith's and William Little's *The Easy Instructor* (1802) and Andrew Law's *Musical Primer*, fourth edition (1803). Smith and Little used a right-angle triangle for *fa*; a circle, or round head, for *sol*; a square for *la*; and a diamond head for *mi*—all on the five-line music staff. Law used the same four shapes with slightly different arrangement. His *fa* was square, his *la* was the right-angle triangle, and he eliminated the use of the staff. It was the Smith and Little pattern of the shape of the noteheads that was used extensively in the Southern folk hymn publications.

The first important collection to contain folk hymns in shaped notation was John Wyeth's *Repository of Sacred Music, Part Second*, published in Harrisburg, Pennsylvania, in 1813. Wyeth's compilation is significant both for the large number of folk tunes that were put into print for the first time (forty-four) and for its influence on the content of the first important Southern collection, the *Kentucky Harmony* of Ananias Davisson.[22]

Southern Shaped-Note Collections   The use of the shaped notes in four-shape notation spread rapidly to the South and West. As evidence of the increasing popularity of these collections, George Pullen Jackson lists thirty-eight tune books published in the first half of the nineteenth century, twenty-one of which were produced by compilers living in the Southern states.[23]

The first significant Southern collection, Davisson's *Kentucky Harmony*, was copyrighted in 1816, but may have been in use for as long as two years before then. The book's 144 tunes were set in four-part harmony—in contrast to the three-voice pattern that was to become characteristic of many of the later Southern compilations—with the melody in the tenor. In this volume, as well as other folk hymn publications, it is difficult to determine the extent of the original contributions of the compiler, who often attached his name to tunes he had harmonized or arranged as well as to those he had composed.

William Caldwell's *Union Harmony* (1837) bears a close relationship to *Kentucky Harmony*. However, its significance lies in the large number of tunes to which Caldwell's name is attached, but with the admission that many are not original, having been collected and harmonized. Thus, Caldwell made an important contribution through his transcription of a number of melodies from oral tradition which then became a part of American Folk hymn literature.

The Southern Harmony (1835), of William Walker of Spartanburg, South Carolina, and *The Sacred Harp* (1844), by B.F. White and E.J. King, of Hamilton, Georgia, were the two most popular oblong tunebooks in the four-shape tradition, in both sales volume and geographical coverage.

Some of the Southern folk tunes which are found in many hymnals today are AMAZING GRACE (76), FOUNDATION (104), MORNING SONG (98), LAND OF REST (102), HOLY MANNA (106), PISGAH (107), KEDRON (90), and BEACH SPRING (78). George Pullen Jackson refers to this body of tunes as "old Baptist Music,"[24] not because the tunes were sung exclusively by Baptists, but because many of the tunes were used for singing from the words-only hymnal collections of Andrew Broaddus, Jesse Mercer, Staunton S. Burdett, and William Dossey. Many of the tunes were pentatonic, in major, natural minor, or other modes. Harmonizations often used open fourths and fifths.

Around the middle of the nineteenth century, a seven-shape notation pattern began to replace the four-shape notation in some circles. Jesse Aikin's *The Christian Minstrel* (1846) established the seven-shape system. When William Walker published his *Christian Harmony* in 1866, he abandoned the four-shape notation in favor of a seven-shape pattern (not identical to the one used by Aikin) and included an article defending the change. However, the editors of the 1869 edition of *Sacred Harp* decided to retain four-shape notation, after considering the seven shapes.

Other Early-Nineteenth-Century Developments

The desire for a more definitely evangelical hymnody among the progressive Presbyterians and the Congregationalists resulted in Asahel Nettleton's *Village Hymns*, 1824. This collection included no tunes, but above each hymn was printed the name of one or more suitable tunes. Nettleton published shortly thereafter *Zion's Harp*, a collection of tunes for his *Village Hymns*. Nettleton's work became immensely popular, and *Village Hymns* ran through several editions in the first three years. Those churches that used Dwight and Worcester for their services found *Village Hymns* most effective for revival meetings, and the popular acceptance of this collection opened the way for similar collections to follow.

Even more evangelical in style and popular in appeal was *The Christian Lyre,* New York, 1831, by Joshua Leavitt, an associate of Charles G. Finney, the noted evangelist. This collection, primarily intended for use in Finney's meetings, was patterned after the work of Nettleton. Yet, Leavitt went considerably beyond his predecessor, since he "aimed to supply the revival need with somewhat lighter and more songlike hymns with rippling rhythms and sometimes 'choruses.' "[25] In addition to the "revival hymns," Leavitt's collection contained several translations of German and Latin hymns, among which was J.W. Alexander's "O Sacred Head! now wounded." The inclusion of these translations marked the first awareness in America of the richness of this heritage for hymnic use. The popularity of *The Christian Lyre* among the evangelicals is evidenced by the fact that it had passed through twenty-six editions by 1846. One of the tunes from this collection is PLEADING SAVIOUR (97).

Benjamin Carr   In the closing part of the eighteenth century and in the early nineteenth century a number of European musicians who came to America contributed significantly to the development of music in such growing cities as Charleston, Philadelphia, New York, and Boston. Among these professional immigrants was Benjamin Carr, who opened Philadelphia's first music store in 1793, and, as a music publisher, exerted great influence in music activities in that city. ADESTE FIDELES (95), SPANISH HYMN, and PLEYEL'S HYMN were introduced into American usage through his efforts.

Lowell Mason   Lowell Mason was the outstanding musician of his day. Having settled in Boston in 1827, Mason became associated with the Bowdoin Street Church, where his church choir earned national recognition for the quality of its singing. In an effort to improve music in both choir and congregation, Mason began music classes for the children of his church and published *The Juvenile Psalmist, or The Child's Introduction to Sacred Music,* 1829. His concern for the improvement of music in the churches was a basic objective of the Boston Academy of Music, which he founded in 1832. By 1838, he had gained approval for the teaching of vocal music in the public schools of Boston in "preparation for making the praise of God glorious in families and churches." In the years that followed, musical conventions became increasingly popular, resulting in 1853 in the formation of the first musical normal institutes. In this later activity Mason was assisted by George F. Root, Thomas Hastings, and William B. Bradbury.

"Lowell Mason carried on his pioneer work in the training of music teachers for nearly twenty-five years, and through teachers' classes, musical conventions, lectures on the pedagogy of music, teachers' institutes, and musical normal institutes, he provided the United States for more than a generation with most of its training of public school music teachers, as well as a large proportion of its trained church musicians and other professional musicians."[26] In her excellent study of the life and contributions of Lowell Mason, Carol A. Pemberton comments: "The finest tribute to Lowell Mason's total career is the enormous public support Americans now extend to music and musicians, support that owes much to his pioneering efforts and timeless ideals."[27]

Mason was prolific in his publication of collections of music in church and school. Pemberton lists eighty-four collections of music with which Mason was associated either as sole compiler or in collaboration with others.[28] These publications show his recognition of the need for better music, his contributions of original tunes, and his adaptation of tunes from other sources, especially European.[29] OLIVET and MISSIONARY HYMN (80) are his best-known original tunes, and ANTIOCH (94), AZMON (108), and HAMBURG (101) are the most widely used of his adaptations or arrangements.

Greatly alarmed by the popularity of Leavitt's *Christian Lyre*, containing what he considered "inferior music," Mason feared that this collection of lighter songs would undo his efforts to improve church music. With the assistance of Thomas Hastings, Mason published *Spiritual Songs for Social Worship*, 1832, to stem the tide of Leavitt's influence. This venture was extremely successful, and this hymnal, designed not for church worship but for religious gatherings and revival meetings, was widely accepted.

ENDNOTES

[1] Charles W. Baird, *History of the Huguenot Emigration to America* (New York: Dodd, Mead & Company, Inc., 1885), I, 68.

[2] Francis Fletcher, "The World Encompassed by Sir Francis Drake," in H.S. Burrage, ed., *Early English and French Voyages* (New York: Charles Scribner's Sons, 1906), p. 163

[3] Quoted in Zoltan Haraszti, *The Enigma of the Bay Psalm Book* (Chicago: University of Chicago Press, 1956), p. 12. This definitive work was published with a facsimile publication of the *Bay Psalm Book*.

[4] The supposition that Thomas Welde, John Eliot, and Richard Mather were the sole authors of the psalm versions appearing in the *Bay Psalm Book*—an idea conveyed for many years in writings concerning early New England psalmody—has been convincingly refuted in Haraszti, pp. 12-18, 31-60.

[5] Quoted in Irving Lowens, *Music and Musicians in Early America* (New York: W.W. Norton & Company, Inc., 1964), p. 31.

[6] See Richard G. Appel, *The Music of the Bay Psalm Book 9th Edition (1698)* (New York: Institute for Studies in American Music Monographs, Brooklyn College, The City University of New York, 1975).

[7] In Gilbert Chase, *America's Music* (New York: McGraw-Hill Book Company, Inc., 1955), pp. 22-40, this development is treated as the emergence of a folk tradition in American church music.

[8] The experiences of one New England precentor, Samuel Sewell, are recounted in Robert Stevenson, *Protestant Church Music in America* (New York: W.W. Norton & Company, Inc., 1966), pp. 16-18, and Henry Wilder Foote, *Three Centuries of American Hymnody* (Cambridge: Harvard University Press, 1940), pp. 94-5.

[9] The early history of Tufts's *Introduction* is treated in Lowens, pp. 39-57.

[10] John Tufts, *An Introduction to the Singing of Psalm-Tunes*, a facsimile reprint of the fifth edition, with foreword by Irving Lowens (Philadelphia: Printed for *Musical Americana* by Albert Saifer, Publisher, 1954).

[11] Tufts, pp. 5-6

[12] For an interesting description of a "typical" singing school, see George Pullen Jackson, *White Spirituals in the Southern Uplands* (New York: Dover Publications, Inc., 1965; reprint of the book first published by University of North Carolina Press, Chapel Hill, 1933), pp. 8-9.

[13] An enlightening essay concerning the origins of the American fuguing tune appears in Lowens, pp. 237-48.

[14] Lester Hostetler, *Handbook to the Mennonite Hymnary* (Newton, Kans.: General Conference of the Mennonite Church of North American Board of Publications, 1949), p. xxx.

[15] *Hymnal and Liturgies of the Moravian Church* (Unitas Fratrum), p. 4.

[16] Henry Wilder Foote, *Three Centuries of American Hymnody* (Cambridge: Harvard University Press, 1940), p. 145.

[17] Louis F. Benson, *The English Hymn* (New York: George H. Doran Company, 1915), p. 196

[18] Charles A. Johnson, *The Frontier Camp Meeting* (Dallas: Southern Methodist University Press, 1955), p. 18.

[19] Johnson, pp. 67-8.

[20] Benson, p. 201

[21] Lowens, pp. 139-40.

[22] A detailed study of the relationship between Wyeth's *Repository of Sacred Music, Part Second,* and Davisson's *Kentucky Harmony* is made in Lowens, pp. 138-55, and in Lowens' new introduction to Ananias Davisson, *Kentucky Harmony* (Harrisonburg, Va.: The Author, 1816; facsimile reprint, Minneapolis: Augsburg Press, 1976).

[23] Jackson, p. 25.

[24] George Pullen Jackson. *The Story of the Sacred Harp 1844-1944* (Nashville: Vanderbilt University Press, 1944), p. 7.

[25] Benson, p. 377.

[26] Arthur Lowndes Rich, *Lowell Mason* (Chapel Hill: The University of North Carolina Press, 1946), pp. 58-59.

[27] Carol A. Pemberton, *Lowell Mason: His Life and Work* (Ann Arbor: UMI Research Press, 1985), pp. 223-5.

[28] Pemberton, p. 213.

[29] For a listing of these tunes, see Henry L. Mason, *Hymn Tunes of Lowell Mason* (Cambridge: The University Press, 1944).

Chapter Seven

AMERICAN HYMNODY, II

The widespread influence of early-nineteenth-century revivals resulted in increased denominational activity in America. The spiritual energy tapped by these revivals found expression in many areas of religious life. A reawakening of great concern for the spreading of the gospel brought about the establishment of various denominational boards to supervise missionary activity both at home and abroad. By 1812 pioneering missionaries had gone forth to such faraway places as India, Ceylon, Africa, and, later, to China and Japan. Opportunities for home missions expanded rapidly as the United States acquired more territory through the Louisiana Purchase, the regions of California, Oregon, and finally, Texas. Before mid-century the boundaries of the United States reached from the Atlantic to the Pacific and from Mexico to Canada.

The idea of Sunday schools, introduced first by the Methodists following the Revolutionary War, was adopted by other groups. But, because of the lack of adequate public schools, these Sunday schools also were used to teach reading and writing. The American Sunday School Union founded in 1824 promoted the spread of Sunday schools and published needed materials for them.

The increase of denominational strength is further seen in the publication of denominational hymnals.

Episcopal With the approval of the 1826 General Convention, *Hymns of the Protestant Episcopal Church of the United States of America,* compiled by William A. Mühlenberg and Henry U. Onderdonck, was published in 1827. Bound with the *Book of Common Prayer,* it became known as the Prayer Book Collection. Watts, Doddridge, Steele, Wesley, and other English hymn writers of the eighteenth century made the major contribution to the 212 hymns in this collection. Also included were hymns by Newton, Cowper, Montgomery, and Heber. In addition to these imports from England and hymns by the compilers, Mühlenberg and Onderdonck, there were hymns by Francis Scott Key, James W. Eastburn, and George Washington Doane.

Methodist   Wesleyan hymns made up the major portion of hymnic material used by the Methodists. Upon the authorization of the Methodist General Conference, *A Collection of Hymns for the use of the Methodist Episcopal Church, principally from the Collection of the Rev. John Wesley* was published in New York in 1821 and slightly revised in 1832. This was the fifth Wesleyan collection produced in America. A sixth edition was published in 1836. These reprints of English Wesleyan collections were largely made up of the hymns of Charles Wesley and did not contain any hymns of American origin, nor any of the camp-meeting hymns so popular among the Methodists of the time.

Unitarian   The most important of several Unitarian collections of the nineteenth century were two compilations by the "two Sams," Samuel Johnson and Samuel Longfellow. *A Book of Hymns*, published in 1846 while both men were fellow students at the Harvard Divinity School, was an effort to produce a collection more in keeping with contemporary theological thought. *Hymns of the Spirit*, 1864, was a collection of theistic hymns, expressive of the compilers' philosophy of universal religion. Included in these collections were works of American Unitarian writers, John Greenleaf Whittier, James Russell Lowell, Jones Very, Theodore Parker, and Harriet Beecher Stowe, as well as hymns by Johnson and Longfellow.

Baptist   Numerous collections were used by Baptist churches in the first half of the nineteenth century. *Winchell's Watts* was generally used throughout the New England states, while *Watts and Rippon* was found in the middle states. Miller's *New Selection*, Cincinnati, 1835, and Buck's *The Baptist Hymnal*, Louisville, 1847, were popular in the South and the West. The finest collection for Baptists was *The Psalmist*, Boston, 1843, compiled by Baron Stow and Samuel F. Smith. Immensely successful in the North, *The Psalmist* met with strong opposition in the South because of the omission of many hymns popular in that area. Richard Fuller and J.B. Jeter published a *Supplement* in 1850, in an attempt to overcome this opposition by the addition of many of the omitted hymns.

Congregational   At mid-century two important hymnals were published for Congregational churches: Henry Ward Beecher's *Plymouth Collection*, 1855, and *The Sabbath Hymn Book*, 1858, compiled by two Andover Theological Seminary professors, Edwards A. Park and Austin Phelps. Beecher's collection, primarily designed for his Plymouth Congregational Church in Brooklyn, New York, was evangelical in character, while the Andover collection was more scholarly in content. Both hymnals were large in size. *The Plymouth Collection* contained 1,374 hymns, and *The Sabbath Hymn Book*, 1,290. These two hymnals mark the transition in the development of hymnody in America from the "psalms and hymns" era to the increasing acceptance of a free and catholic hymnody drawn from all available sources. Here were the forerunners of the modern church hymnal.

John Zundel, organist at Plymouth Church, and Charles Beecher served as music editors for the *Plymouth Collection*. This was the first church hymnal to print the tune above the words on the same page. No doubt the success and popularity of *The Christian Lyre* and *Spiritual Songs for Social Worship* led Henry Ward Beecher to adopt this format for his hymnal. With both words and tunes in the hands of the worshipers, congregational participation in hymn singing took on increased interest and significance in the service.

Mennonite   Throughout most of the nineteenth century, many Mennonite congregations retained their German language hymnals. The *Ausbund* continued in use, and the *Gesangbuch* (1856), brought to this country by Swiss and South German Mennonites, enjoyed widespread usage, becoming the first official hymnbook of the General Conference Mennonite Church. The first American Mennonite hymnal in English was published in Harrisonburg, Virginia, in 1847. Joseph Funk, significant in developments related to shape-note tunebooks in the Shenandoah Valley, was a member of the hymnal committee.[1]

Moravian   The first original hymnal for the Moravian church in America was published in 1851, revised in 1876. In this initial effort, the Moravians relied heavily on Moravian hymnals published in England, adding little of significance from their own congregations. These compilers boldly maintained the hymnody of Moravian tradition, yet there is increasing evidence of the infiltration of hymns and tunes from non-Moravian English and American sources.

Lutheran   Before the late 1800's, most Lutheran hymnals in America were published as two separate books: the hymnal, which contained only the texts, and the chorale book, which included the tunes and was intended to be used by the organist.

> In the course of its youthful years, Lutheran churches in America seemingly did very little to influence the use of Lutheran hymns and chorales in other denominations. Furthermore, instead of creating their own unique hymnody, English-speaking congregations relied on the use of their American neighbors.[2]

One of the earliest English hymnals for American Lutherans was the 1795 *A Hymn and Prayer Book*, prepared by John Christopher Kunze. The first American Lutheran Hymnal of widespread significance was the *Church Book*, published in 1868 for the use of Evangelical Lutheran Congregations.

New Sects   In addition to the expansion and growth of denominational groups, a further outgrowth of the early-nineteenth-century revivals was the appearance of new sects. The most important of these were the Shakers, the Adventists, and the Mormons—all of which had their beginnings in New York or New England. In the activities of these groups and the propagating of their beliefs, hymn singing was a constant aid. Aggressive, intense sectarianism characterized the hymnody of each group.

Shakers, the common name of the United Society of Believers in Christ's Second Appearing, established the first community at New Lebanon, New York, in 1787. Eighteen Shaker villages had been set up in eight states by 1826. Twenty Shaker hymnals were published between 1813 and 1908, and because of this, an extensive body of hymnic literature developed. The hymns of the Shakers expressed belief in the mystical union of the believer with God's Holy Spirit, and in God as a dual person, both male and female. A *Sacred Repository of Anthems and Hymns for Devotional Worship and Praise* (Canterbury, New Hampshire, 1852), was the first hymnal to include music. In their desire for simplicity and practicality, the compilers used alphabet notation for the music without any staff. The last collection, *Shaker Hymnal* (Canterbury, New Hampshire, 1908), contained 225 hymns and 23 anthems.[3]

The Seventh-day Adventists, which began in mid-nineteenth century, were encouraged to sing by their early leaders. The early hymns they wrote reflect the strong faith of this group in the imminent second coming of Christ. The first Adventist compilation was *Hymns for God's Peculiar People That Keep the Commandments of God and the Faith of Jesus*, 1849. For this collection, James White (1821-1881), one of the early leaders, drew freely from existing hymnals of Methodists, Baptists, and others. Early Adventist authors were well represented in this and subsequent hymnals published in 1869 and 1886.

The Mormons, the Church of Jesus Christ of Latter-Day Saints, began in Manchester, New York, in 1827. Three years later, Joseph Smith published his *Book of Mormon*. Smith's wife, Emma, published *A Collection of Sacred Hymns*, in New York, 1836, and again in Nauvoo, Illinois, 1841. To this first hymnal she contributed 90 hymns. Many of these hymns tell of the glories of Mormon history—the revelation to Joseph Smith, the trials and tribulations of the westward journey, and the joyful anticipation of reaching the "promised land" of Utah. The best-known Mormon hymn is William Clayton's "Come, come, ye saints" (99), written in 1846.[4]

The Emergence of the Gospel Song

The issue of slavery became the first major political issue to confront the rapidly expanding nation in the nineteenth century. The revivals early in the century had produced strong opposition to slavery at the grass-roots level. The churches of America were caught in the maelstrom of this upheaval, and major splits resulted in the three most influential groups—Methodists, Baptists, and Presbyterians—prior to the outbreak of war between the states. Of increasing significance was the growth and popularity of the Sunday school movement and the expanding influence of the Young Men's Christian Association (founded in England in 1844, with an organized branch in Boston in 1851). However, by mid-century, the enthusiasm for missions had waned, and in the business prosperity of the decade 1845-1855, interest in churches declined in the towns and cities. In 1857 the third great panic in American history caused thousands of businessmen to close their doors, as banks failed and railroads went into bankruptcy. A new wave of revivalism followed, known as the Second Great Awakening. This reappearance of evangelical fervor found its greatest expression in the interdenominational noon-day prayer meetings held daily in churches and theaters. For use in these noon-day meetings, the Sunday School Union published *Union Prayer Meeting Hymns*, 1858, largely a collection of familiar hymns. The revivalism that immediately preceded the Civil War did much to prepare the way for Moody, Whittle, Pentecost, and other evangelists who appeared later.

Expansion of the Frontier   The population expansion westward continued the movement of the American frontier. The religious activity along this frontier was fervently evangelical in nature and largely led by Methodists, Baptists, and small splinter sects. There were no metropolitan areas of culture, no influential educational centers. In the struggling frontier settlements, the music used in the religious services consisted of folk and camp-meeting hymns. Itinerant evangelists imported the gospel songs to these areas as they became popular in the East and Midwest.

Music Copyrights   Music copyrights played no small role in the development of American hymnody, as legal developments provided protection for music compositions.[5] The Copyright Act of 1831 was the first to include music. This became increasingly significant after the Civil War, when the Registry of Copyrights office was opened about 1870 at Washington in the Library of Congress. Prior to this, the registry of music was handled in the various districts of the states. Owners' refusals to grant permission or their demand for exorbitant fees reduced the number of copyrighted tunes in many hymnals. As a result, the compilers imported an increasing number of public-domain tunes from England. Quite frequently that which was musically superior was at the same time less expensive to use.

The Gospel Song   Perhaps most phenomenal of the developments of Christian song in the second half of the nineteenth century was the appearance and widespread popularity of the gospel song. Neither the name nor the type of these songs was new, but this label was attached to the songs popularized in the Moody-Sankey revivals. In 1874, P.P. Bliss compiled a small collection, *Gospel Songs*, which was published by the John Church Company, Cincinnati. That title became the generic label by which all subsequent songs of this type became known.

Antecedents   The gospel song had its roots in American folk hymnody, which emerged at the turn of the century in Jeremiah Ingalls' *Christian Harmony*, 1805, and the evangelical collections of Asahel Nettleton and Joshua Leavitt. Of equal importance were the camp-meeting collections, the singing-school tune books, and the songs designed for use in the Sunday school movement. All these forces met, merged, and contributed to the development of the gospel song.

The use of the gospel song in the evangelistic movement from about 1870 on had its immediate roots in at least four lines of development: (1) the "praise services" of Eben Tourjee (1834-1890); (2) the hearty singing of large groups attending the annual national conventions of the YMCA and the Sunday School Union; (3) the "services of song" led by Philip Phillips (1834-1895) at Sunday school conventions and evangelistic campaigns both in America and around the world[6] and (4) the influence of Philip P. Bliss (1838-1876) in connection with Moody's early work in Chicago. Tourjee, who founded the New England Conservatory of Music in 1867, began holding "praise services," or "sings," in his home in Warren, Rhode

Island, as early as 1851. The popularity of these meetings increased, and Tourjee's reputation as a musical leader became widely known.

> When the great revival meetings commenced at the Tabernacle in Boston, Dr. Tourjee came forward with a choir of about two thousand voices...In no city have the revivalists been sustained by better music than in Boston; and it is certainly most gratifying to see the accomplished director of the largest musical conservatory in the world thus lending his own personal influence to swell the tide of song that rises from the mighty concourse to the praise of the Redeemer.[7]

Sunday School Songs The enormous output of Sunday school collections beginning in the twenties and continuing into the seventies had much to do with cultivating a taste for a lighter type of religious song among young people. Leaders in publication of these were William B. Bradbury, George F. Root, Silas J. Vale, Asa Hull, William H. Doane, and Robert Lowry. Many of the familiar gospel songs found in denominational hymnals today, such as "What a friend we have in Jesus," "He leadeth me, O blessed thought," "All the way my Savior leads me," and "To God be the glory" (96) first appeared in these collections.

The Revivalist One of the numerous evangelical collections that immediately preceded Bliss and Sankey was *The Revivalist*, 1868, compiled by Joseph Hillman, with Lewis Hartsough as music editor. This collection ran through eleven editions within a few years following its appearance and was most popular among the Methodists in New York. John W. Dadmun, William Hunter, William Mac-Donald, and William G. Fischer were among the more significant contributors to this collection and its subsequent editions.

Philip P. Bliss Bliss was one of the most widely known and best loved musicians of his day. His activities in music-school teaching and in musical conventions took him from New York to Wisconsin and from Michigan to Alabama. For several years he was associated with Root and Cady, a well-known music-publishing firm in Chicago for whom he wrote many songs and which he also represented in his travels in music-convention work. Later, he was associated with the John Church Company of Cincinnati, which published four of his books: *The Charm*, 1871; *The Song Tree*, 1872; *Sunshine*, 1873; and *Gospel Songs*, 1874. Bliss first met Dwight L. Moody in Chicago during the summer of 1869. When he was at home in Chicago between engagements, he frequently sang in Moody's services. The effectiveness of Bliss's singing in these services first brought to Moody an awareness of the real value of music in his work. At Moody's insistence, Bliss abandoned his teaching in 1874 and became song leader for Major D.W. Whittle, a prominent evangelist. Bliss was a prolific songwriter, usually providing both words and music. One of his best-known gospel songs is "Sing them over again to me" (111).

Sankey's "Sacred Songs and Solos" After several years as a YMCA worker, Ira D. Sankey (1840-1908) began his work as songleader and soloist with Dwight L. Moody (1837-1899) in 1870, following their first meeting at a YMCA convention in Indianapolis. In 1872, Moody and Sankey visited England, where Sankey used Philip Phillips' *Hallowed Songs*, with some additional songs in manuscript he had picked up in Chicago before his departure. The demand in England for these manuscript songs prompted him to request the publishers of *Hallowed Songs* to bring out a new edition to which his songs might be appended. When this request was refused, an English publisher, Morgan and Scott, published a twenty-four-page pamphlet of Sankey's songs in 1873, entitled, *Sacred Songs and Solos*. Additional songs were put into subsequent editions, until the 1903 edition contained 1,200 songs. The sales of this collection reflect its extraordinary popularity in England, for in the first fifty years after its publication more than eighty million copies had been sold.[8]

The "Gospel Hymns" Series   Upon his return to America, Sankey discovered *Gospel Songs*, 1874, by Bliss and suggested that they merge their materials and publish a joint collection. *Gospel Hymns and Sacred Songs* appeared in 1875 and was followed by *Gospel Hymns No. 2* in 1876; *No. 3* in 1878; *No. 4* in 1883; *No. 5* in 1887; and *No. 6* in 1891. These six editions were jointly published by Biglow and Main, New York and Chicago, and the John Church Company, New York and Cincinnati. The strange coincidence of copublication no doubt added greatly to the distribution and popularity of these books.

The combination of the two compilers, Bliss and Sankey, and the two publishers, Biglow and Main and the John Church Company, explains to a large degree the dominant role played by this series of gospel song books. Biglow and Main (Sankey's publisher) was founded in 1868 primarily to publish the collections of William B. Bradbury. This firm was familiar to churches as a publisher of Sunday school song books prior to the Bliss and Sankey series. The John Church Company (Bliss's publisher), organized in 1859, was well-established in general music publishing, specializing in vocal and piano music as well as Sunday school collections. They had developed a successful merchandising operation through local retail music dealers, as well as a nation-wide mail-order business. No better plan for merchandising and promoting this book could have been available for Bliss and Sankey. After the death of Bliss in 1876, Sankey was assisted in the later editions of *Gospel Hymns* by James McGranahan and George C. Stebbins

The mainstream of gospel hymnody followed *Gospel Hymns*, and this series remained unchallenged to the end of the century. Gospel songs which first appeared in other collections later became immensely popular through their inclusion in one of these six editions. This series culminated in *Gospel Hymns Nos. 1-6 Complete*, 1894, containing 739 hymns.[9]

Moody Bible Institute   For the training of evangelists and song leaders, Dwight L. Moody founded Moody Bible Institute in Chicago in 1890. This institution has played a major role in gospel hymnody in America. Daniel B. Towner, noted gospel song composer, served as head of the music department from 1893 until his death in 1919. In this strategic position, he exerted a wide influence throughout the nation as he trained evangelical church music leaders.

Fanny J. Crosby   The author of "All the way my Savior leads me" and "To God be the glory" (96) was by far the most prolific writer of gospel song texts. Beginning in the early 1830's, Fanny Crosby's hymn writing continued at a phenomenal rate until shortly before her death in 1915 at the age of ninety-five. An estimate of the number of hymns she wrote has been placed at 8,000. Though blind from infancy, Fanny Crosby lived a radiant life and, to a greater extent than any other person, captured the spirit of literary expression of the gospel song era. While most of her writing was for the Biglow and Main Company, she supplied texts for such composers as Bradbury, Root, Doane, Lowry, Sankey, Sweney, Kirkpatrick, and others.

Distinguishing Characteristics   Simple expressions of Christian experience and salvation characterize these gospel songs.

> The American Gospel Hymn is nothing if it is not emotional. It takes a simple phrase and repeats it over and over again. There is no reasoning, nor are the lines made heavy with introspection. "Tell me the story simply, as to a little child." The feelings are touched; the stiffest of us become children again.[10]

These songs, which appealed to the masses of people, were used most effectively in services of evangelistic emphasis. The tunes were simple, popular melodies, which usually included a refrain. They were quickly learned and easily remembered by the common people. The melodic line was supported by simple harmonic structure with infrequent changes of harmony.

> The old hymn-tune, with fundamental harmony at each beat, moved with the stride and strength of a giant, while the attenuated effect of those American tunes is largely due to their changing the harmony but once in a bar.[11]

Nonetheless, in spite of texts that are light and lacking in lyrical beauty or doctrinal strength and tunes that are melodically trite and harmonically dull, the gospel songs continue after a century of usage, strongly favored by evangelical Christians around the world.

> Gospel hymnody has the distinction of being America's most typical contribution to Christian song. Gospel hymnody has been a plough digging up the hardened surfaces of pavemented minds. Its very obviousness has been its strength. Where delicacy or dignity can make no impress, gospel hymnody stands up triumphing. In an age when religion must win mass approval in order to survive, in an age when religion must at least win a majority vote from the electorate, gospel hymnody is inevitable. Sankey's songs are true folk music of the people. Dan Emmett and Stephen Foster only did in secular music what Ira D. Sankey and P.P. Bliss did as validly and effectively in sacred music.[12]

Translation into Other Languages   American missionaries, carrying the gospel of Christ to other nations, have translated gospel songs into the language of the people and have used them as effective tools of missionary enterprise. An examination of evangelical hymnals from many countries today, in both the eastern and western hemispheres, reveals a surprisingly large number of the songs of Sankey and his followers.

Late-Nineteenth-Century Hymnals

Gospel hymnody had the least influence in those denominational groups that had an authorized hymnal compiled and sanctioned by ecclesiastical authority. This was especially true of the Episcopalians.

Episcopal An American edition of *Hymns Ancient and Modern* was issued in 1862 and was licensed for use in some dioceses. In spite of the fact that this hymnal was not widely used, it left an indelible imprint upon subsequent Episcopal hymnals. *The Hymnal*, 1871-1874, contained no tunes, but five musical editions were published: Goodrich and Gilbert, 1875; Hall and Whiteley; Hutchins, 1872; Pearce, 1872 (?); and Tucker and Rousseau, 1875.

The next revision of *The Hymnal*, 1892, likewise contained no tunes. Six musical editions were published: Messiter, 1893; Tucker and Rousseau, 1894; Hutchins, 1894; Darlington, 1897; Parker, 1903; and Helfenstein, 1909. Of these six musical editions, the one prepared by Hutchins was the most popular and the most widely used.

The Hymnal, 1916, was followed by an authorized music edition entitled *The New Hymnal*, 1918, the first Episcopal hymnal since 1785 to contain tunes and the first effort of the Episcopal Church to standardize the tunes used to the hymns of the official hymnal.

Methodist A number of Methodist hymnals appeared during the nineteenth century published by the three branches of American Methodism. The Methodist Episcopal church issued hymnals in 1849 and again in 1878. The Methodist Protestant Church issued hymnals in 1838 and 1859. *Tribute of Praise and Methodist Protestant Hymnal*, 1882, was a combination of Eben Tourjee's *Tribute of Praise*, 1874, with revision of previous Methodist hymnals, and was the first hymnal by the Methodist Protestants to contain tunes. The last official hymnal of this group was published in 1901.

The Methodist Episcopal Church, South, published its first hymnal in 1847. This collection was amplified in 1851 by *Songs of Zion*. The first tune book for this group, *Wesleyan Hymn and Tune Book*, 1859, contained the hymns of the 1847 collection, with suitable tunes selected by L.C. Everett. In response to the demand for a smaller and less expensive collection, the *New Hymn Book* was issued in 1881. The last official hymnal of this group appeared in 1889.

The first merging of hymnic endeavors among Methodists occurred with the joint publication of the *Methodist Hymnal*, 1905, by the Methodist Episcopal Church and the Methodist Episcopal church, South. The commission that compiled this hymnal had the musical assistance of Peter C. Lutkin, who served as music editor.

Presbyterian Presbyterian hymnals in the last half of the nineteenth century reflected strong influences of *Hymns Ancient and Modern*. The Presbyterian *Hymnal*, 1870, drew heavily on the new translations of Latin hymns, and even to a greater extent on the tunes of Monk and his fellow composers. This collection was replaced by the *Hymnal*, 1895, prepared with great care and effort by the Board of Publication, Philadelphia.

> The whole field of Hymnody was freshly studied with the resources of the new Hymnology; the hymns were chosen in the interests of devotion as distinguished from homiletics, and their text was determined with scrupulousness that had been more common in literature than in Hymnody.[13]

In addition to the tunes of the English composers, the committee selected tunes by American composers which had appeared in the musical editions of the Episcopal *Hymnal* of 1892. Because of its increased popularity, this Presbyterian hymnal established a measure of uniformity in the hymn singing of Presbyterian churches. A revision was made in 1911.

While denominational hymnals were gaining in importance, independent collections were still widely used. A well-known Presbyterian minister, Charles S. Robinson, published no less than fifteen collections, of which the most significant were: *Songs of the Church*, 1862; *Songs for the Sanctuary*, 1865; *Psalms and Hymns and Spiritual Songs*, 1875; *Laudes Domini*, 1885; and *In Excelsis*, 1897. While Robinson included contemporary material in his collections, his hymnals were not as advanced as the denominational collections. Much of the popularity of these books can be attributed to the use of popular tunes by Mason, Hastings, Bradbury, Root, and Greatorex, as well as the work of Joseph P. Holbrook, music editor for most of Robinson's collection.

The southern branch of American Presbyterianism was more conservative and, at the same time, more evangelical than the northern branch and was less influenced by Anglican hymnody. Robinson's *Psalms and Hymns and Spiritual Songs*, 1875, was officially adopted by this group. In 1901, *New Psalms and Hymns* was authorized and published in Richmond.

Congregationalists While many Congregational churches used hymnals compiled by Robinson, there were efforts within the denomination to produce hymnals for these churches. The two most important of this type published in the last half of the nineteenth century were *Hymns of the Faith with Psalms*, Boston, 1887; and Lyman Abbott's *Plymouth Hymnal*, 1893. While both of these collections reveal strong influences of Anglican hymnody, the latter was the more advanced in this respect.

Baptists The only new Baptist collection to appear during the Civil War was William B. Bradbury's *Devotional Hymn and Tune Book*, published by the American Baptist Publication Society, Philadelphia, 1864. Among the new material in this collection was Bradbury's SOLID ROCK (103).

Of the major denominational groups, the Baptists were least affected by the influences of the Oxford Movement and the liturgical hymn. In this period, the most widely used collections, particularly in the North, were: *The Service of Song for Baptist Churches*, 1871, compiled by S.L. Caldwell and A.J. Gordon; *The Calvary Selection of Spiritual Songs*, 1878, a Baptist edition of Robinson's *Psalms and Hymns and Spritual Songs*, 1875, edited by R.S. MacArthur, pastor of the Calvary Baptist Church, New York; and *The Baptist Hymnal*, 1883. William H. Doane's work as one of the music editors of this hymnal is evidence of the growing popularity of his gospel songs among Baptists and of an effort on the part of the denomination to meet the competition of commercially published collections. Hymns by Anglican writers were included, along with seventeen hymns by Fanny J. Crosby. Tunes by Barnby and Dykes were outnumbered by those of Mason and Doane.

The finest Baptist collection of this period was *Sursum Corda*, 1898, edited by E.H. Johnson and published by the American Baptist Publication Society. This hymnal reveals Johnson's disinterest in the gospel song and his greater enthusiasm for Anglican hymns. In an effort to promote Anglican hymn tunes, Johnson included 1,346 tunes for the 856 hymns in this collection. Apparently *Sursum Corda* was too advanced for its day, for it did not approach the popular acceptance of the *Baptist Hymnal*. Regarding Johnson's efforts to raise the standards of hymnody among Baptists, Benson comments:

> It is indeed easier to plan, within the walls of a Seminary, the elevation of the literary and musical standards of a Church's devotion, than to change the habits and tastes of a great body of people who do not share the Seminary's advantages.[14]

Baptist churches in the South used a varied assortment of hymnals during this period. The collections mentioned above, together with more evangelical collections independently published, were used in some churches. Collections then issued in the South, and most popular in the areas where they were produced, were: *The Southern Psalmist*, Nashville, 1858, edited by J.R. Graves and J.M. Pendleton; J.M.D. Cates's *The Sacred Harp*, Nashville, 1867; J.R. Graves's *The New Baptist Psalmist*, Memphis, 1873; and A.B. Cates's *Baptist Songs, with Music*, Louisville, 1879.

Hymns and Hymn Writers   American authors contributed new hymns to many hymnals that appeared in the last half of the nineteenth century. Among the more important of these are John White Chadwick's "Eternal Ruler of the ceaseless round," 1864 (45); John Greenleaf Whittier's "Immortal love, forever full," 1866; Phillips Brooks's "O little town of Bethlehem," 1868; Mary Ann Thomson's "O Zion, haste, thy mission high fulfilling," 1868 (115); Fanny J. Crosby's "To God be the glory, great things he hath done," 1875 (96); Daniel C. Roberts' "God of our fathers, whose almighty hand," 1876; Mary A. Lathbury's "Break thou the bread of life," 1877; Washington Gladden's "O Master, let me walk with thee," 1879 (68); Ernest W. Shurtleff's "Lead on, O King Eternal," 1887; Katherine Lee Bates's "O beautiful for spacious skies," 1893; and Louis F. Benson's "O sing a song of Bethlehem," 1899 (79).

Expansion of Southern Shaped-Note Singing

Following the Civil War shape-note singing expanded throughout the South. The "fasola singing" of the four-shape notation diminished as the popularity of the seven-shape notation rapidly increased. As early as 1816, Joseph Funk (1778-1862), the Mennonite publisher in the Shenandoah Valley of Virginia, published a shape-note collection entitled *Choral Music* for the German-speaking communities of Pennsylvania. His English collection, *Harmonia Sacra*, 1851, jokingly called the "Hominy Soaker," was most popular in Virginia and North Carolina. After the Civil War, Joseph Funk's grandson, Aldine S. Kieffer (1840-1904), established the Ruebush-Kieffer Music Company in Dayton, Virginia. B.C. Unseld (1843-?) of New York, a student of Eben Tourjee and Theodore F. Seward, was invited to teach the first normal music school in Virginia in 1874. To promote the schools and the new music publications, Kieffer began in 1870 a monthly periodical, *Musical Million*,[15] which continued until 1915.

Among the more prominent music teachers that came from Unseld's normal schools in Virginia were Samuel W. Beasley, D.M. Click, A.B. Funk, E.P. Hauser, J.H. Hall, E.T. Hildebrand, George B. Holsinger, A.J. Showalter, and W.M. Weakley. In the years that followed, normal music schools were conducted in Virginia, West Virginia, North and South Carolina, Georgia, Alabama, Kentucky, Tennessee, Louisiana, Arkansas, Missouri, Texas, and Oklahoma (then Indian Territory).

As the popularity of these schools spread, the demand for new songs and new collections grew, and the singing of the seven-shape notation moved westward across the South. A.J. Showalter (1858-1924), a descendent of the Funks of Pennsylvania and an associate of Kieffer, established a music publishing company in Dalton, Georgia, in 1885. James D. Vaughan (1864-1941) and R.E. Winsett (1876-1952) became successful music publishers in Tennessee. Vaughan's first shape-note book appeared in 1900,[16] and Winsett's first book appeared in 1903. E.M. Bartlett (1884-1941) began the Hartford Music Company in Hartford, Arkansas, about 1922. In Texas, the Stamps-Baxter Music and Printing Company (beginning in 1925) and the Stamps Quartet Company (beginning in 1945) became the most influential publishers of shape-note songbooks in the Southwest.

Largely a rural activity, singing conventions have been most popular among Baptist, Methodist, Nazarene, Church of God, Pentecostal, and Holiness groups. In addition to the annual publications of one or two "convention" books, most music publishers produced a shape-note hymnal for churches. To the well-known standard hymns and gospel songs, the "convention" songs that had become favorites were added. One of these was "Farther Along" (113).

The popularity of convention singing reached its peak in the 1930's and early 1940's. The years that followed World War II saw a gradual decline. The urbanization of the South, the closing of rural community schools in favor of consolidated district schools, the mechanization of farm operation, and the technological advances in transportation and communication all contributed to this change. The tradition of gospel singing in the South no longer involved people in singing. Rather they had become spectators to listen to the singing and purchase the record albums and tapes of the performers. The contemporary sound of traditional groups such as the Speer Family, the Masters Five, the Imperials, the Happy Goodmans and others has roots in the heritage of Funk, Kieffer, Showalter, Vaughan, Bartlett, Stamps, and others.[17] But the distinctive technique for teaching music reading so long identified with this musical tradition in America has all but disappeared.

Twentieth-Century Hymnals

Remarkable progress has characterized American hymnody in the twentieth century. Strict denominational lines have given way to a merging of many traditions, as hymnal committees have drawn on the resources of a common heritage for congregational singing. A common core of hymnody has emerged as each new publication has borrowed freely from previous hymnals of other faiths. Editorial standards have steadily risen, resulting in hymnals far superior to those of the previous century. Of particular significance have been the joint efforts of denominational groups in compiling and publishing hymnals. Three major branches of Methodism joined in compiling the *Methodist Hymnal*, 1935. Four Presbyterian groups cooperated in the compilation of *The Hymnbook*, 1955, and the *Service Book and Hymnal*, 1958, was the cooperative effort of eight different Lutheran groups in America.

During recent decades, more well-edited hymnals have been published than in any other period of American hymnody. To make a critical comparative study of these hymnals would be unrealistic and inappropriate. A denominational hymnal is prepared, not for competition or comparison with hymnals of other denominational groups, but solely as a collection of hymns for congregational use in churches of that denomination. While a common core of hymnody is increasingly evident, there remain major distinctive characteristics of the denominational groups themselves. These characteristics, having to do with differences in forms of worship, hymnological heritage, and cultural and economic backgrounds of the people, are inevitable factors in hymnal compilation, Those denominations whose constituency encompasses the full scope of economic, cultural, and geographical distribution encounter the greatest difficulty in providing an acceptable hymnal. In those evangelical groups where local congregations are autonomous, or subject to little ecclesiastical control, acceptability of a hymnal by local congregations becomes of major concern. Acceptability by the people becomes of less concern to groups who by historical tradition have used without question the hymnals prepared by ecclesiastical leadership. This practice usually has produced hymnals of high literary and musical quality.[18]

African Methodist Episcopal   *The A.M.E.C. Bicentennial Hymnal*, 1984, commemorates the two-hundredth anniversary of the African Methodist Episcopal Church. Bishop Vinton Randolph Anderson was chairman of The Commission on Worship and Liturgy, and Robert O. Hoffelt was hymnal editor. The more than 650 hymns in the book encompass a great diversity of material drawn from many sources. Traditional spirituals and black gospel songs are well represented.

Baptist   *Christian Worship*, 1941, was jointly compiled by the Disciples of Christ and the Northern Baptist Convention, now the American Baptist Churches. The same two groups published *The Hymnbook for Christian Worship*, 1970, edited by Charles H. Heaton. It contained much new material, including twenty new texts which came from the Hymn Society of America's search for new hymns. The Association of Free Will Baptists, organized in 1935, and headquartered in Nashville, Tennessee, published the *Free Will Baptist Hymn Book*, 1964.

Southern Baptists have never had an official hymnal. *The Broadman Hymnal*, 1940, compiled by B.B. McKinney, contained forty-one of his original gospel songs, and was widely accepted. So extensive was its use that it became, more than any previous collection, the most generally used hymnal among Southern Baptists. As such, it was a unifying force in congregational singing and gradually displaced other collections.

In 1956, *Baptist Hymnal*, edited by W. Hines Sims, the first hymnal since 1883 with that title, reflected the evangelical spirit of Southern Baptists. Added to the body of gospel songs, the hymnal included many hymns of historic tradition. *Baptist Hymnal*, 1975, edited by William J. Reynolds, was the most eclectic hymnal ever compiled for Southern Baptists. Among new material in the hymnal were plainsong melodies, tunes by Ralph Vaughan Williams, Erik Routley, Eric H. Thiman, Moravian and Lutheran hymn tunes, sacred folk songs from many nations, and songs of the folk and "pop" culture of the late 1960's. Fifty-five twentieth-century Southern Baptist authors and composers contributed to the hymnal.

The New National Baptist Hymnal, 1977, prepared under the leadership of T.B. Boyd, Jr., has provided National Baptist churches with a great variety of hymns for congregational singing.

Church of Christ   *Great Songs of the Church, No. 2*, 1976, and *Gospel Songs & Hymns*, 1978, have been widely used by Churches of Christ. *Great Songs of the Church, Revised*, 1986, is a significant hymnal. Forrest M. McCann, general editor, and Jack Boyd, music editor, have prepared a hymnal that maintains the evangelical spirit of these churches, and includes both historical and contemporary hymnody.

Church of Jesus Christ of Latter-Day Saints   *Hymns for the Church of Jesus Christ of Latter-Day Saints*, 1985, was published in Salt Lake City, Utah. Among its 341 hymns are twenty-six hymns by Emma Smith, which appeared in the 1836 hymnal she compiled.

Church of the Nazarene   Beginning late in the nineteenth century, the present organization dates from 1908, when several scattered holiness groups merged.[19] Since 1904, forty-two collections of hymns and songs have been published for these churches; since 1923, these have borne the imprint of the Lillenas Publishing Company. Three of these hymnals have been authorized by the General Board of the Church of the Nazarene: *Glorious Gospel Hymns*, 1931, *Praise and Worship*, 1953, and *Worship in Song*, 1972. A basic core of 253 hymns have been common to all three hymnals, and reflect the churches' beliefs concerning holiness, Christ, love, heaven, missionary zeal, and salvation.[20]

Covenant The Swedish Evangelical Mission Covenant Church, organized in 1885, had its roots in the Protestant Reformation, the Lutheran State Church of Sweden, and the spiritual awakenings of the nineteenth century. The designation "Swedish" was dropped in 1929, and in 1957 the church took the name The Evangelical Covenant Church of America. The hymnals published by this fellowship over the last hundred years have emphasized hymns of Swedish evangelical tradition such as "Thanks to God for my Redeemer" (126). *The Covenant Hymnal*, 1973, is evidence that The Evangelical Covenant Church of America has grown from "a small emigrant church to a denomination with full stature in the world community."[21]

Episcopal *The Hymnal 1940*, authorized in that year and published in 1943, was considered an important landmark in the development of American hymnals. The scholarly influence of Winfred Douglas made this hymnal significant, not only for the literary quality of its hymns, but also for the character of its tunes. Plainsong melodies and a large number of tunes of American origin were distinctive features. The absence of meter signatures on all the hymn tunes reflects the influence of rhythmically free plainsong. The resources of English hymn tunes were used extensively, and this became a trend in future hymnal compilations.

The Hymnal 1982, the work of the Standing Commission on Church Music of the Episcopal Church, is a distinctive hymnal for this church. Larger in size by 128 pages than the previous hymnal, there was adequate space to reflect the pluralistic nature of the Church. Some new tunes were provided for old texts, and some new texts were mated to old tunes. The result will enrich congregational song in the coming years. Russell Schulz-Widmar served as music editor, and his insights and understandings are reflected in the judgments that were made. New hymns and tunes of English and American authors and composers enrich and enhance the hymnal. This hymnal appeared in 1985, and the acceptance it has achieved assures it a distinguished place in the development of American hymnody for the Episcopal Church.

Lutheran *Service Book and Hymnal*, 1958, was a joint undertaking by eight synodical Lutheran groups—a cooperative effort that produced the most catholic hymnal Lutheran congregations had ever used. Beginning in 1965, the Inter-Lutheran Commission on Worship began work on another hymnal, and the *Lutheran Book of Worship* was published in 1978. The Lutheran Church—Missouri Synod published *Lutheran Worship* in 1982. Both of these hymnals are excellent volumes, carefully compiled and edited and providing the churches with a great body of hymns. Both hymnals emphasize the rich heritage of Lutheran hymnody but present it in different and distinctive ways.

Mennonite *The Mennonite Hymnal*, 1969, was a joint project of the (Old) Mennonite Church and the General Conference Mennonite Church with a committee made up of representatives from both groups. This hymnal is the successor to two earlier collections, *Church Hymnal*, 1927, and *The Mennonite Hymnary*, 1940. Vernon H. Neufeld was chairman of the joint committee, Mary Oyer, executive secretary. *Worship Hymnal*, 1971, edited by Paul Wohlgemuth, published by the General Conference of Mennonite Brethren Churches, is the successor to the Canadian *The Hymn Book*, 1960, and the *Mennonite Brethren Hymnal*, 1953, used in the United States.

Methodist   *The Methodist Hymnal*, 1935, edited by Robert G. McCutchan, was jointly prepared by three major Methodist groups. A genuine effort was made to prepare a collection suitable for congregations both large and small, urban and rural. Primarily for the benefit of rural churches in the South, a shaped-note edition was provided for several years. Harry Emerson Fosdick's "God of grace and God of glory" (72) appeared for the first time with John Hughes's CWM RHONDDA in this hymnal, and McCutchan's judgment in pairing the two has been validated by the fact that this union is now almost exclusively used.

The *Methodist Hymnal*, 1966, was later renamed *The Book of Hymns*. The Methodist Church and the Evangelical United Brethren Church merged to become the United Methodist Church. With Carlton R. Young serving as editor, the Commission on Worship compiled a hymnal that maintained an excellent balance between broad historical and ecumenical representation, and between the richness of the Methodist tradition (there are 77 hymns by Charles Wesley) and contributions of the twentieth century. Among the new tunes first appearing in this hymnal are Lloyd Pfautsch's WALDA and Katherine K. Davis's MASSACHUSETTS (131).

The 1984 General Conference of the United Methodist Church created the Hymnal Revision Committee and instructed it to bring a report to the 1988 General Conference. In the summer of 1985, an unofficial hymnal revision survey was conducted by the *United Methodist Reporter*, a national weekly publication. More than 3,000 respondents indicated that from the 1966 hymnal, the three hymns they most wished to retain were "How great Thou art," "Amazing grace," and "O for a thousand tongues to sing." In response to an inquiry as to additional hymns they desired to find in the new hymnal that were not in the 1966 hymnal, respondents listed as the three top hymns "In the garden," "Because He lives," and "Great is thy faithfulness." In the months that followed in 1985 and 1986, as the Commission continued its work, news releases by the media kept the Methodists and the general public informed. Surely this hymnal in preparation received more publicity in both the secular and religious press than any other hymnal in Christian history. In the *United Methodist Reporter*, John A. Lovelace reported that the committee was reminded by the survey that the hymnal should be for congregations, not for choirs or professional singers, and that the singing needs of small congregations should be kept in mind.

One respondent advised the committee's editor, Dr. Carlton R. Young, "Don't pay any attention to all the acrimonious letters to the editor, and just give us a decent selection that you feel appropriate to honest liturgical expression as we enter the 21st century." Another advised, "Ignore the cranks who write letters to this paper."

Cranks, organists, choir directors, activists, feminists or just plain church members—whoever they are, some 3,000 of them took the time to speak their minds about the proposed revision of the United Methodist hymnal. One thing is sure: They care about it.[22]

Moravian   The 1969 *Hymnal and Liturgies of the Moravian Church*, published by authority of the provincial synods of The Moravian Church in America, replaced the 1923 publication bearing the same title. The most recent hymnal, like its predecessor, draws heavily upon its European chorale heritage. However, the 1969 hymnal includes some of the chorale melodies in their early rhythmic versions (instead of the isometric adaptations of later centuries) for the first time in an American Moravian hymnal. Of the 623 hymns contained, 191 are from Moravian sources.

Presbyterian   *The Hymnal*, 1933, was published by the Presbyterian Church, U.S.A. Clarence Dickinson served as editor, and his experienced judgment as a church musician is reflected in the high quality of the hymns and tunes included. While this has been referred to as a "musician's hymnal" and has been widely used, it has not been a popular collection with the more evangelical congregations in Presbyterianism. This fact was revealed at the time of the compilation of the 1955 *Hymnbook*, when regional groups requested a more functional hymnal, less high church in character.

The Hymnbook, 1955, was jointly prepared by the Presbyterian Church in the United States, the Presbyterian Church in the United States of America, the United Presbyterian Church of North America, and the Reformed Church in America. The need to satisfy the particular demands of these groups accounts for the inclusion of a body of metrical psalms for the Reformed Church and the evangelistic hymns for the Southern Presbyterians. *The Hymnbook* was ably edited by David Hugh Jones.

The Worshipbook, 1972, was produced for the Cumberland Presbyterian Church, the Presbyterian Church in the United States, and the United Presbyterian Church in the U.S.A. The organization of content is interesting, in that the hymns are arranged alphabetically by first line. As many as 122 of the hymns have either text or tune from the twentieth century.

In 1985, a committee was appointed to prepare a new hymnal for the Presbyterian Church (U.S.A.), with a planned release date in 1990.

Reformed Church in America   *Rejoice in the Lord: A Hymn Companion to the Scriptures*, 1985, edited by Erik Routley, is basically the work of one man. Born, reared, educated, and ordained in England, Routley pastored and taught there for many years. At the age of 58, he came to the United States to teach at Westminster Choir College. He was already a highly respected hymnologist, church musician, and author. His prolific writings about hymns and church music were widely circulated. The Hymnbook Committee appointed by the General Synod of the Reformed Church in America chose him to serve as editor and followed his guidance and judgment. The compilation had been completed at the time of his death, October 8, 1982. The hymnal's title, organization, and hymns and

tunes reflect the inventiveness of the editor, and many of his ideas will be ex-
amined, borrowed, adapted, and implemented by subsequent editors and hymnal
committees.

Reorganized Church of Jesus Christ of Latter-Day Saints   *Hymns of the Saints,*
1981, was published in Independence, Missouri. Introduced in a worshp and hymnody institute in Independence in 1981, the hymnal is being used in the United
States, Canada, Australia, New Zealand, and Great Britain. In addition to the
many hymns distinctive to this church, new material was drawn from many sources.

Roman Catholic   Prior to the Second Vatican Council, hymn texts that were
sung as part of the Mass were all drawn from the Roman Missal. Vatican II approved the celebration of the Mass in the vernacular of the people, and some
freedom to use texts outside the Roman Missal was allowed. Such changes resulted
in much diversity among parishes. Latin hymn texts became obsolete, and Catholic
churches sought other options for English texts. The absence of an official Catholic
publisher in the United States has resulted in several independent publishing ventures to provide materials as aids to participation. The need for participation of
the people in the rites of the Church resulted in supplementary hymn bulletins
and leaflets, usually involving some hymns of Protestant tradition. Perhaps the
most widely used early collection to respond to this need was *People's Mass Book,*
1964, revised 1984. By extensive emendation, the compilers of this collection
sought to "Catholicize" hymns by non-Catholic authors. Of the more than a dozen
hymnals published by independent publishers for Catholic churches, three of these
are *Hymns, Psalms, and Spiritual Canticles,* 1983, *Glory and Praise,* 1984, and *Worship III,* 1985. Numerous small paperback booklets, called missalettes, have been
published that include all the Mass texts and music for a month, or a liturgical
season. Robert J. Batastini, president of the Hymn Society of America, 1986-88,
has provided creative leadership in developing contemporary Catholic hymnody
in America. He has sought out authors and composers to provide new hymns
and tunes appropriate for Catholic churches. Two new Eucharist hymns are "You
satisfy the hungry heart" (154) and "I am the Bread of Life" (153).

Seventh-day Adventist   *The Church Hymnal,* 1941, was published for the
churches by the Review and Herald Publishing Association, Washington, D.C.,
and has been used faithfully for more than four decades. A representative committee with C.L. Brooks, and Wayne Hooper, excutive secretary, prepared a new
compilation, *The Seventh-day Adventist Hymnal,* 1985, that will serve the churches
well. The international character of the Seventh-day Adventist Church dictated
that patriotic hymns tied to a single nation be eliminated. The addition of a
number of American folk hymns, Negro spirituals, German chorales, and psalm
tunes has been welcomed. New works by Adventist authors and composers are
included.

United Church of Christ   The union of the Evangelical and Reformed Church
and the General Council of Congregational Christian Churches occurred in 1957.
Prior to this the Evangelical and Reformed Church had published *The Hymnal,*

1940, and the General Council of Congregational Christian Churches had published *The Pilgrim Hymnal*, 1958, edited by Ethel and Hugh Porter. Successor to
these hymnals was *The Hymnal of the United Church of Christ*, 1974, edited by
John Ferguson and William Nelson. Every effort was made to prepare a hymnal
consonant with the ecumenical spirit of the United Church of Christ.

Other Hymnals   Significant hymnals have come from independent publishing
interests unaffiliated with any denominational fellowship. Among the more worthy
of these compilations are:

> *Hymns of the Living Church*, Donald P. Hustad, editor. Carol Stream, IL: Hope
>   Publishing Co., 1974.
> *The New Church Hymnal*, Ralph Carmichael, editor. Woodland Hills, CA: Lex-
>   icon Music, Inc., 1976.
> *Hymns for the Family of God*, Fred Bock, editor. Nashville: Paragon Associates,
>   Inc., 1976.
> *Praise! Our Songs and Hymns*, John W. Peterson and Norman Johnson, compilers.
>   Grand Rapids, MI: Singspiration Music, 1979.
> *Hymns of Faith.* Wheaton, IL: Tabernacle Publishing Company, 1980.
> *The Singing Church.* Carol Stream, IL: Hope Publishing Company, 1985.
> *The Hymnal for Worship and Celebration*, Tom Fettke, editor. Waco, TX: Word Music,
>   1986.
> *Worship His Majesty*, Fred Bock, editor. Alexandria, IN: Gaither Music Co., 1987.

American Hymnal Companions

Of invaluable worth has been the willingness of various denominations to provide handbooks or companion books for their hymnals. Accurate information
of genuine interest relative to both hymn and tune, together with biographical
sketches of authors and composers, all help to broaden understanding. A page-
by-page study of a hymnal and its handbook is a most rewarding adventure in
Christian song.

The first significant American handbook of our century was Robert G.
McCutchan's *Our Hymnody*, 1937, prepared as a manual for the 1935 *Methodist
Hymnal.* McCutchan's painstaking research, his love and concern for congregational song, and his familiarity with hymnic literature are revealed in the pages
of his handbook. Leonard Ellinwood's *The Hymnal 1940 Companion*, 1949, and
Armin Haeussler's *The Story of Our Hymns*, 1952 (Evangelical and Reformed
Church *Hymnal*, 1941), were scholarly works in the finest tradition, bringing to
light the most recent hymnological discoveries of the time. Other hymnal companions produced around the mid-century were W.G. Polack's *The Handbook to
the Lutheran Hymnal*, 1942, and *Handbook to the Mennonite Hymnary*, 1949, by
Lester Hostetler.

Guide to the Pilgrim Hymnal, 1966, by Albert C. Ronander and Ethel K. Porter,
was a companion to the 1958 hymnal. The collaboration of Fred D. Gealy, Austin
C. Lovelace, and Carlton R. Young, under the general editorship of Emory Stevens

Bucke, resulted in *Companion to the Hymnal*, 1970, for the Methodist *Book of Hymns*, 1966. Arthur N. Wake's *Companion to Hymnbook for Christian Worship*, 1970, was for the hymnal jointly compiled for the Christian (Disciples of Christ) and American Baptist churches. *Hymns of Our Faith*, 1964, for the 1956 *Baptist Hymnal*, and the *Companion to Baptist Hymnal*, 1976, for the 1975 hymnal, were written by William J. Reynolds. Rather than serving as a companion to a single hymnal, J. Vincent Higginson's *Handbook of American Catholic Hymnals*, 1976, deals with texts and tunes from Catholic hymnals in common use through 1964, prior to Vatican Council II.

Donald P. Hustad's *Dictionary-Handbook to Hymns for the Living Church*, 1978, is a helpful companion to the hymnal for which he served as editor in 1974. The historical essay by George H. Shorney, Jr., on Hope Publishing Company, its divisions and affiliates, is a significant contribution to American hymnody. Erik Routley's *An English-Speaking Hymnal Guide*, 1979, was designed as a companion to twenty-six selected hymnals from 1906 to 1975. Those hymns that appeared in at least four of the hymnals were included, and only texts and authors were discussed.

The finest companion of this century is Marilyn Kay Stulken's *Hymnal Companion to the Lutheran Book of Worship*, 1981. The historical essays and the discussions of the hymns, tunes, authors, composers, and sources are the result of careful scholarship. This companion will be the standard by which future companions are measured.

Twentieth-Century Texts and Tunes

Hymns representative of the first half of the twentieth century by American writers show the evidence of diverse hymnic styles and emphases. Among those which seem to have enduring quality are Julia Cady Cory's "We praise you, O God, our Redeemer, Creator," 1902 (116); Frank Mason North's "Where cross the crowded ways of life," 1903 (66); Jay T. Stocking's "O Master Workman of the race," 1912; J. Edgar Park's "We would see Jesus; lo, his star is shining, 1913 (151); Harry Emerson Fosdick's "God of grace and God of glory," 1930 (72); and Georgia Harkness, "Hope of the world, thou Christ of great compassion," 1954 (34).

In recent decades, hymn writing has continued, providing contemporary expression for congregational song. Some examples of hymns found in recent hymnals are: Sybil Leonard Armes's "How gracious are thy mercies, Lord" (150); Herbert Brokering's "Earth and all stars"; Carl P. Daw, Jr.'s "Like the murmur of the dove's song" (145); F. Samuel Janzow's "From shepherding of stars that gaze" (138); Jeffrey Rowthorn's "Creating God, your fingers trace" (136); Suzanne Toolan's "I am the Bread of Life" (153); F. Bland Tucker's "Awake, O sleeper, rise from death" (146); Jaroslav J. Vajda's "Now the silence, now the peace" (144); Omer Westendorf's "You satisfy the hungry heart" (154); W. Nantlais Williams' "Jesus, friend of thronging pilgrims" (148); and Kate Wilkins Woolley's "Free to be me, God, I really am free" (130).

Many fine hymn tunes have been composed in recent years to add to the repertoire of contemporary Christian song. Some examples of these are A.L. Butler's ADA (53); Katherine K. Davis' MASSACHUSETTS (131); Richard W. Dirksen's VINEYARD HAVEN (152); Richard W. Hillert's SHEPHERDING (138); David N. Johnson's EARTH AND ALL STARS; Robert E. Kreutz's BICENTENNIAL (154); Phillip Landgrave's SEMINARY (147); Max Miller's MARSH CHAPEL (146); Daniel Moe's CITY OF GOD (119); Milburn Price's PAX IAM (137); Carl Schalk's NOW (144); Reginald S. Thatcher's WILDERNESS (136); Suzanne Toolan's BREAD OF LIFE (153); and Heinz Werner Zimmerman's CARPENTER 1970 (132).

Influences in Twentieth-Century Developments

The development of hymnody in America has been greatly enriched by the contribution of scholars who have devoted a large share of their time and energies to this area of understanding. One of the most prominent among these contributors was Louis F. Benson—hymnologist, hymn writer, hymnal editor, author, and lecturer. He excelled in many areas, including the writing of hymn texts such as "The light of God is falling." His persistent, careful scholarship has resulted in the writing of *The English Hymn* and *The Hymnody of the Christian Church*, which are important landmarks in American hymnological activity.

The numerous people cited earlier in this chapter for their role in the development of twentieth-century hymnals and hymnal companions have been a vital part of the movement bringing about the continuing enrichment of the American hymn tradition. To this list must be added the names of scholars whose research and writing have contributed valuable insight into specialized areas of hymnology. Included among these are Ruth Ellis Messenger (1884-1964), for her work in Latin hymnody, George Pullen Jackson (1874-1953), who was a pioneer in the since-productive field of research into American folk hymnody, and Henry Wilder Foote, for his writings concerning American hymnody.

The most prolific and provocative hymnologist of the twentieth century was Erik Routley (1917-1982). He was a distinguished scholar, whose writings of more than three decades included fifty books and monographs that he authored, eighteen hymnals and collections of hymns that he edited, plus 546 articles, thirty-four hymns, ninety-eight hymn tunes, and a vast assortment of other miscellaneous works of his creation.[23] These writings provide a scholarly treatment of historical material and gave a penetrating insight into contemporary developments and trends.

The Hymn Society of America   One of the most vital forces currently engaged in promoting the interest of hymnody in the United States is The Hymn Society of America. Founded in 1922 to promote hymn singing, hymn writing, and hymnological research, the Society has grown steadily across the years. The headquarters are now located on the campus of Texas Christian University, Fort Worth,

Texas. W. Thomas Smith, executive director since 1976, has provided excellent leadership in the expanding activities of the Society. *The Hymn*, a quarterly publication has experienced distinguished recognition through the diligent efforts of editors Harry Eskew (1976-84) and Paul Westermeyer (since 1985). The annual conferences sponsored by the Society have been of great value and have been well attended by ministers, church musicians, and lay persons interested in hymnody. The Society's "hymn searches" have resulted in some fine hymnic expressions as capable persons have been motivated to write hymns. Local chapters have been organized throughout the nation, and hymn festivals have been encouraged.[24]

Experimental Collections   As interest in the folk collections diminished, other collections appeared giving exposure to new texts and tunes. *Ecumenical Praise*, 1977, contained some new folk material but introduced new hymn tunes that were most venturesome. Carlton R. Young was the executive editor, assisted by Austin C. Lovelace, Erik Routley, and Alec Wyton. This collection, probably not designed for regular church services, was widely used in conferences, workshops, retreats, festivals, and other places where persons with a vibrant interest in Christian song gathered. They dared to sing new texts and tunes and found them singable. Two collections of Afro-American spirituals were published by Abingdon Press (Methodist) and The Church Hymnal Corporation (Episcopal). *Songs of Zion*, 1981 (Methodist), and *Lift Every Voice*, 1981 (Episcopal), were attempts to preserve in song the culture of Black Americans, and to make this material more available for congregational usage. *Hymnal Supplement*, 1984, offered an excellent collection of hymns and tunes by today's choice authors and composers. The work of outstanding British writers Fred Pratt Green, Fred Kaan, Erik Routley, and Brian Wren is prominently displayed.

Contemporary Trends

Christian song is never static, never quite the same from one generation to another. When viewed from two or three decades the changes may appear rather small. However, a backward look of fifty years reveals more distinct differences, and these differences become more sharply defined over a passing century. The last hundred years have witnessed a marked change in the concept of worship as reflected in American hymnody. The increasing significance of corporate worship, the shifting of emphasis from the fear and awe of God and impending judgment to an expression of love and gratitude to God, and the meaning and comfort of worship to the individual, all are reflected in succeeding hymnal compilations. Hymnic expressions yearning for the "Promised Land" have given way to hymns revealing a desire for a more abundant life in this world. Hymns of missionary emphasis sing of sharing the gospel with persons across the street and across the world, but do not refer to them as "pagans" or "heathen." Texts of nineteenth-century English missionary hymns have been carefully pruned to remove expressions reflecting British colonialism. Hymns of vital Christian living emphasizing active service and the welfare of humanity are replacing those speaking only of passive, pious Christian living.

Watts and Wesley are both well-represented in our hymnals today, but not in the proportion of a century ago. Hymns of the eighteenth century have rapidly declined in number during the last century as many literary expressions of that era have become obsolete and meaningless in Christian experience. The quantity of nineteenth-century English hymnody in today's hymnals has diminished. Archaic language, meaningless expressions, and imagery related to a rural agrarian society have little impact in church services of a nation whose technological and urban development has been dynamic.

While contemporary denominational hymnals reveal certain denominational characteristics, these have become less sharply defined. Hymnic material from the Reformation and pre-Reformation traditions, as well as Wesleyan, Anglican, and Evangelical influences, make up a common body of hymnody which can be found in the hymnals of all major denominations.

This merging of influence is also seen in hymn tunes. Plainsong melodies, once the sole property of the Roman Catholic Church, may now be found in Protestant hymnals, along with Lutheran chorale melodies and French and English psalm tunes. On the other hand, the gospel song, a product of American revivalism, appears in hymnals of liturgical tradition, which in years past have paid scant attention to this area.

Hymn Tune Developments Among the specific trends in our time, the decline of many tunes popular from fifty to a hundred years ago is readily apparent. Only the most hearty of the victorian tunes are surviving in the critical atmosphere of the late-twentieth century. A renewed interest in plainsong explains the presence of such tunes as DIVINUM MYSTERIUM and VENI CREATOR in several Protestant hymnals. EIN' FESTE BURG, NUN DANKET, NEUMARK, and PASSION CHORALE are among the numerous Lutheran chorale melodies that commonly appear in hymnals outside the Lutheran tradition. Lutheran, Congregational, and Presbyterian hymnals now include a number of gospel songs, recognizing the popularity of these songs among these denominational groups.

Unison singing has become inceasingly popular, and strong unison tunes, such as LASST UNS ERFREUEN (25), SINE NOMINE (75), and SLANE (77) are regularly found in most collections. American composers have contributed to the growing repertoire of unison melodies with vigorous tunes such as WALDA and MASSACHUSETTS (131). Several splendid tunes from European sources have been added to our musical repertoire as hymnal editors have diligently searched for worthy material. One such example is the Norwegian tune KIRKEN DEN ER ET (125), which remained for almost a century exclusively in Lutheran usage. Other Scandinavian tunes have greatly enriched our musical treasures of Christian song.

While English and European folk material have long been standard fare, American hymnal compilers have now discovered the rich heritage of our own native folk song. Most of these are of Southern origin and include such tunes as MORNING SONG (98), KEDRON (90), FOUNDATION (104), and AMAZING GRACE (76). Negro spirituals have become increasingly popular for hymnal usage during the last three decades. "Were you there" (105) and "Lord, I want to be a Christian" (117) are among the spirituals most frequently found in current hymnals.

One of the most interesting developments in the hymnody of our time is the appearance in American hymnals of hymns and tunes of Far East origin. During the last century and a half missionaries journeyed to India, China, and many other remote places. Now Christian hymns return from these mission fields, reflecting the literary and musical culture of these distant places. From Chinese sources have come such hymns as "Father, long before creation," "The bread of life" (122), and "Rise to greet the sun" (120). CHINESE MELODY (114), SHENG EN (122) and LE P'ING (120) illustrate tunes from Oriental sources. Recent hymnals have also included tunes from Thailand, Nigeria, Korea, and Indonesia. The international interchange of hymnic ideas, both texts and tunes, has been significantly aided by the four editions (1924, 1930, 1951, and 1974) of *Cantate Domino*, the hymnal published by the World Student Christian Federation.

Folk and "Pop" Musical Influences   In the mid-1960's, there emerged a growing body of song literature for group singing that was written to appeal to the musical tastes of young people. Utilizing melodic and harmonic materials associated with folk music and the various styles of "pop" music, the sounds of "youth music" began to appear with increasing frequency in the church. Youth musicals—semidramatic productions designed both for presentation within the church and as a vehicle for taking the message of faith outside of the church into secular society—became quite popular. After a decade this trend began to diminish, and few of the songs associated with this experience have remained.

Other Developments   The influence of the gospel song of the late-nineteenth century has continued through the twentieth century. This is evident not only in the continued use of this material, but also in its effect upon a subsequent style of writing of contemporary Christian songs. Beginning in the 1940's, the songs of John W. Peterson were widely known and extremely popular. Twenty years later, the music of Bill Gaither reached an even wider market, as he, with his wife, Gloria, their singers and instrumentalists, toured the nation annually singing their songs to throngs of people. The Gaithers contributed thirty songs to *Hymns for the Family of God*, 1976.

New translations of the Bible and their use in church services has influenced the language of hymnic literature. The American Bible Society published the New Testament in "Today's English Version" in 1966, and the Old Testament in 1976. In this context, for many people the "thee-thou-thy" language of many hymns seemed awkward. Authors of new hymns avoided such usage. Some hymnal editors attempted to carefully alter eighteenth- and nineteenth-century hymns by using "you-your" language. Some difficulties have occurred in weakened lyric lines and destroyed rhyme. Other hymnal editors have retained the original words in the traditional hymns, but accepted contemporary language in new hymns. The mixing of "thee-thou-thy" and "you-your" seems acceptable in the same hymnal, but not in the same hymn.

Of greater concern in contemporary hymnody is the awareness of the need for "inclusive language." In many existing hymns "man" is used to mean "people" or "all humanity," not merely a male person. But early hymn writers who used the words "brethren" and "sons" probably intended a masculine connotation. Editors of recent hymn collections have sought to substitute inclusive words and avoid exclusive terminology if at all possible, and this practice will likely continue in the future.

Greater interest in the lectionary began in the 1970's. Churches in the mainstream of Protestant tradition began to rely on it for service planning. While the lectionary speaks to the minister, it also has implications for the church musician. One helpful aid to churches has been Horace T. Allen's *A Handbook for the Lectionary*, designed to provide church leaders with suggestions for the Church Year. Developed by the Joint Office of Worship of the Presbyterian Church in the United States and the United Presbyterian Church in the United States of America, Allen's work includes collects, readings, psalms, hymns, and anthems for each Sunday and special day in the Church Year. Specific titles for five or six hymns are listed for each day, enabling the worship planners to select the hymns that could best be used with a given congregation. Such resource materials are most helpful in providing guidance for selecting hymns for congregational singing.

Of unusual interest is a hymnal published in 1985 by the China Christian Council and the National Committee of The Three-Self Movement of the Protestant Churches in China. Christians in China emerged from the Cultural Revolution with a strong desire to be heard and believed. The impetus for the hymnal originated in the Third National Christian Conference late in 1980, and in a few months a hymnal committee was established. An announcement that the committee was soliciting new Christian songs brought an enthusiastic response from nearly every province, municipality, and autonomous region in China. Of the 400 hymns in the new hymnal, almost 300 are hymns previously used in Chinese churches. These hymns reflect the strong Western influence of traditional eighteenth- and nineteenth-century hymnic material from England and America. Of unusual significance is the fact that 102 hymns have either words or melodies composed by Chinese Christians or are adaptations of indigenous Chinese melodies. Of these, 46 date from the early 1930's, and 56 were written since 1980. That the committee included so much of this material represents concern for indigenous Christian song, and that they retain so much western hymnody indicates their desire for identification with the worldwide Christian community.

The stream of our hymnody continues to widen as each succeeding generation expresses its judgment on its hymnic inheritance and makes its own contribution of new material. The hymnody of today encompasses a far wider range of material— both texts and tunes—than ever before in Christian history. The richness of our heritage and the creative activity of the present should enable contemporary congregations to become involved in meaningful hymn singing to a degree unparalleled in the history of the church's song.

ENDNOTES

[1] Harry Lee Eskew, "Shape-Note Hymnody in the Shenandoah Valley, 1816-1860"(unpublished Ph.D. dissertation, Tulane University, 1966), p. 98.

[2] Dale Eugene Warland, "The Music of Twentieth-Century Lutheran Hymnody in America" (unpublished D.M.A. dissertation, University of Southern California, 1965), p. 7.

[3] See Roger L. Hall, "Shaker Hymnody: An American Communal Tradition," *The Hymn*, Vol. 27, No. 1 (January 1976), p. 22-9. Also, Daniel W. Patterson, *The Shaker Spiritual* (Princeton, N.J.: Princeton University Press, 1979).

[4] J. Spencer Cornwall, *A Century of Singing* (Salt Lake City: Deseret Book Company, 1958), pp. 303-4.

[5] See the discussion of music copyright law in Burton, "Copyright and the Creative Arts," in Paul H. Lang, *One Hundred Years of Music in America* (New York: G. Schirmer, Inc., 1961), pp. 282-301.

[6] For a detailed description see Philip Phillips, *Song Pilgrimage Around the World* (Chicago: Fairbanks, Palmer & Co., 1880).

[7] Elias Nason and J. Frank Beale, Jr., *Lives and Labors of Eminent Divines* (Philadelphia: John E. Potter & Co., 1895), p. 298.

[8] *The Ira D. Sankey Centenary* (New Castle, Pa., 1941), p. 15.

[9] The six collections of *Gospel Hymns* have been reprinted in Ira D. Sankey et al., *Gospel Hymns Nos. 1 to 6*, new introduction by H. Wiley Hitchcock (New York: Da Capo Press, 1972).

[10] John Spencer Curwen, *Studies in Worship Music*, 2d series (London: J. Curwen & Sons, 1885), p. 40.

[11] Curwen, p. 39.

[12] Robert M. Stevenson, *Patterns of Protestant Church Music* (Durham, N.C.: Duke University Press, 1953), p. 162.

[13] Louis F. Benson, *The English Hymn* (New York: George H. Doran Company, 1915), p. 555.

[14] Benson, p. 559.

[15] See Paul M. Hall, "The *Musical Million*: A Study and Analysis of the Periodical Promoting Music Reading Through Shape-Notes in North America from 1870 to 1914" (unpublished Ph.D. dissertation, Catholic University of America, 1970).

[16] Jo Lee Fleming, "James D. Vaughan, Music Publisher, Lawenceburg, Tennessee, 1912-1964" (unpublished D.S.M. dissertation, Union Theological Seminary, 1972), p. 51.

[17] The James D. Vaughan interests and copyrights are owned by the Tennessee Music company, Cleveland, Tennessee. The Stamps Quartet Company interests and copyrights are owned by the Blackwood Brothers and J.D. Sumner, Memphis, Tennessee. The Hartford Music Company interests and copyrights are owned by Albert Brumley, Powell, Missouri. The Stamps-Baxter Music and Printing Company interests and copyrights are owned by the Zondervan Corporation, Grand Rapids, Michigan.

[18] For a comprehensive listing of hymnals, see Harry Eskew, "Bibliography of Hymnals in Use in American and Canadian Churches," *The Hymn*, Vol. 37, No. 2 (April 1986), pp. 25-30.

[19] Fred A. Mund, *Keep the Music Ringing: A Short History of the Church of the Nazarene* (Kansas City: Nazarene Publishing House, 1979), p. 2.

[20] Mund, p. 27.

[21] J. Irving Erickson, *Twice-Born Hymns* (Chicago: Covenant Press, 1976), p. 12.

[22] John A. Lovelace, "Hymn Survey Draws Loud Chorus of Reader Response," *The United Methodist Reporter*, 23 August 1985, p. 2.

[23] See Robin A. Leaver and James H. Litton (editors), *Duty and Delight: Routley Remembered* (Carol Stream, IL: Hope Publishing Company, 1985), pp. 241-304.

[24] Information concerning membership and publications of the Society may be obtained from The Hymn Society of America, National Headquarters, Texas Christian University, P.O. Box 30854, Fort Worth, TX 76129; (817) 921-7608; W. Thomas Smith, executive director.

SUGGESTIONS FOR SUPPLEMENTARY STUDY

Introduction
Buszin, Walter E. "Theology and Church Music as Bearers of the *Verbum Dei.*" *The Musical Heritage of the Church VI*, ed. Theodore Hoelty-Nickel. St. Louis: Concordia Publishing House, 1964. Pp. 17-31.

Doran, Carol, and Thomas H. Troeger. "Writing Hymns as a Theologically Informed Artistic Discipline," *The Hymn*, Vol. 36, No. 2 (April 1985), pp. 7-11.

Eskew, Harry, and Hugh L. McElrath. *Sing with Understanding.* Nashville: Broadman Press, 1980. Pp. 45-71.

Giles, William Brewster. "Christian Theology and Hymnody," *The Hymn*, Vol. 14, No. 1 (January 1963), pp. 9-12.

Grant, John Webster. "The Hymn as Theological Statement," *The Hymn*, Vol. 37, No. 4 (October 1986), pp. 1-10.

Leaver, Robin. "The Hymns and the Old Testament," *Bulletin of the Hymn Society of Great Britain and Ireland*, No. 141 (January 1978), pp. 14-16.

Schilling, S. Paul. *The Faith We Sing.* Philadelphia: The Westminister Press, 1983.

Wren, Brian. "Sexism in Hymn Language," *The Hymn*, Vol. 34, No. 4 (October 1983), pp. 227-32.

Chapter 1 - Early Church Song
Apel, Willi. *Gregorian Chant.* Bloomington: Indiana University Press, 1958.

Binder, A.W. *Bibical Chant.* Philosophical Library, 1959.

Britt, Dom Matthew (ed.). *The Hymns of the Breviary and Missal.* New York: Benziger Brothers, 1948.

Douglas, Winfred. *Church Music in History and Practice.* Revised with additional material by Leonard Ellinwood. New York: Charles Scribner's Sons, 1962. Pp. 124-54.

Julian, John. *A Dictionary of Hymnology.* 2 vols. New York: Dover Publications, 1957 (reprint of the Second Rev. Ed., 1907). Articles on "Greek Hymnody," "Latin Hymnody," "Sequence," and individual hymns listed under their Latin and Greek titles.

Messenger, Ruth. "Christian Hymns of the First Three Centuries," *Papers of the Hymn Society of America*, No. IX, 1942.

————. "Latin Hymns of the Middle Ages," *Papers of the Hymn Society of America*, No. XIV, 1948.

————. *The Medieval Latin Hymn.* Washington: Capital Press, 1953.

Patrick, Millar. *The Story of the Church's Song.* Rev. ed. by James Rawlings Sydnor. Richmond: John Knox Press, 1962. Pp. 11-69.

Reese, Gustave. *Music in the Middle Ages.* New York: W. W. Norton & Co., 1940. Pp. 57-197.

Sanders, J.T. *The New Testament Christological Hymns.* Cambridge: Cambridge University Press, 1971.

Wellesz, Egon. *A History of Byzantine Music and Hymnography.* Second Ed. Oxford: Clarendon Press, 1962.

Werner, Eric. *The Sacred Bridge.* New York: Columbia University Press. Pp. 1-49; 207-72.

Chapter 2 - The Lutheran Chorale
Bailey, Albert E. *The Gospel in Hymns.* New York: Scribner's, 1950. Pp. 308-46.

Blume, Friedrich, ed. *Protestant Church Music.* New York: W.W. Norton & Co., 1974. Pp. 3-105, 127-61, 236-45, 251-62, 593-607.

Duerksen, Rosella Reimer. "Anabaptist Hymnody of the Sixteenth Century." Unpublished D.S.M. dissertation. Union Theological Seminary, 1956.

Hewitt, Theodore Brown. *Paul Gerhardt as a Hymn Writer and His Influence on English Hymnody.* 2nd ed. St.Louis: Concordia Publishing House, 1976.

Jenny, Markus. "The Hymns of Zwingli and Luther: a Comparison," in *Cantors at the Crossroads.* Ed. Johannes Riedel. St. Louis: Concordia Publishing House, 1967. Pp. 45-63.

Julian. *A Dictionary of Hymnology*, articles on "German Hymnody" and individual hymn writers.

Leaver, Robin A. "Bach, Hymns and Hymnbooks," *The Hymn*, Vol. 36, No. 4 (October 1985), pp. 7-13.

Leupold, Ulrich S., ed. *Liturgy and Hymns.* Vol. 53 of *Luther's Works.* Philadelphia: Fortress Press, 1965.

Liemohn, Edwin. *The Chorale, Through 400 Years of Musical Development as a Congregational Hymn.* Philadelphia: Muhlenburg Press, 1953.

Reed, Luther D. "Luther and Congregational Song," *Papers of the Hymn Society of America*, No. XII, 1947.

Riedel, Johannes. *The Lutheran Chorale: Its Basic Traditions.* Minneapolis: Augsburg Publishing House, 1967.

Routley, Erik. *Christian Hymns Observed.* Princeton: Prestige Publications, 1982. Pp. 15-23.

—————. *The Music of Christian Hymns.* Chicago: G.I.A. Publications, Inc., 1981. Pp. 21-7, 59-67.

Chapter 3 - Psalmody

Anderson, Ronald Eugene. "Richard Alison's Psalter (1599) and Devotional Music in England to 1640." Unpublished Ph.D. dissertation. 2 vols. University of Iowa, 1974.

Bailey, *The Gospel in Hymns*, pp. 2-17.

Blankenburg, Walter. "Church Music in Reformed Europe," in *Protestant Church Music.* Ed. Friedrich Blume. New York: W.W. Norton & Co., 1974. Pp. 509-90.

Douen, E.O. *Clement Marot et le Psautier Huguenot.* Paris: L'Imprimerie Nationale, 1878-1879.

Frost, Maurice. *English and Scottish Psalm and Hymn Tunes.* London: S.P.C.K. and Oxford University Press, 1953.

Julian. *A Dictionary of Hymnology*, articles on "Psalters, English," "Psalters, French," and "Old Version."

New Grove Dictionary of Music and Musicians, 1986 ed. See "Psalmody," Vol. 15, pp. 337-47; "Psalms, Metrical," Vol. 15, pp. 347-82.

Patrick. *The Story of the Church's Song*, pp. 86-113.

Patrick, Millar. *Four Centuries of Scottish Psalmody.* London: Oxford University Press, 1950.

Pidoux, Pierre. *Le Psautier Huguenot du XVIe Siecle.* 2 vols. Basel: Edition Barenreiter, 1962.

Pratt, Waldo Selden. *The Music of the French Psalter of 1562.* New York: AMS Press, 1966 (reprint of edition of Columbia University Press, New York, 1939).

Prothero, Rowland E. *The Psalms in Human Life.* London: Thomas Nelson & Sons, 1903. Pp. 168-267.

Reese, Gustave. *Music in the Renaissance.* Rev. ed. New York: W.W. Norton & Co., 1959. Pp. 355-62, 501-06.

Roper, Cecil Mizelle. "The Strasbourg French Psalters, 1539-1553." Unpublished D.M.A. dissertation. University of Southern California, 1972.

Routley. *Christian Hymns Observed*, pp. 23-54.

—————.*The Music of Christian Hymns*, pp. 21-58.

Stroud, William Paul. "The Ravenscroft Psalter (1621): The Tunes, with a Background on Thomas Ravenscroft and Psalm Singing in His Time." Unpublished D.M.A. dissertation. University of Southern California, 1959.

Chapter 4 - English Hymnody, I

Bailey, *The Gospel in Hymns*, pp. 18-140.

Benson, Louis F. *The English Hymn.* Richmond: John Knox press, 1962 (reprinted from the 1915 edition published by the George H. Doran Company, New York). Pp. 19-357.

—————. *The Hymnody of the Christian Church*, pp. 86-95, 105-38.

—————. "The Hymns of John Bunyan," *Papers of the Hymn Society of America*, No. 1, 1930.

Bishop, Selma L., ed. *Isaac Watts: Hymns and Spiritual Songs, 1707-1748*. London: The Faith Press, 1962.

Escott, Harry. *Isaac Watts, Hymnographer*. London: Independent Press, 1962.

Fountain, David. *Isaac Watts Remembered*. Worthington, Eng.: Henry E. Walter, 1974.

Haas, Alfred Burton. "Charles Wesley," *Papers of the Hymn Society of America*, No. XXII, 1957.

Johansen, John Henry. "The Olney Hymns," *Papers of The Hymn Society of America*, No. XX, 1956.

Manning, Bernard L. *The Hymns of Wesley and Watts*. London: Epworth Press, 1942.

Martin, Hugh. *They Wrote Our Hymns*. Naperville, IL: Alec R. Allenson, 1961. Pp. 1-56.

Parks, Edna. *The Hymns and Hymn Tunes Found in the English Metrical Psalters*. New York: Coleman-Ross Company, 1966.

Patrick, *The Story of the Church's Song*, pp. 114-41.

Pollack, John. *Amazing Grace: John Newton's Story*. New York: Harper & Row, 1981.

Routley, Erik. *Hymns and Human Life*. London: John Murray, 1952. Pp. 63-125.

————— . *The Music of Christian Hymns*, pp. 68-77; 83-8.

————— . *The Musical Wesleys*. London: Herbert Jenkins, 1968. Pp. 1-42.

Stevenson, Robert M. *Patterns of Protestant Church Music*. Durham, N.C.: Duke University Press, 1953. Pp. 93-138.

Young, Robert H. "The History of Baptist Hymnody in England from 1612 to 1800." Unpublished D.M.A. dissertation. University of Southern California, 1959.

Chapter 5 - English Hymnody, II

Bailey, *The Gospel in Hymns*, pp. 141-210; 347-476.

Benson, *The English Hymn*, pp. 435-60; 493-543.

Dearmer, Percy. *Songs of Praise Discussed*. London: Oxford University Press, 1933.

Higginson, J. Vincent. "John Mason Neale and the 19th-Century Hymnody: His Work and Influence," *The Hymn*, Vol. 16, No. 4 (October 1965), pp. 101-1117.

Julian, *A Dictionary of Hymnology*, articles on "England Hymnody, Church of," and individual hymns and hymn writers.

Kaan, Fred. "Saturday Night and Sunday Morning," *The Hymn*, Vol. 27, No. 4 (October 1976), pp. 100-108.

Leaver, Robin A. *Catherine Winkworth: The Influence of Her Translations on English Hymnody*. St.Louis: Concordia Publishing House, 1978.

Lock, William. "Six Hymns from Olney," *Journal of Church Music* (November 1975), pp. 8-10.

Martin, Hugh, ed. *The Baptist Hymn Book Companion* (Rev. ed., R.W. Thomson, ed.). London: Psalms and Hymns Trust, 1967.

————— . *They Wrote Our Hymns*. London: SCM Press, 1961.

New Grove Dictionary of American Music, 1986 ed. S.v. "Hymnody," Vol. II, p. 447.

Parry. K.L., and Erik Routley. *Companion to Congregation Praise*. London: Independent Press, 1953.

Patrick, *The Story of the Church's Song*, pp. 142-65.

Routley, *Christian Hymns Observed*, pp. 53-60; 71-86.

————— . *Hymns and Human Life*, pp. 129-223.

————— . "Hymn Writers of the New English Renaissance," *The Hymn* Vol. 28, No. 1 (January 1977), pp. 6-10.

————— . *The Music of Christian Hymns*, pp. 80-120; 140-70.

Temperley, Nicholas, and Charles G. Manns. *Fuguing-Tunes in the Eighteenth Century*. Detroit Studies in Music Bibliography, No. 49. Detroit: Information Coordinators, 1983.

Westermeyer, Paul. "The Hymnal Noted: Theological and Music Intersections," *Church Music*, Vol. 73, No. 2, pp. 1-9.

Chapter 6 - American Hymnody, I

Barbour, J. Murray. *The Church Music of William Billings*. East Lansing: Michigan State University Press, 1960.

Benson, *The English Hymn*, pp. 161-204; 280-314; 358-434.

Britton, Allen P. "Theoretical Introductions in American Tune-Books to 1800." Unpublished Ph.D. dissertation. University of Michigan, 1949.

Chase, Gilbert. *America's Music: From the Pilgrims to the Present.* Rev. ed. New York: McGraw-Hill Book Company, 1966. Pp. 3-64; 123-63; 183-258.

Cobb, Buell. *The Sacred Harp: A Tradition and Its Music.* Athens: The University of Georgia Press, 1978.

Davisson, Ananias. *Kentucky Harmony.* New introduction by Irving Lowens. Minneapolis: Augsburg Press, 1976 (facsimile reprint of the 1816 edition published in Harrisonburg, Va.).

Downey, James Cecil. "The Music of American Revivalism." Unpublished Ph.D. dissertation. Tulane University, 1968.

Ellinwood, Leonard. *The History of American Church Music.* New York: Morehouse-Gorham Company, 1953. Pp. 3-52; 67-71; 101-9.

Eskew, Harry Lee. "Shape-Note Hymnody in the Shenandoah Valley, 1816-1860." Unpublished Ph.D. dissertation. Tulane University, 1966.

Foote, Henry Wilder. *Three Centuries of American Hymnody.* Cambridge, Mass.: Harvard University Press, 1940. Pp. 3-202; 373-86.

Haraszti, Zoltan. *The Enigma of the Bay Psalm Book.* Chicago: University of Chicago Press, 1956.

Horn, Dorothy D. *Sing to Me of Heaven: A Study of Folk and Early American Materials in Three Old Harp Books.* Gainesville: University of Florida Press, 1970.

Jackson, George Pullen. *Another Sheaf of White Spirituals.* Gainesville: University of Florida Press, 1952.

_____ . *Down-East Spirituals and Others.* 2nd ed. Locust Valley, N.Y.: J.J. Augustin, 1953.

_____ . *Spiritual Folk-Songs of Early America.* New York: J.J. Augustin, 1937. Reprint New York: Dover Publications, 1975.

_____ . *White Spirituals in the Southern Uplands.* Chapel Hill: University of North Carolina Press, 1933. Reprint eds. Hatboro, Pa.: Folklore Associates, 1964. New York: Dover Publications, 1965.

Kroeger, Karl. "William Billings and the Hymn-Tune," *The Hymn,* Vol. 37, No. 3 (July 1986), pp. 19-26.

Lowens, Irving. *Music and Musicians in Early America.* New York: W.W. Norton & Co., 1964.

Lyon, James. *Urania: A Choice Collection of Psalm-Tunes, Anthems, and Hymns.* New preface by Richard Crawford. New York: Da Capo Press, 1974 (unabridged republication of the first edition published in Philadelphia, 1761).

MacDougall, Hamilton C. *Early New England Psalmody: An Historical Appreciation, 1620-1820.* Brattleboro: Stephen Daye Press, 1940.

McCurry, John G. *The Social Harp.* Philadelphia, 1855. Reprint ed. by Daniel W. Patterson and John F. Garst. Athens: University of Georgia Press, 1973.

McKay, David P., and Richard Crawford. *William Billings of Boston.* Princeton: Princeton University Press, 1975.

Mason, Henry Lowell. "Lowell Mason: An Appreciation of his Life and Work," *Papers of the Hymn Society of America,* No. VIII, 1941.

New Grove Dictionary of American Music, 1986 ed. "Spirituals, white," Vol.IV, pp. 284-6; "Spiritual, black," Vol. IV, pp. 286-90.

Pemberton, Carol A. *Lowell Mason: His Life and Work.* Ann Arbor: UMI Research Press, 1985.

Sims, John N. "The Hymnody of the Camp-Meeting Tradition." Unpublished D.S.M. dissertation. Union Theological Seminary, 1960.

Stevenson, Robert. *Protestant Church Music in America.* New York: W.W. Norton & Co., 1966. Pp. 3-105.

White, B.F. and E.J. King. *The Sacred Harp.* 3rd ed. Philadelphia, 1859. Reprint ed. Nashville: Broadman Press, 1968.

Wyeth, John. *Wyeth's Repository of Sacred Music, Part Second.* Harrisburg, Pa., 1820. Reprint ed. New York: Da Capo Press, 1964.

Chapter 7 - American Hymnody, II

Bailey, *The Gospel in Hymns,* pp. 482-577.

Benson, *The English Hymn*, pp. 460-92; 543-90.

Brink, Emily R. "Psalm Singing in the Christian Reformed Church," *The American Organist* (November 1986), pp. 32-3.

Daniels, Harold M. "Presbyterians and the Psalms," *The American Organist* (December 1986), p. 51.

Eskew, Harry. "Bibliography of Hymnals in Use in American and Canadian Churches," *The Hymn*, Vol. 37, No. 2 (April 1986), pp. 25-30.

_____ . *Sing with Understanding*, pp. 170-92.

Erickson, J. Irving. *Twice-Born Hymns*. Chicago: Covenant Press, 1976.

Jost, Walter James. "The Hymn Tune Tradition of the General Conference Mennonite Church." Unpublished D.M.A. dissertation. University of Southern California, 1966.

Linder, Michael. "William Evander Penn: His Contribution to Church Music," Unpublished D.M.A. dissertation. Southwestern Baptist Theological Seminary, 1985.

Loewen, Alice, Harold Moyer, and Mary Oyer. *Exploring the Mennonite Hymnal: Handbook*. Scottdale, Pa.: Mennonite Publishing House, 1983.

Lorenz, Ellen Jane. *Glory, Hallelujah! The Story of the Campmeeting Spiritual*. Nashville: Abingdon Press, 1980.

New Grove Dictionary of American Music, 1986 ed. S.v. "Hymnody, 1800-1850," Vol. II, pp. 447-55; "Gospel Music," Vol. II, pp. 248-61.

New Grove Dictionary of Music and Musicians, 1986 ed. S.v. "Hymns, Protestant," Vol. 8, pp 846-51.

Noyes, Morgan P. "Louis F. Benson, Hymnologist," *Papers of the Hymn Society of America*, No. XIX, 1955.

Oyer, Mary. *Exploring the Mennonite Hymnal: Essays*. Scottdale, Pa.,: Mennonite Publishing House, 1980.

Patrick, *The Story of the Church's Song*, pp. 166-92.

Reed, Luther D. *Worship: A Study of Corporate Devotion*. Philadelphia: Muhlenberg Press, 1959. Pp, 150-57; 230-39.

Routley, *Christian Hymns Observed*, pp. 93-107.

Sankey, Ira. D. *Sankey's Story of the Gospel Hymns*. Philadelphia: The Sunday School Times Company, 1906.

Schulz-Widmar, Russell. "American Hymnody: A View of the Current Scene," *The Hymn*, Vol. 33, No. 3 (July 1982), pp. 134-58.

Stevenson, *Protestant Church Music in America*, pp. 106-32.

Warland, Dale Eugene. "The Music of Twentieth-Century Lutheran Hymnody in America." Unpublished D.M.A. dissertation. University of Southern California, 1965.

Weight, Newell Bryan. "An Historical Study of the Origin and Character of Indigenous Hymn Tunes of the Latter-Day Saints." Unpublished D.M.A. dissertation. University of Southern California, 1961.

Wohlgemuth, Paul W. "Mennonite Hymnals Published in the English Language." Unpublished D.M.A. dissertation. University of Southern California, 1958.

Zuiderveld, Rudolf. "Some Musical Traditions in Dutch Reformed Churches in America," *The Hymn*, Vol. 36, No. 3 (July 1985), pp. 23-5.

Illustrative
Hymns

1 O Splendor of God's Glory Bright

1. O Splen-dor of God's glo-ry bright, O thou that bring-est
2. O thou true Sun, on us thy glance Let fall in roy-al
3. The Fa-ther, too, our prayers im-plore, Fa-ther of glo-ry
4. To guide what-e'er we no-bly do, With love all en-vy

light from light, O Light of light, light's liv-ing spring,
ra-di-ance; The Spir-it's sanc-ti-fy-ing beam
ev-er-more, The Fa-ther of all grace and might,
to sub-due; To make ill-for-tune turn to fair,

O Day, all days il-lu-min-ing,
Up-on our earth-ly sen-ses stream.
To ban-ish sin from our de-light:
And give us grace our wrongs to bear. A-men.

WORDS: Latin, *Splendor paternae gloriae;* St. Ambrose, 340-397;   SPLENDOR PATERNAE
        tr. Robert S. Bridges, 1899   L.M.
MUSIC: Melody from *Sarum Plainsong,* Mode I

Christians, to the Paschal Victim 2

1. Chris-tians, to the Pas-chal vic-tim Of-fer your thank-ful prais-es!

2. A lamb the sheep re-deem-eth: Christ, who on-ly is sin-less,

Re-con-cil-eth Sin-ners to the Fa-ther. 3. Death and life have con-tend-ed

6. Bright an - gels at - test - ing, The shroud and nap - kin rest - ing.

7. Yea, Christ my hope is a - ris - en: To Gal - i - lee he goes be -

fore you." 8. Christ in - deed from death is ris-en, Our new life ob-tain-ing

Have mer - cy, vic - tor King, ev - er reign - ing! A - men.

WORDS: Ascribed to Wipo, d.c. 1050; tr. Anonymous
MUSIC: Ascribed to Wipo, d.c. 1050

VICTIMAE PASCHALI
Irregular meter

3   Of the Father's Love Begotten

Unison

1. Of the Fa-ther's love be-got-ten, Ere the worlds be-gan to be,
2. O that birth for-ev-er bless-ed, When the Vir-gin, full of grace,
3. O ye heights of heav'n, a-dore Him; An-gel hosts, His prais-es sing,
4. Christ, to Thee with God the Fa-ther, And, O Ho-ly Ghost, to Thee,

He is Al-pha and O-me-ga, He the Source, the End-ing He,
By the Ho-ly Ghost con-ceiv-ing, Bare the Sav-ior of our race;
Pow'rs, do-min-ions, bow be-fore Him, And ex-tol our God and King;
Hymn and chant and high thanks-giv-ing And un-wea-ried prais-es be:

Of the things that are, that have been, And that fu-ture
And the Babe, the world's Re-deem-er, First re-vealed His
Let no tongue on earth be si-lent, Ev-ery voice in
Hon-or, glo-ry, and do-min-ion, And e-ter-nal

years shall see, Ev-er-more and ev-er-more!
sa-cred face, Ev-er-more and ev-er-more!
con-cert ring, Ev-er-more and ev-er-more!
vic-to-ry, Ev-er-more and ev-er-more! A-men.

WORDS: Aurelius C. Prudentius, 4th century;   DIVINUM MYSTERIUM
        tr. John M. Neale, 1854, and Henry W. Baker, 1859   8.7.8.7.8.7.7
MUSIC: Plainsong, 13th century; arr. C. Winfred Douglas, 1916

Come, Holy Ghost, Our Souls Inspire 4

Unison

1. Come, Ho - ly Ghost, our souls in - spire And light-en with ce -
2. Thy bless - ed unc - tion from a - bove Is com-fort, life, and
3. A - noint and cheer our soil - ed face With the a - bun - dance
4. Teach us to know the Fa - ther, Son, And thee, of both, to

les - tial fire; Thou the a - noint - ing spir - it art
fire of love; En - a - ble with per - pet - ual light
of thy grace; Keep far our foes, give peace at home;
be but one; That through the a - ges all a - long

After last stanza

Who dost thy seven - fold gifts im - part.
The dull - ness of our blind - ed sight.
Where thou art guide no ill can come.
This may be our end - less song: Praise to thy e -

ter - nal mer - it, Fa - ther, Son, and Ho - ly Spir-it. A - men.

WORDS: Latin, 9th century; tr. John Cosin, 1627
MUSIC: Plainsong, *Vesperale Romanum* (Mechlin), 1848

VENI CREATOR
L.M.

5 A Mighty Fortress Is Our God

Unison

1. A might - y   for - tress is   our   God,
2. With might of   ours   can naught   be   done,
3. Though dev - ils   all   the world   should fill,
4. The Word they   still   shall let   re - main

A trust - y   shield and weap -   on;
Soon were   our   loss   ef - fect -   ed;
All ea - ger   to   de - vour   us,
Nor an - y   thanks have for   it;

He helps   us   free   from ev - 'ry   need
But for   us   fights the val - iant   One,
We trem - ble   not,   we fear   no   ill,
He's by   our   side   up - on   the   plain

That hath   us   now   o'er - tak -   en.
Whom God   him - self   e - lect -   ed.
They shall   not   o - ver - pow'r   us.
With his   good   gifts and Spir -   it.

1. The old e - vil foe Now means dead - ly woe; Deep guile and great might Are his dread arms in fight; On earth is not his e - qual.
2. Ask ye, Who is this? Je - sus Christ it is, Of sab - a - oth Lord, And there's none oth - er God; He holds the field for ev - er.
3. This world's prince may still Scowl fierce as he will, He can harm us none, He's judged; the deed is done; One lit - tle word can fell him.
4. And take they our life, Goods, fame, child, and wife, Though these all be gone, Our vic - t'ry has been won; The King - dom ours re - main - eth.

WORDS: Martin Luther, 1529; tr. composite
MUSIC: Martin Luther, 1529

EIN' FESTE BURG
8.7.8.7.5.5.5.6.7

6 Out of the Depths I Cry to You

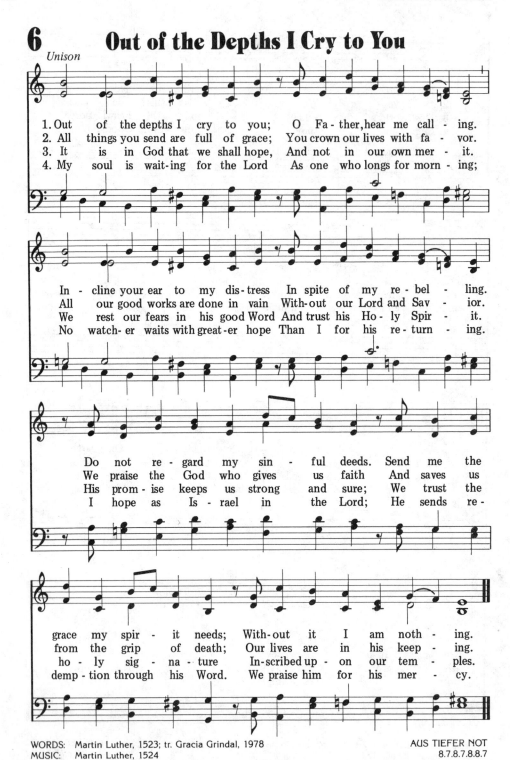

1. Out of the depths I cry to you; O Fa-ther, hear me call-ing.
2. All things you send are full of grace; You crown our lives with fa-vor.
3. It is in God that we shall hope, And not in our own mer-it.
4. My soul is wait-ing for the Lord As one who longs for morn-ing;

In-cline your ear to my dis-tress In spite of my re-bel-ling.
All our good works are done in vain With-out our Lord and Sav-ior.
We rest our fears in his good Word And trust his Ho-ly Spir-it.
No watch-er waits with great-er hope Than I for his re-turn-ing.

Do not re-gard my sin-ful deeds. Send me the
We praise the God who gives us faith And saves us
His prom-ise keeps us strong and sure; We trust the
I hope as Is-rael in the Lord; He sends re-

grace my spir-it needs; With-out it I am noth-ing.
from the grip of death; Our lives are in his keep-ing.
ho-ly sig-na-ture In-scribed up-on our tem-ples.
demp-tion through his Word. We praise him for his mer-cy.

WORDS: Martin Luther, 1523; tr. Gracia Grindal, 1978   AUS TIEFER NOT
MUSIC: Martin Luther, 1524   8.7.8.7.8.8.7

All Glory Be to God on High

7

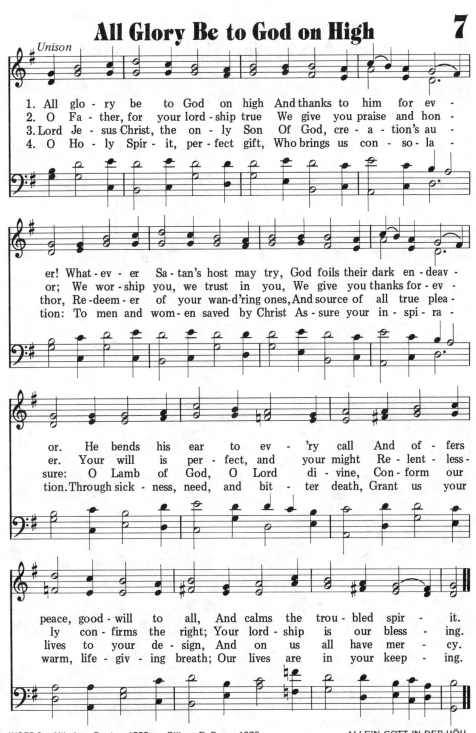

Unison

1. All glo - ry be to God on high And thanks to him for ev - er! What - ev - er Sa - tan's host may try, God foils their dark en - deav - or. He bends his ear to ev - 'ry call And of - fers peace, good - will to all, And calms the trou - bled spir - it.

2. O Fa - ther, for your lord - ship true We give you praise and hon - or; We wor - ship you, we trust in you, We give you thanks for - ev - er. Your will is per - fect, and your might Re - lent - less - ly con - firms the right; Your lord - ship is our bless - ing.

3. Lord Je - sus Christ, the on - ly Son Of God, cre - a - tion's au - thor, Re - deem - er of your wan - d'ring ones, And source of all true plea - sure: O Lamb of God, O Lord di - vine, Con - form our lives to your de - sign, And on us all have mer - cy.

4. O Ho - ly Spir - it, per - fect gift, Who brings us con - so - la - tion: To men and wom - en saved by Christ As - sure your in - spi - ra - tion. Through sick - ness, need, and bit - ter death, Grant us your warm, life - giv - ing breath; Our lives are in your keep - ing.

WORDS: Nikolaus Decius, 1525; tr. Gilbert E. Doan, 1978
MUSIC: Attr. Nikolaus Decius, c. 1485 - aft. 1546

ALLEIN GOTT IN DER HÖH
8.7.8.7.8.8.7

8 Wake, Awake, for Night Is Flying

1. Wake, a-wake, for night is fly - ing, The watch-men on
Mid - night hears the wel-come voic - es And at the thrill-

the heights are cry - ing, A-wake, Je - ru - sa - lem, at last!
ing cry re - joic - es: Come forth, ye vir - gins, night is past!

The Bride-groom comes, a-wake, Your lamps with glad-ness take; Al-le - lu - ia!

And for his mar-riage feast pre-pare, For ye must go to meet him there. A-men.

2. Zion hears the watchmen singing,
   And all her heart with joy is springing,
     She wakes, she rises from her gloom;
   For her Lord comes down all-glorious,
   The strong in grace, in truth victorious,
     Her star is risen, her Light is come.

   Ah come, thou blessèd one,
   God's own belovèd Son,
     Alleluia!
   We follow till the halls we see
   Where thou hast bid us sup with thee.

WORDS: Philipp Nicolai, 1599; tr. Catherine Winkworth, 1858
MUSIC: Philipp Nicolai, 1599

WACHET AUF
Irregular meter

Wake, Awake, for Night is Flying

9

1. Wake, a-wake, for night is fly - ing, The watch-men on the
   Mid-night hears the wel-come voic - es And at the thrill-ing

Wake a-wake, for

heights are cry - ing, A - wake, Je - ru - sa - lem, at last!
cry re - joic - es: Come forth, ye vir-gins, night is past! The Bride-groom

comes, a - wake, Your lamps with glad - ness take; Al - le - lu - ia! And for his

mar-riage feast pre-pare, For ye must go to meet him there. A-men.

3. Now let all the heavens adore thee,
   And men and angels sing before thee,
   With harp and cymbal's clearest tone;
   Of one pearl each shining portal,
   Where we are with the choir immortal
   Of angels round thy dazzling throne;

Nor eye hath seen, nor ear
Hath yet attained to hear
What there is ours;
But we rejoice, and sing to thee
Our hymn of joy eternally.
Amen.

WORDS: Philipp Nicolai, 1599; tr. Catherine Winkworth, 1858
MUSIC: Philipp Nicolai, 1599; adapt. and harm. J. S. Bach, 1731

WACHET AUF
Irregular meter

10 O Morning Star, How Fair and Bright

1. O Morn-ing Star, how   fair and bright Thou beam-est forth in
2. Thou heaven-ly Bright-ness! Light di-vine! O   deep with-in my

truth and light! O Sov-ereign meek and low - ly! Thou Root of Jes - se,
heart now shine, And make thee there an al - tar! Fill me with joy and

Da-vid's Son, My Lord and Mas-ter,   thou hast won My heart to serve thee
strength to be Thy mem-ber, ev - er   joined to thee In love that can-not

sole - ly! Thou art ho - ly, Fair and glo-rious, all vic-to-rious,
fal - ter; Toward thee long-ing Doth pos-sess me; turn and bless me;

Rich in bless - ing, Rule and might o'er all pos - sess - ing.
Here in sad - ness Eye and heart long for thy glad-ness! A-men.

WORDS: Philipp Nicolai, 1599; tr. Catherine Winkworth, 1858
MUSIC: Melody by Philipp Nicolai, 1599; harm. J. S. Bach, 1685-1750

WIE SCHÖN LEUCHTET
8.8.7.8.8.7.4.8.4.8

While Shepherds Watched Their Flocks 11

1. While shep - herds watched their flocks by night, All
2. "Fear not," said he, for might - y dread Had
3. "To you, in Da - vid's town, this day Is
4. "The heaven - ly babe you there shall find To

seat - ed on the ground, The an - gel of the
seized their trou - bled mind, "Glad ti - dings of great
born of Da - vid's line The Sav - ior, who is
hu - man view dis - played. All mean - ly wrapped in

Lord came down, And glo - ry shone a - round.
joy I bring To you and all man - kind.
Christ the Lord; And this shall be the sign:
swath - ing bands, And in a man - ger laid." A - men.

5. Thus spake the seraph; and forthwith
   Appeared a shining throng
Of angels praising God, who thus
   Addressed their joyful song:

6. "All glory be to God on high,
   And to the earth be peace;
Good will henceforth from heaven to men
   Begin and never cease."

WORDS: Nahum Tate, 1700
MUSIC: Thomas Este's *Whole Book of Psalms*, 1592

WINCHESTER OLD
C.M.

12 O Sacred Head, Now Wounded

1. O sa-cred Head, now wound-ed, With grief and shame weighed down,
2. What Thou, my Lord, hast suf-fered Was all for sin-ners' gain;
3. What lan-guage shall I bor-row To thank Thee, dear-est friend,

Now scorn-ful-ly sur-round-ed With thorns, Thine on-ly crown:
Mine, mine was the trans-gres-sion, But Thine the dead-ly pain.
For this Thy dy-ing sor-row, Thy pit-y with-out end?

O sa-cred Head, what glo-ry, What bliss till now was Thine!
Lo, here I fall, my Sav-ior! 'Tis I de-serve Thy place;
O make me Thine for-ev-er; And should I faint-ing be,

Yet, though de-spised and go-ry, I joy to call Thee mine.
Look on me with Thy fa-vor, Vouch-safe to me Thy grace.
Lord, let me nev-er, nev-er Out-live my love to Thee. A-men.

WORDS: Attr. Bernard of Clairvaux, 12th century; tr. (German) Paul Gerhardt, 1656;
        tr. (English) James W. Alexander, 1830
MUSIC: Hans Leo Hassler, 1601; arr. J. S. Bach, 1729

PASSION CHORALE
7.6.7.6 D.

Gentle Mary Laid Her Child 13

1. Gen-tle Ma-ry laid her Child Low-ly in a man-ger;
2. An-gels sang a-bout His birth; Wise Men sought and found Him;
3. Gen-tle Ma-ry laid her Child Low-ly in a man-ger;

There He lay, the un-de-filed, To the world a stran-ger:
Heav-en's star shone bright-ly forth, Glo-ry all a-round Him:
He is still the un-de-filed, But no more a stran-ger:

Such a Babe in such a place, Can He be the Sav-ior?
Shep-herds saw the won-drous sight, Heard the an-gels sing-ing;
Son of God, of hum-ble birth, Beau-ti-ful the sto-ry;

Ask the saved of all the race Who have found His fa-vor.
All the plains were lit that night, All the hills were ring-ing.
Praise His name in all the earth, Hail the King of glo-ry!

WORDS: Joseph S. Cook, 1919
MUSIC: *Piae Cantiones*, 1582; arr. Ernest Macmillan, 1930

TEMPUS ADEST FLORIDUM
7.6.7.6 D.

14   **Unto Us a Boy Is Born**

Unison

1. Un - to us a boy is born! The King of all cre-
2. Cra - dled in a stall was he With sleep - y cows and
3. Her - od then with fear was filled: "A prince," he said, "in
4. Now may Mar - y's son, who came So long a - go to

a - tion, Came he to a world for - lorn, The
ass - es; But the ver - y beasts could see That
Jew - ry!" All the lit - tle boys he killed At
love us, Lead us all with hearts a - flame Un-

Lord of ev - ery na - tion.
he all men sur - pass - es.
Beth - lem in his fu - ry.
to the joys a - bove - us.

5. Alpha and Omega he!
Let the organ thunder,
While the choir with peals of glee
Doth rend the air asunder.

WORDS: Latin carol, 15th century; tr. Percy Dearmer, 1928   PUER NOBIS
MUSIC: *Piae Cantiones*, 1582; arr. Geoffrey Shaw, 1928   7.7.7.7

All Glory, Laud and Honor   15

WORDS: Theodulph of Orleans, c. 800; tr. John M. Neale, 1854
MUSIC: Melchior Teschner, c.1613

ST. THEODULPH
7.6.7.6 D.

16   Lo! How a Rose E'er Blooming

1. Lo! how a rose e'er bloom - ing From ten - der stem hath
2. I - sa - iah 'twas fore - told it, The rose I have in
3. This flower, whose fra - grance ten - der With sweet - ness fills the

sprung! Of Jes - se's lin - eage com - ing As men of old have
mind; With Mar - y we be - hold it, The vir - gin moth - er
air, Dis - pels with glo - rious splen - dor The dark - ness ev - ery -

sung. It came, a flow - eret bright, A - mid the
kind. To show God's love a - right She bore to
where. True man, yet ver - y God, From sin and

cold of win - ter, When half - spent was the night.
men a Sav - ior, When half - spent was the night.
death He saves us And light - ens ev - ery load.

WORDS: German carol, 16th century; Sts. 1, 2, tr. Theodore Baker, 1894;   ES IST EIN' ROS' ENTSPRUNGEN
         St. 3, tr. Harriet Krauth Spaeth, 1875   Irregular meter
MUSIC: *Geistliche Kirchengesäng*, 1599; harm. Michael Praetorius, 1609

Jesus, Priceless Treasure 17

1. Je - sus, price - less treas - ure, Source of pur - est pleas - ure, Tru - est
2. In thine arm I rest me; Foes who would mo - lest me Can - not
3. Hence, all thoughts of sad - ness! For the Lord of glad - ness, Je - sus,

friend to me, Long my heart hath pant - ed, Till it well - nigh
reach me here. Though the earth be shak - ing, Ev - ery heart be
en - ters in; Those who love the Fa - ther, Though the storms may

faint - ed, Thirst - ing aft - er thee. Thine I am, O spot - less Lamb,
quak - ing, God dis - pels our fear; Sin and hell in con - flict fell
gath - er, Still have peace with - in; Yea, what - e'er we here must bear,

I will suf - fer nought to hide thee, Ask for nought be - side thee.
With their heav - iest storms as - sail us; Je - sus will not fail us.
Still in thee lies pur - est pleas - ure, Je - sus, price - less treas - ure! A - men.

WORDS: Johann Franck, 1653; tr. Catherine Winkworth, 1863
MUSIC: Traditional German melody; adapt. Johann Crüger, 1653

JESU, MEINE FREUDE
6.6.5.6.6.5.7.8.6

18 Ah, Holy Jesus, How Hast Thou Offended?

1. Ah, ho-ly Je-sus, how hast Thou of-fend-ed,
2. Who was the guilt-y? Who brought this up-on Thee?
3. For me, kind Je-sus, was Thy in-car-na-tion,
4. There-fore, kind Je-sus, since I can-not pay Thee,

That man to judge Thee hath in hate pre-tend-ed? By foes de-
A-las, my trea-son, Je-sus, hath un-done Thee! 'Twas I, Lord
Thy mor-tal sor-row, and Thy life's ob-la-tion; Thy death of
I do a-dore Thee, and will ev-er pray Thee, Think on Thy

rid-ed, by Thine own re-ject-ed, O most af-flict-ed!
Je-sus, I it was de-nied Thee; I cru-ci-fied Thee.
an-guish and Thy bit-ter pas-sion, For my sal-va-tion.
pit-y and Thy love un-swerv-ing, Not my de-serv-ing. A-men.

WORDS: Johann Heermann, c. 1630; tr. Robert S. Bridges, 1899;
based on Jean de Fecamp. d.1078
MUSIC: Johann Crüger, 1640

HERZLIEBSTER JESU
11.11.11.5

19 If You Will Only Let God Guide You

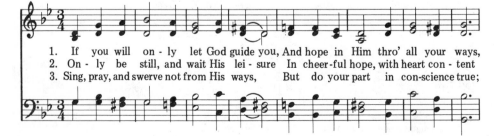

1. If you will on-ly let God guide you, And hope in Him thro' all your ways,
2. On-ly be still, and wait His lei-sure In cheer-ful hope, with heart con-tent
3. Sing, pray, and swerve not from His ways, But do your part in con-science true;

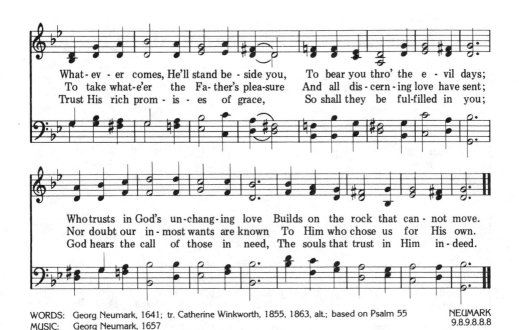

What-ev-er comes, He'll stand be-side you,   To bear you thro' the e-vil days;
To take what-e'er   the Fa-ther's plea-sure   And all dis-cern-ing love have sent;
Trust His rich prom-is-es   of grace,   So shall they be ful-filled in you;

Who trusts in God's un-chang-ing love Builds on the rock that can-not move.
Nor doubt our in-most wants are known To Him who chose us for His own.
God hears the call   of those in   need, The souls that trust in Him   in-deed.

WORDS: Georg Neumark, 1641; tr. Catherine Winkworth, 1855, 1863, alt.; based on Psalm 55   NEUMARK
MUSIC: Georg Neumark, 1657   9.8.9.8.8.8

God Moves in a Mysterious Way 20

1. God moves in   a   mys-te-rious way His won-ders   to   per-form;
2. You fear-ful   saints, fresh cour-age   take; The clouds you   so   much dread
3. Judge not   the Lord   by   fee-ble   sense, But trust Him   for   His grace;
4. His pur-pos-es   will rip-en   fast, Un-fold-ing   ev-ery   hour:
5. Blind   un-be-lief   is   sure   to   err, And scan His work   in   vain:

He plants His foot-steps in   the   sea, And rides up-on   the storm.
Are big with mer-cy, and shall break In bless-ings   on   your head.
Be-hind   a frown-ing prov-i-dence He hides a   smil-ing face.
The bud may have a   bit-ter taste, But sweet will   be   the flower.
God is   His own in-ter-pret-er, And He   will make it plain. A-men.

WORDS: William Cowper, 1774   DUNDEE
MUSIC: Thomas Ravenscroft's Psalmes, 1621   C.M.

21 Ye Servants of God, Your Master Proclaim

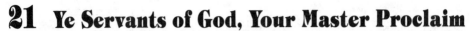

1. Ye serv-ants of God, your Mas-ter pro-claim, And pub-lish a-
2. God rul-eth on high, al-might-y to save; And still He is
3. Sal-va-tion to God who sits on the throne, Let all cry a-
4. Then let us a-dore and give Him His right, All glo-ry and

broad His won-der-ful name; The name all vic-to-rious of
nigh— His pres-ence we have; The great con-gre-ga-tion His
loud, and hon-or the Son; The prais-es of Je-sus the
pow'r, all wis-dom and might; All hon-or and bless-ing, with

Je-sus ex-tol; His king-dom is glo-rious, He rules o-ver all.
tri-umph shall sing, As-crib-ing sal-va-tion to Je-sus our King.
an-gels pro-claim, Fall down on their fac-es and wor-ship the Lamb.
an-gels a-bove, And thanks nev-er ceas-ing, and in-fi-nite love. A-men.

WORDS: Charles Wesley, 1744
MUSIC: William Croft, 1708

HANOVER
10.10.11.11

22 Stand Up and Bless the Lord

1. Stand up and bless the Lord, Ye
2. Though high a-bove all praise, A-
3. God is our strength and song, And
4. Stand up and bless the Lord, The

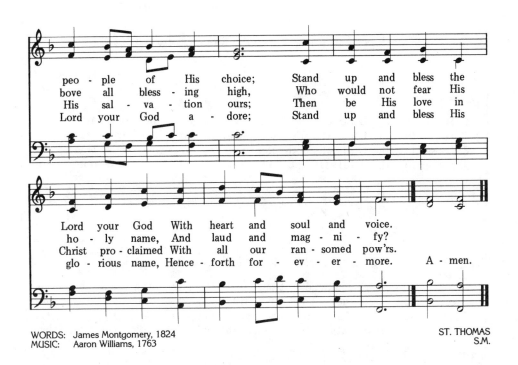

peo - ple of His choice; Stand up and bless the
bove all bless - ing high, Who would not fear His
His sal - va - tion ours; Then be His love in
Lord your God a - dore; Stand up and bless His

Lord your God With heart and soul and voice.
ho - ly name, And laud and mag - ni - fy?
Christ pro - claimed With all our ran - somed pow'rs.
glo - rious name, Hence - forth for - ev - er - more. A - men.

WORDS: James Montgomery, 1824
MUSIC: Aaron Williams, 1763

ST. THOMAS
S.M.

The Head That Once Was Crowned 23

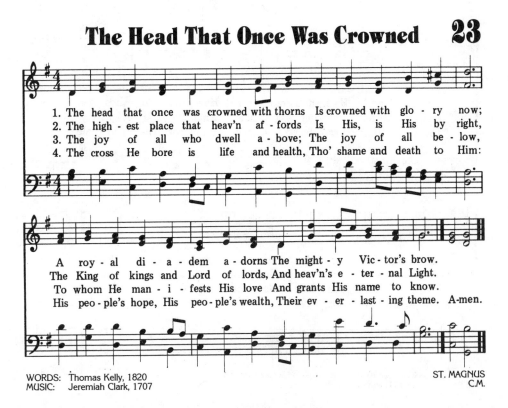

1. The head that once was crowned with thorns Is crowned with glo - ry now;
2. The high - est place that heav'n af - fords Is His, is His by right,
3. The joy of all who dwell a - bove; The joy of all be - low,
4. The cross He bore is life and health, Tho' shame and death to Him:

A roy - al di - a - dem a - dorns The might - y Vic - tor's brow.
The King of kings and Lord of lords, And heav'n's e - ter - nal Light.
To whom He man - i - fests His love And grants His name to know.
His peo - ple's hope, His peo - ple's wealth, Their ev - er - last - ing theme. A-men.

WORDS: Thomas Kelly, 1820
MUSIC: Jeremiah Clark, 1707

ST. MAGNUS
C.M.

24 Praise to the Lord, the Almighty

1. Praise to the Lord, the Al-might-y, the King of cre-a-
2. Praise to the Lord, who o'er all things so won-drous-ly reign-
3. Praise to the Lord, who doth pros-per thy work and de-fend
4. Praise to the Lord! O let all that is in me a-dore

tion! O my soul, praise Him, for He is thy health and sal-
eth, Shel-ters thee un-der His wings, yea, so gen-tly sus-
thee; Sure-ly His good-ness and mer-cy here dai-ly at-
Him! All that hath life and breath, come now with prais-es be-

va-tion! All ye who hear, Now to His tem-ple draw
tain-eth! Hast thou not seen How thy de-sires e'er have
tend thee. Pon-der a-new What the Al-might-y can
fore Him! Let the A-men Sound from His peo-ple a-

near; Join me in glad ad-o-ra-tion!
been Grant-ed in what He or-dain-eth?
do, If with His love He be-friend thee.
gain: Glad-ly for aye we a-dore Him. A-men.

WORDS: Joachim Neander, 1680; tr. Catherine Winkworth, 1863   LOBE DEN HERREN
MUSIC: *Stralsund Gesangbuch*, 1665   14.14.4.7.8

All Creatures of Our God and King 25

1. All crea-tures of our God and King, Lift up your voice and with us sing
2. Thou rush-ing wind that art so strong, Ye clouds that sail in heav'n a - long,
3. Thou flow-ing wa - ter, pure and clear, Make mu-sic for thy Lord to hear,
4. And all ye men of ten- der heart, For-giv - ing oth - ers, take your part,
5. Let all things their Cre-a - tor bless, And wor-ship Him in hum-ble - ness,

Al -le - lu - ia, Al-le - lu - ia! Thou burn-ing sun with gold - en beam,
O praise Him, Al-le - lu - ia! Thou ris - ing morn in praise re - joice,
Al-le - lu - ia, Al-le - lu - ia! Thou fire so mas - ter - ful and bright,
O sing ye, Al-le - lu - ia! Ye who long pain and sor - row bear,
O praise Him, Al-le - lu - ia! Praise, praise the Fa - ther, praise the Son,

Thou sil - ver moon with soft - er gleam, O praise Him, O praise Him,
Ye lights of eve - ning, find a voice, O praise Him, O praise Him,
That giv - est man both warmth and light, O praise Him, O praise Him,
Praise God and on Him cast your care, O praise Him, O praise Him,
And praise the Spir - it, three in one, O praise Him, O praise Him,

Al-le - lu - ia, al - le - lu - ia, al - le - lu - ia!
Al-le - lu - ia, al - le - lu - ia, al - le - lu - ia!
Al-le - lu - ia, al - le - lu - ia, al - le - lu - ia!
Al-le - lu - ia, al - le - lu - ia, al - le - lu - ia!
Al-le - lu - ia, al - le - lu - ia, al - le - lu - ia! A-men.

WORDS: St. Francis of Assisi, 1225; tr. William H. Draper, 1926
MUSIC: *Geistliche Kirchengesäng*, Cologne, 1623

LASST UNS ERFREUEN
L.M. Alleluias

26 Open Now Thy Gates of Beauty

1. O - pen now thy gates of beau - ty, Zi - on, let me en - ter there,
2. Gra - cious God, I come be - fore thee, Come thou al - so un - to me;

Where my soul in joy - ful du - ty, Waits for him who an - swers prayer.
Where we find thee and a - dore thee, There a heaven on earth must be.

O how bless - ed is this place, Filled with sol - ace, light, and grace!
To my heart O en - ter thou, Let it be thy tem - ple now.

WORDS: Benjamin Schmolck, 1732; tr. Catherine Winkworth, 1863   UNSER HERRSCHER
MUSIC: Joachim Neander, 1680   8.7.8.7.7.7

27 O for a Closer Walk with God

1. O for a clos - er walk with God, A calm and heaven - ly frame,
2. Where is the bless - ed - ness I knew When first I saw the Lord?
3. Re - turn, O ho - ly dove, re - turn, Sweet mes - sen - ger of rest!
4. The dear - est i - dol I have known, What-e'er that i - dol be,
5. So shall my walk be close with God, Calm and se - rene my frame;

A light to shine up - on the road That leads me to the Lamb!
Where is the soul - re - fresh- ing view Of Je - sus and his word?
I hate the sins that made thee mourn And drove thee from my breast.
Help me to tear it from thy throne, And wor-ship on - ly thee.
So pur - er light shall mark the road That leads me to the Lamb. A-men.

WORDS: William Cowper, 1772
MUSIC: *Scottish Psalter, 1635*

CAITHNESS
C.M.

Jesus, the Very Thought of Thee 28

1. Je - sus, the ver - y thought of thee
2. Nor voice can sing, nor heart can frame,
3. O hope of ev - ery con - trite heart,

With sweet-ness fills my breast; But sweet - er far thy
Nor can the mem - ory find, A sweet - er sound than
O joy of all the meek, To those who fall, how

face to see, And in thy pres-ence rest.
thy blest name, O Sav - ior of man - kind!
kind thou art! How good to those who seek!

WORDS: Latin, 12th century; tr. Edward Caswall, 1849, alt.
MUSIC: Jeremiah Clark, 1707

KING'S NORTON
C.M.

29 Spread, O Spread, Thou Mighty Word

1. Spread, O spread, thou might-y word, Spread the king-dom of the Lord, That to earth's re-mot-est bound Men may heed the joy-ful sound;

2. Word of how the Fa-ther's will Made the world, and keeps it, still; How his on-ly Son he gave, Man from sin and death to save;

3. Word of how the Sav-ior's love Earth's sore bur-den doth re-move; How for-ev-er, in its heav'n-ly life to save; Word through whose all-ho-ly need, Through his death the world is freed;

4. Might-y word God's Spir-it gave, Man for which the na-tions long, Spread a-broad, un-til from might Man can will and do the right;

5. Word of life, most pure and strong, Word for night All the world a-wakes to light.

WORDS: Jonathan Friedrich Bohnmaier, 1827; tr. Catherine Winkworth, 1858, alt.   GOTT SEI DANK
MUSIC: Freylinghausen's *Gesangbuch*, 1704   7.7.7.7

Sing Praise to God Who Reigns Above 30

1. Sing praise to God who reigns a - bove, The God of all cre - a - tion, The God of pow'r, the God of love, The God of our sal - va - tion; With heal - ing balm my soul He fills, And ev - ery faith - less mur-mur stills: To God all praise and glo - ry.

2. What God's al - might - y pow'r hath made His gra-cious mer - cy keep - eth; By morn-ing glow or eve-ning shade His watch-ful eye ne'er sleep - eth; With - in the king - dom of His might, Lo! all is just and all is right: To God all praise and glo - ry.

3. The Lord is nev - er far a - way, But, through all grief dis - tress-ing, An ev - er - pres - ent help and stay, Our peace, and joy, and bless - ing; As with a moth - er's ten - der hand, He leads His own, His cho-sen band: To God all praise and glo - ry.

4. Thus, all my glad - some way a - long, I sing a - loud Thy prais - es, That men may hear the grate-ful song My voice un - wea - ried rais - es, Be joy - ful in the Lord, my heart, Both soul and bod - y bear your part: To God all praise and glo - ry. A - men.

WORDS: Johann J. Schütz, 1675; tr. Frances E. Cox, 1864   MIT FREUDEN ZART
MUSIC: Bohemian Brethren's *Kirchengesänge*, Berlin, 1566   8.7.8.7.8.8.7

31 Christian Hearts, in Love United

1. Chris-tian hearts, in love u-nit-ed, Seek a-lone in Je-sus rest;
2. Come then, come, O flock of Je-sus, Cov-e-nant with Him a-new;
3. Grant, Lord, that with Thy di-rec-tion, "Love each oth-er," we com-ply,
4. O that such may be our u-nion, As Thine with the Fa-ther is,

Has He not your love ex-cit-ed? Then let love in-spire each breast;
Un-to Him, Who con-quered for us, Pledge we love and ser-vice true;
Aim-ing with un-feigned af-fec-tion Thy love to ex-em-pli-fy;
And not one of our com-mun-ion E'er for-sake the path of bliss;

Mem-bers on our Head de-pend-ing Lights re-flect-ing Him, our Sun,
And should our love's u-nion ho-ly Firm-ly linked no more re-main,
Let our mu-tual love be glow-ing, Thus will all men plain-ly see,
May our light 'fore men with bright-ness, From Thy light re-flect-ed, shine;

Breth-ren His com-mands at-tend-ing, We in Him, our Lord, are one.
Wait ye at His foot-stool low-ly, Till He draw it close a-gain.
That we, as on one stem grow-ing, Liv-ing branch-es are in Thee.
Thus the world will bear us wit-ness, That we, Lord, are tru-ly Thine. A-men.

WORDS: Nicolaus L. von Zinzendorf, 1725; tr. Frederich W. Foster, 1789
MUSIC: German melody

CASSELL
8.7.8.7 D.

Jesus Makes My Heart Rejoice 32

1. Je - sus makes my heart re - joice, I'm His sheep, and
2. Trust - ing His mild staff al - ways, I go in and
3. Should not I for glad - ness leap, Led by Je - sus

know his voice; He's a Shep - herd, kind and gra - cious,
out in peace; He will feed me with the treas - ure
as his sheep? For when these blest days are o - ver,

And His past - ures are de - li - cious; Con - stant love to
Of His grace in rich - est meas - ure; When a thirst to
To the arms of my dear Sav - ior I shall be con -

me He shows, Yea, my ve - ry name He knows.
Him I cry, Liv - ing wa - ter He'll sup - ply.
veyed to rest: A - men, yea, my lot is blest. A - men.

WORDS: Henriette Luise von Hayn, 1778; tr. Frederick W. Foster, 1789
MUSIC: *Herrnhuter Choralbuch*, 1735

HAYN
7.7.8.8.7.7

33 The Day Thou Gavest, Lord, Is Ended

1. The day thou gav - est, Lord, is end - ed,
2. We thank thee that thy Church, un - sleep - ing,
3. As o'er each con - ti - nent and is - land
4. The sun that bids us rest is wak - ing,
5. So be it, Lord; thy throne shall nev - er,

The dark - ness falls at thy be - hest;
While earth rolls on - ward in - to light,
The dawn leads on an oth - er day,
Our breth - ren 'neath the west - ern sky,
Like earth's proud em - pires, pass a - way;

To thee our morn - ing hymns as - cend - ed,
Through all the world her watch is keep - ing,
The voice of prayer is nev - er si - lent,
And hour by hour fresh lips are mak - ing
Thy king - dom stands, and grows for - ev - er,

Thy praise shall sanc - ti - fy our rest.
And rests not now by day or night.
Nor dies the strain of praise a - way.
Thy won - drous do - ings heard on high.
Till all thy crea - tures own thy sway. A - men.

WORDS: John Ellerton, 1870, alt.   LES COMMANDEMENS DE DIEU
MUSIC: Attr. Louis Bourgeois, c. 1510-c. 1561; *Genevan Psalter*, 1543   9.8.9.8

Hope of the World

34

Unison

1. Hope of the world, Thou Christ of great com - pas - sion,
2. Hope of the world, God's gift from high - est heav - en,
3. Hope of the world, a - foot on dust - y high - ways,
4. Hope of the world, Who by Thy cross didst save us
5. Hope of the world, O Christ o'er death vic - to - rious,

Speak to our fear - ful hearts by con - flict rent.
Bring - ing to hun - gry souls the bread of life,
Show - ing to wan - dering souls the path of light;
From death and dark de - spair, from sin and guilt;
Who by this sign didst con - quer grief and pain,

Save us, Thy peo - ple, from con - sum - ing pas - sion,
Still let Thy Spir - it un - to us be giv - en
Walk Thou be - side us lest the tempt - ing by - ways
We ren - der back the love Thy mer - cy gave us;
We would be faith - ful to Thy gos - pel glo - rious:

Who by our own false hopes and aims are spent.
To heal earth's wounds and end her bit - ter strife.
Lure us a - way from Thee to end - less night.
Take Thou our lives, and use them as Thou wilt.
Thou art our Lord! Thou dost for - ev - er reign! A-men.

WORDS: Georgia E. Harkness, 1954   VICAR
MUSIC: V. Earle Copes, 1963   11.10.11.10

35   Jesus, Still Lead On

1. Je - sus, still lead on, Till our rest be won, And, al - though the
2. If the way be drear, If the foe be near, Let not faith - less
3. When we seek re - lief From a long - felt grief, When op-pressed by
4. Je - sus, still lead on, Till our rest be won; Heav'n - ly lead - er,

way be cheer - less, We will fol - low, calm and fear - less;
fears o'er - take us, Let not faith and hope for - sake us;
new temp - ta - tions, Lord, in - crease and per - fect pa - tience;
still di - rect us, Still sup - port, con - sole, pro - tect us,

Guide us by Thy hand To our fa - ther - land.
For, through man - y a woe, To our home we go.
Show us that bright shore Where we weep no more.
Till we safe - ly stand In our fa - ther - land. A - men.

WORDS: Nikolaus L. von Zinzendorf, 1721;   SEELENBRÄUTIGAM
        tr. Jane L. Borthwick, 1846   5.5.8.8.5.5
MUSIC: Adam Drese, 1698

36   All People That on Earth Do Dwell

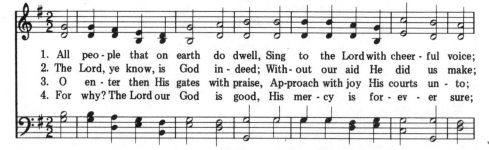

1. All peo - ple that on earth do dwell, Sing to the Lord with cheer - ful voice;
2. The Lord, ye know, is God in - deed; With - out our aid He did us make;
3. O en - ter then His gates with praise, Ap-proach with joy His courts un - to;
4. For why? The Lord our God is good, His mer - cy is for - ev - er sure;

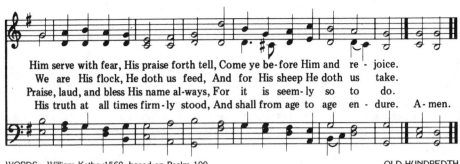

Him serve with fear, His praise forth tell, Come ye be-fore Him and re - joice.
We are His flock, He doth us feed, And for His sheep He doth us take.
Praise, laud, and bless His name al-ways, For it is seem-ly so to do.
His truth at all times firm-ly stood, And shall from age to age en - dure. A-men.

WORDS: William Kethe, 1560; based on Psalm 100
MUSIC: *Genevan Psalter*, 1551, ed. Louis Bourgeois

OLD HUNDREDTH
L.M.

Angels from the Realms of Glory 37

1. An - gels from the realms of glo - ry, Wing your flight o'er all the earth;
2. Shep-herds in the fields a - bid - ing, Watch-ing o'er your flocks by night,
3. Sag - es, leave your con - tem - pla - tions, Bright-er vi - sions beam a - far;
4. Saints be - fore the al - tar bend - ing, Watch-ing long in hope and fear,

Ye who sang cre - a - tion's sto - ry, Now pro-claim Mes - si - ah's birth:
God with man is now re - sid - ing, Yon - der shines the in - fant Light:
Seek the great De - sire of na - tions, Ye have seen His na - tal star:
Sud - den - ly the Lord, de - scend - ing, In His tem - ple shall ap - pear:

Refrain

Come and wor-ship, come and wor-ship, Wor-ship Christ, the new-born King. A-men.

WORDS: James Montgomery, 1816
MUSIC: Henry T. Smart, 1867

REGENT SQUARE
8.7.8.7.8.7

38 Jesus Shall Reign Where'er the Sun

1. Je - sus shall reign wher-e'er the sun Does his suc - ces - sive jour-neys run;
2. From north to south the na - tions meet To pay their hom - age at His feet;
3. To Him shall end - less prayer be made, And end - less prais - es crown His head;
4. Peo - ple and realms of ev - ery tongue Dwell on His love with sweet-est song,

His king-dom spread from shore to shore, Till moons shall wax and wane no more.
While west-ern em - pires own their Lord, And east-ern lands at-tend His word.
His name like sweet per - fume shall rise With ev - ery morn - ing sac - ri - fice.
And in-fant voic - es shall pro-claim Their ear - ly bless - ings on His name.

WORDS: Isaac Watts, 1719, alt.; based on Psalm 72
MUSIC: John Hatton, 1793

DUKE STREET
L.M.

39 Lord Jesus, Think on Me

1. Lord Je - sus, think on me And purge a - way my sin;
2. Lord Je - sus, think on me, With care and woe op - pressed;
3. Lord Je - sus, think on me Nor let me go a - stray;
4. Lord Je - sus, think on me, That when the flood is past,

From earth-born pas - sions set me free And make me pure with - in.
Let me Thy lov - ing serv - ant be And gain Thy prom - ised rest.
Thro' dark - ness and per - plex - i - ty Point Thou the heav'n - ly way.
I may th' e - ter - nal bright-ness see And share Thy joy at last. A-men.

WORDS: Synesius of Cyrene, c. 410; tr. Allen W. Chatfield, 1876
MUSIC: William Damon's *Psalms*, 1579

SOUTHWELL
S.M.

Comfort, Comfort Ye My People 40

1. Com - fort, com - fort ye my peo - ple, Speak ye peace, thus saith our God;
2. Hark, the voice of one that cri - eth In the des - ert far and near,
3. Make ye straight what long was crook - ed, Make the rough - er pla - ces plain;

Com - fort those who sit in dark - ness Mourn - ing 'neath their sor - rows' load.
Bid - ding all men to re - pent - ance Since the king - dom now is here.
Let your hearts be true and hum - ble, As be - fits his ho - ly reign.

Speak ye to Je - ru - sa - lem Of the peace that waits for them;
Oh, that warn - ing cry o - bey! Now pre - pare for God a way;
For the glo - ry of the Lord Now o'er earth is shed a - broad;

Tell her that her sins I cov - er, And her war - fare now is o - ver.
Let the val - leys rise to meet him And the hills bow down to greet him.
And all flesh shall see the to - ken That his word is nev - er bro - ken. A - men.

WORDS: Based on Isaiah 40: 1-8; Johannes Olearius, 1671; tr. Catherine Winkworth, 1863, alt. PSALM 42
MUSIC: *Genevan Psalter*, 1551   8.7.8.7.7.7.8.8

41   All Praise to Thee, My God

1. All praise to thee, my God, this night, For
2. For - give me, Lord, for thy dear Son, The
3. O may my soul on thee re - pose, And
4. Praise God, from whom all bless - ings flow; Praise

all the bless - ings of the light! Keep me, O keep me,
ill that I this day have done, That with the world, my -
with sweet sleep mine eye - lids close, Sleep that may me more
him, all crea - tures here be - low; Praise him a - bove, ye

King of kings, Be - neath thine own al - might - y wings!
self, and thee, I, ere I sleep, at peace may bè.
vig - orous make To serve my God when I a - wake.
heaven - ly host; Praise Fa - ther, Son, and Ho - ly Ghost. A - men.

WORDS: Thomas Ken, 1674, alt.
MUSIC: Thomas Tallis, 1560

TALLIS' CANON
L.M.

42   When All Thy Mercies, O My God

1. When all thy mer cies, O my God, My ris - ing soul sur - veys, Trans-
2. Un - num-bered com-forts to my soul Thy ten - der care be-stowed, Be-
3. Ten thou-sand thou-sand pre-cious gifts My dai - ly thanks em - ploy; Nor
4. Through all e - ter - ni - ty to thee A joy - ful song I'll raise; For,

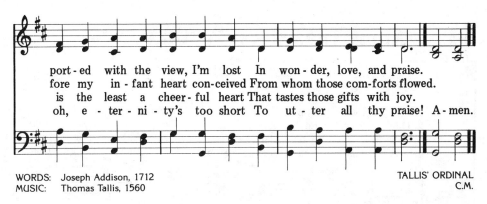

port-ed with the view, I'm lost In won-der, love, and praise.
fore my in-fant heart con-ceived From whom those com-forts flowed.
is the least a cheer-ful heart That tastes those gifts with joy.
oh, e-ter-ni-ty's too short To ut-ter all thy praise! A-men.

WORDS: Joseph Addison, 1712
MUSIC: Thomas Tallis, 1560

TALLIS' ORDINAL
C.M.

O Gladsome Light 43

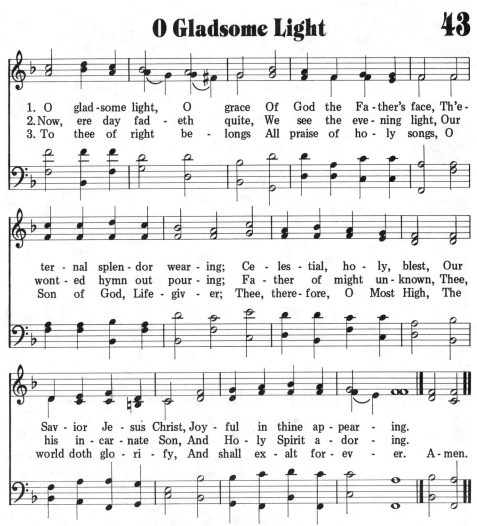

1. O glad-some light, O grace Of God the Fa-ther's face, Th'e-
2. Now, ere day fad-eth quite, We see the eve-ning light, Our
3. To thee of right be-longs All praise of ho-ly songs, O

ter-nal splen-dor wear-ing; Ce-les-tial, ho-ly, blest, Our
wont-ed hymn out pour-ing; Fa-ther of might un-known, Thee,
Son of God, Life-giv-er; Thee, there-fore, O Most High, The

Sav-ior Je-sus Christ, Joy-ful in thine ap-pear-ing.
his in-car-nate Son, And Ho-ly Spirit a-dor-ing.
world doth glo-ri-fy, And shall ex-alt for-ev-er. A-men.

WORDS: Greek: *Phōs hilaron*, 3rd century?; tr. Robert S. Bridges, 1899
MUSIC: Attr. Louis Bourgeois, 1549; harm. adapt. Claude Goudimel, 1551

NUNC DIMITTIS
6.6.7.6.6.7

44 Alone Thou Goest Forth, O Lord

1. A - lone thou go - est forth, O Lord, In
2. Our sins, not thine, thou bear - est, Lord, Make
3. This is earth's dark - est hour, but thou Dost
4. Give us com - pas - sion for thee, Lord, That,

sac - ri - fice to die; Is this thy sor - row
us thy sor - row feel, Till through our pit - y
light and life re - store; Then let all praise be
as we share this hour, Thy cross may bring us

naught to us Who pass un - heed - ing by?
and our shame Love an - swers love's ap - peal.
giv - en thee Who liv - est ev - er - more.
to thy joy And res - ur - rec - tion power. A - men.

WORDS: Peter Abelard, 1079-1142; tr. F. Bland Tucker, 1940
MUSIC: William Tans'ur, 1734

BANGOR
C.M.

45 Eternal Ruler of the Ceaseless Round

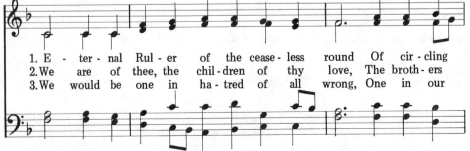

1. E - ter - nal Rul - er of the cease - less round Of cir - cling
2. We are of thee, the chil - dren of thy love, The broth - ers
3. We would be one in ha - tred of all wrong, One in our

WORDS: John W. Chadwich, 1864
MUSIC: Orlando Gibbons, 1623

SONG 1
10.10.10.10.10.10

46 Print Thine Image Pure and Holy

1. Print Thine im - age pure and ho - ly On my heart, O
2. So that noth - ing high or low - ly Thy blest like - ness

Lord of Grace;
can ef - face, Let the clear in - scrip - tion be: Je - sus,

cru - ci - fied for me, And the Lord of all cre - a -

tion, Be my ref - uge and sal - va - tion. A - men.

WORDS: Thomas Hansen Kingo, 1689; tr. Jens Christian Aaberg   PSALM 42 (FREU DICH SEHR)
MUSIC: *Genevan Psalter*, 1551; adapt. and harm. J. S. Bach, 1769   8.7.8.7.7.7.8.8

Rise, My Soul, and Stretch Thy Wings 47

1. Rise my soul, and stretch thy wings, Thy bet - ter por - tion trace;
2. Riv - ers to the o - cean run, Nor stay in all their course;
3. Cease, my soul, then, cease to mourn, Press on - ward to the prize;

Rise from tran - si - to - ry things Toward heaven, thy des - tined place.
Fire as - cend - ing seeks the sun; Both speed them to their source:
Soon the Sav - ior will re - turn Tri - um - phant in the skies:

Sun and moon and stars de - cay, Time shall soon this earth re - move;
So my soul, de - rived from God, Longs to view His glo - rious face,
Yet a sea - son, and we know Hap - py en - trance will be given,

Rise, my soul, and haste a - way To seats pre - pared a - bove.
For - ward tends to His a - bode, To rest in His em - brace.
All our sor - rows left be - low, And earth ex - changed for heaven. A - men.

WORDS: Robert Seagrave, 1742
MUSIC: John Wesley's *The Foundry Collection*, 1742

AMSTERDAM
7.6.7.6.7.7.7.6

48 Christ the Lord Is Risen Today

1. Christ the Lord is risen to-day, Al - le - lu - ia!
2. Lives a - gain our glo - rious King; Al - le - lu - ia!
3. Love's re - deem-ing work is done, Al - le - lu - ia!
4. Soar we now where Christ has led, Al - le - lu - ia!

Sons of men and an - gels say: Al - le - lu - ia!
Where, O death, is now thy sting? Al - le - lu - ia!
Fought the fight, the bat - tle won; Al - le - lu - ia!
Fol-lowing our ex - alt - ed Head; Al - le - lu - ia!

Raise your joys and tri - umphs high, Al - le - lu - ia!
Dy - ing once, He all doth save: Al - le - lu - ia!
Death in vain for - bids Him rise; Al - le - lu - ia!
Made like Him, like Him we rise; Al - le - lu - ia!

Sing, ye heav'ns, and earth re - ply, Al - le - lu - ia!
Where thy vic - to - ry, O grave? Al - le - lu - ia!
Christ has o - pened Par - a - dise. Al - le - lu - ia!
Ours the cross, the grave, the skies. Al - le - lu - ia! A-men.

WORDS: Charles Wesley, 1739
MUSIC: Arr. from *Lyra Davidica*, London, 1708

EASTER HYMN
7.7.7.7 Alleluias

The God of Abraham Praise 49

1. The God of A-braham praise, Who reigns en-throned a-bove;
2. He by Him-self hath sworn, I on His oath de-pend;
3. The God who reigns on high The great arch-an-gels sing,
4. The whole tri-um-phant host Give thanks to God on high;

An-cient of ev-er-last-ing days, And God of love.
I shall, on ea-gles' wings up-borne, To heav'n as-cend;
And "Ho-ly, ho-ly, ho-ly" cry, "Al-might-y King!"
"Hail, Fa-ther, Son and Ho-ly Ghost!" They ev-er cry.

Je-ho-vah, great I AM, By earth and heav'n con-fessed:
I shall be-hold His face, I shall His pow'r a-dore,
Who was and is the same, And ev-er-more shall be:
Hail, A-braham's God and mine! I join the heav'n-ly lays;

I bow and bless the sa-cred name For-ev-er blest.
And sing the won-ders of His grace For-ev-er-more.
Je-ho-vah, Fa-ther, great I AM, We wor-ship Thee.
All might and maj-es-ty are Thine, And end-less praise. A-men.

WORDS: Thomas Olivers, 1770; based on Jewish *Doxology*
MUSIC: Synagogue melody; arr. Meyer Lyon, 1770

LEONI
6.6.8.4 D.

50   All Hail the Power of Jesus' Name

1. All hail the power of Je - sus' name! Let an - gels pros - trate fall;
2. Ye cho - sen seed of Is - rael's race, Ye ran - somed from the fall,
3. Let ev - ery kin - dred, ev - ery tribe, On this ter - res - trial ball,
4. O that with yon - der sa - cred throng We at His feet may fall!

Bring forth the roy - al di - a - dem, And crown Him Lord of all;
Hail Him who saves you by His grace, And crown Him Lord of all;
To Him all maj - es - ty as - cribe, And crown Him Lord of all;
We'll join the ev - er - last - ing song, And crown Him Lord of all;

Bring forth the roy - al di - a - dem, And crown Him Lord of all!
Hail Him who saves you by His grace, And crown Him Lord of all!
To Him all maj - es - ty as - cribe, And crown Him Lord of all!
We'll join the ev - er - last - ing song, And crown Him Lord of all!

WORDS: Edward Perronet, 1779; adapt. John Rippon, 1787   CORONATION
MUSIC: Oliver Holden, 1792   C.M. Repeats

(Second Tune)

1. All hail the power of Je - sus' name! Let angels pros - trate fall; Bring forth the roy - al

di - a - dem, And crown Him, crown Him, crown Him, Crown Him Lord of all!

WORDS: Edward Perronet, 1779; adapt. John Rippon, 1787   MILES LANE
MUSIC: William Shrubsole, 1779   C.M. Repeats

Glorious Things of Thee Are Spoken 51

1. Glo - rious things of thee are spo - ken, Zi - on, cit - y of our God;
2. See the streams of liv - ing wa - ters, Spring-ing from e - ter - nal love,
3. Round each hab - i - ta - tion hov-ering, See the cloud and fire ap - pear
4. Sav - ior, if of Zi - on's cit - y, I through grace a mem-ber am,

He whose word can - not be bro - ken Formed thee for His own a - bode;
Well sup - ply thy sons and daugh - ters, And all fear of want re - move:
For a glo - ry and a cov - ering, Show - ing that the Lord is near!
Let the world de - ride or pit - y, I will glo - ry in Thy name;

On the Rock of A - ges found - ed, What can shake thy sure re - pose?
Who can faint, while such a riv - er Ev - er will their thirst as - suage?
Thus de - riv - ing from their ban - ner Light by night and shade by day;
Fad - ing is the world's best pleas-ure, All its boast - ed pomp and show;

With sal - va - tion's walls sur-round-ed, Thou mayst smile at all thy foes.
Grace which, like the Lord, the Giv - er, Nev - er fails from age to age.
Safe they feed up - on the man - na Which He gives them when they pray.
Sol - id joys and last - ing treas - ure None but Zi - on's chil-dren know. A-men.

WORDS: John Newton, 1779
MUSIC: Franz Joseph Haydn, 1797

AUSTRIAN HYMN
8.7.8.7 D.

52   All Hail the Power of Jesus' Name

1. All hail the pow'r of Je-sus' name! Let an-gels pros-trate fall, Let an-gels pros-trate fall; Bring forth the roy-al di-a-dem, And crown Him, crown Him, crown Him, crown Him, And crown Him Lord of all. A-men.
2. Ye cho-sen seed of Is-rael's race, Ye ran-somed of the fall, Ye ran-somed of the fall; Hail Him who saves you by His grace,
3. Let ev-ery kin-dred, ev-ery tribe, On this ter-res-trial ball, On this ter-res-trial ball; To Him all maj-es-ty as-cribe,
4. O that with yon-der sa-cred throng We at His feet may fall, We at His feet may fall! We'll join the ev-er-last-ing song,

WORDS: Edward Perronet, 1779; adapt. John Rippon, 1787
MUSIC: James Ellor, 1838

DIADEM
C.M. Ref.

Redeemed, How I Love to Proclaim It 53

1. Re-deemed, how I love to pro-claim it! Re-deemed by the blood of the Lamb; Re-deemed thro' His in-fi-nite mer-cy, His child, and for-ev-er, I am.
2. Re-deemed and so hap-py in Je-sus, No lan-guage my rap-ture can tell; I know that the light of His pres-ence With me doth con-tin-ual-ly dwell.
3. I think of my bless-ed Re-deem-er, I think of Him all the day long; I sing, for I can-not be si-lent; His love is the theme of my song.

Refrain

Re-deemed, re-deemed, Re-deemed by the blood of the Lamb; Re-deemed thro' His in-fi-nite mer-cy, His child, and for-ev-er, I am.

WORDS: Fanny J. Crosby, 1882
MUSIC: A. L. Butler, 1966

ADA
9.8.9.8 Ref.

54 And Can It Be That I Should Gain

1. And can it be that I should gain An in - t'rest in the
2. 'Tis mys - tery all! Th'Im - mor - tal dies! Who can ex - plore His
3. He left His Fa - ther's throne a - bove, So free, so in - fi -
4. Long my im - pris - oned spir - it lay Fast bound in sin and
5. No con - dem - na - tion now I dread; Je - sus, and all in

Sav - ior's blood? Died He for me, who caused His pain? For me, who
strange de - sign? In vain the first - born ser - aph tries To sound the
nite His grace; Emp - tied Him - self of all but love, And bled for
na - ture's night; Thine eye dif - fused a quick - 'ning ray, I woke, the
Him, is mine! A - live in Him, my liv - ing Head, And clothed in

Him to death pur - sued? A - maz - ing love! how can it be That
depths of love di - vine! 'Tis mer - cy all! let earth a - dore, Let
Ad - am's help - less race; 'Tis mer - cy all, im - mense and free; For,
dun - geon flamed with light; My chains fell off, my heart was free; I
right - eous - ness di - vine, Bold I ap - proach th'e - ter - nal throne, And

Refrain

Thou, my God, shouldst die for me?
an - gel minds in - quire no more.
O my God, it found out me. A - maz - ing love! how
rose, went forth and fol - lowed Thee.
claim the crown, through Christ my own. A - maz - ing love!

can   it   be   That Thou,   my   God, shouldst die for me. A - men.
How can it be   That Thou, my God,

WORDS: Charles Wesley, 1738   SAGINA
MUSIC: Thomas Campbell, 1825   8.8.8.8.8.8 Ref.

Jesus, Thou Joy of Loving Hearts **55**

1. Je - sus, Thou Joy of lov - ing hearts, Thou Fount of
2. Thy   truth un - changed hath ev - er stood; Thou sav - est
3. We   taste Thee, O Thou liv - ing Bread, And long to
4. Our   rest - less spir - its yearn for Thee, Where - e'er our
5. O   Je - sus, ev - er with us stay, Make all our

life, Thou Light of men, From the best bliss that earth im -
those that on Thee call; To them that seek Thee, Thou art
feast up - on Thee still; We drink of Thee, the Foun - tain -
change - ful lot is cast; Glad, when Thy gra - cious smile we
mo - ments calm and bright; Chase the dark night of sin a -

parts, We turn un - filled to Thee a - gain.
good, To them that find Thee, all in all.
head, And thirst our souls from Thee to fill.
see, Blest, when our faith can hold Thee fast.
way, Shed o'er the world Thy ho - ly light. A - men.

WORDS: Attr. Bernard of Clairvaux, c.1150; tr. Ray Palmer, 1858   QUEBEC
MUSIC: Henry Baker, 1854   L.M.

56 "Welcome, Happy Morning!"

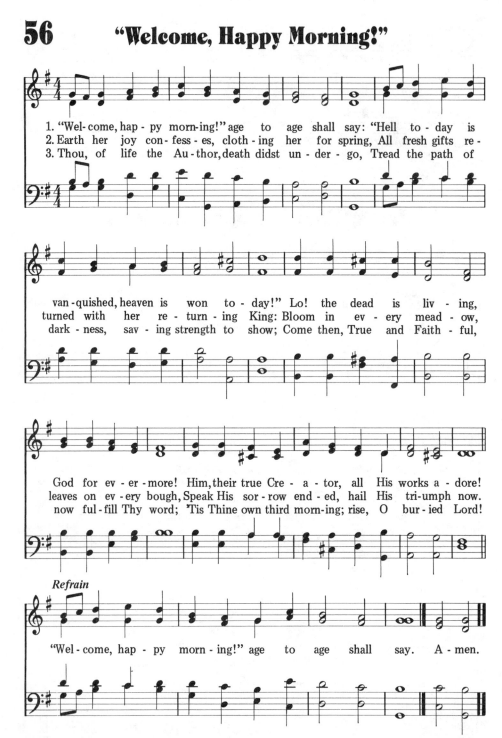

1. "Wel-come, hap-py morn-ing!" age to age shall say: "Hell to-day is
2. Earth her joy con-fess-es, cloth-ing her for spring, All fresh gifts re-
3. Thou, of life the Au-thor, death didst un-der-go, Tread the path of

van-quished, heaven is won to-day!" Lo! the dead is liv-ing,
turned with her re-turn-ing King: Bloom in ev-ery mead-ow,
dark-ness, sav-ing strength to show; Come then, True and Faith-ful,

God for ev-er-more! Him, their true Cre-a-tor, all His works a-dore!
leaves on ev-ery bough, Speak His sor-row end-ed, hail His tri-umph now.
now ful-fill Thy word; 'Tis Thine own third morn-ing; rise, O bur-ied Lord!

Refrain

"Wel-come, hap-py morn-ing!" age to age shall say. A-men.

WORDS: Venantius Fortunatus, 530-609; John Ellerton, 1826-1893   FORTUNATUS
MUSIC: Arthur S. Sullivan, 1842-1900   11.11.11.11 Ref.

O Come, O Come, Emmanuel

57

Unison

1. O come, O come, Em - man - u - el, And ran - som cap - tive
2. O come, Thou Rod of Jes - se, free Thine own from Sa - tan's
3. O come, Thou Day-spring, come and cheer Our spir - its by Thine
4. O come, Thou Key of Da - vid, come, And o - pen wide our
5. O come, De - sire of na - tions, bind All peo - ples in one

Is - ra - el, That mourns in lone - ly ex - ile here
tyr - an - ny; From depths of hell Thy peo - ple save
ad - vent here; And drive a - way the shades of night,
heav'n - ly home; Make safe the way that leads on high,
heart and mind; Bid en - vy, strife and quar - rels cease;

Un - til the Son of God ap - pear.
And give them vic - t'ry o'er the grave.
And pierce the clouds and bring us light! Re - joice! re - joice! Em-
And close the path to mis - er - y.
Fill all the world with heav - en's peace.

man - u - el Shall come to thee, O Is - ra - el! A - men.

WORDS: Latin hymn; tr. John M. Neale, 1851; St. 5, Henry Sloane Coffin, 1916   VENI EMMANUEL
MUSIC: Thomas Helmore, 1854; based on plainsong phrases   8.8.8.8.8.8

58   The Day of Resurrection

1. The day of res-ur-rec-tion! Earth, tell it out a-broad;
2. Our hearts be pure from e-vil, That we may see a-right
3. Now let the heav'ns be joy-ful! Let earth her song be-gin!

The Pass-o-ver of glad-ness, The Pass-o-ver of God.
The Lord in rays e-ter-nal Of res-ur-rec-tion light;
The world re-sound in tri-umph, And all that is there-in;

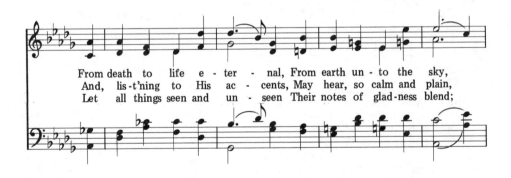

From death to life e-ter-nal, From earth un-to the sky,
And, lis-t'ning to His ac-cents, May hear, so calm and plain,
Let all things seen and un-seen Their notes of glad-ness blend;

Our Christ hath brought us o-ver With hymns of vic-to-ry.
His own "All hail!" and, hear-ing, May raise the vic-tor strain.
For Christ the Lord hath ris-en, Our Joy that hath no end.

WORDS: John of Damascus, 8th Century; tr. John M. Neale, 1862   LANCASHIRE
MUSIC: Henry T. Smart, 1835   7.6.7.6 D.

The Church's One Foundation 59

1. The Church's one foun-da-tion Is Je-sus Christ her Lord;
2. E-lect from ev-ery na-tion, Yet one o'er all the earth,
3. Though with a scorn-ful won-der Men see her sore op-pressed,
4. 'Mid toil and trib-u-la-tion, And tu-mult of her war,
5. Yet she on earth hath un-ion With God, the Three in One,

She is His new cre-a-tion, By wa-ter and the word:
Her char-ter of sal-va-tion, One Lord, one faith, one birth;
By schisms rent a-sun-der, By her-e-sies dis-tressed:
She waits the con-sum-ma-tion Of peace for-ev-er-more;
And mys-tic sweet com-mun-ion With those whose rest is won:

From heav'n He came and sought her To be His ho-ly bride;
One ho-ly name she bless-es, Par-takes one ho-ly food,
Yet saints their watch are keep-ing, Their cry goes up, "How long?"
Till with the vi-sion glo-rious Her long-ing eyes are blest,
O hap-py ones and ho-ly! Lord, give us grace that we,

With His own blood He bought her, And for her life He died.
And to one hope she press-es, With ev-ery grace en-dued.
And soon the night of weep-ing Shall be the morn of song.
And the great Church vic-to-rious Shall be the Church at rest.
Like them, the meek and low-ly, On high may dwell with Thee. A-men.

WORDS: Samuel J. Stone, 1868
MUSIC: Samuel S. Wesley, 1864

AURELIA
7.6.7.6 D.

60 Jerusalem the Golden

1. Je - ru - sa - lem the gold - en, With milk and hon - ey blest!
2. They stand, those halls of Zi - on, All ju - bi - lant with song,
3. There is the throne of Da - vid; And there, from care re - leased,
4. O sweet and bless - ed coun - try, The home of God's e - lect!

Be - neath thy con - tem - pla - tion Sink heart and voice op - pressed;
And bright with many an an - gel, And all the mar - tyr throng;
The song of them that tri - umph, The shout of them that feast;
O sweet and bless - ed coun - try That ea - ger hearts ex - pect!

I know not, O I know not What joys a - wait me there;
The Prince is ev - er in them, The day - light is se - rene;
And they, who with their Lead - er Have con - quered in the fight,
Je - sus, in mer - cy bring us To that dear land of rest;

What ra - dian - cy of glo - ry, What bliss be - yond com - pare!
The pas - tures of the bless - ed Are decked in glo - rious sheen.
For - ev - er and for - ev - er Are clad in robes of white.
Who art, with God the Fa - ther, And Spir - it, ev - er blest. A - men.

WORDS: Bernard of Cluny, c.1145; tr. John M. Neale, 1851, and others
MUSIC: Alexander Ewing, 1853

EWING
7.6.7.6. D.

Hark! the Herald Angels Sing 61

1. Hark! the her - ald an - gels sing, "Glo - ry to the new - born King:
2. Christ, by high - est heav'n a - dored; Christ, the ev - er - last - ing Lord!
3. Hail the heav'n - born Prince of Peace! Hail the Sun of Right - eous - ness!

Peace on earth, and mer - cy mild, God and sin - ners rec - on - ciled!"
Late in time be - hold Him come, Off - spring of the Vir - gin's womb:
Light and life to all He brings, Ris'n with heal - ing in His wings.

Joy - ful, all ye na - tions, rise, Join the tri - umph of the skies;
Veiled in flesh the God - head see; Hail th'in - car - nate De - i - ty,
Mild He lays His glo - ry by, Born that man no more may die,

With th'an - gel - ic host pro - claim, "Christ is born in Beth - le - hem!"
Pleased as man with men to dwell, Je - sus, our Em - man - u - el.
Born to raise the sons of earth, Born to give them sec - ond birth.

Hark! the her - ald an - gels sing, "Glo - ry to the new - born King." A - men.

WORDS: Charles Wesley, 1739
MUSIC: Felix Mendelssohn, 1840; arr. William H. Cummings, 1856

MENDELSSOHN
7.7.7.7 D. Ref.

62 Come, Ye Thankful People, Come

1. Come, ye thank-ful peo - ple, come, Raise the song of har - vest-home:
2. All the world is God's own field, Fruit un - to His praise to yield;
3. For the Lord our God shall come, And shall take His har - vest home;
4. E - ven so, Lord, quick - ly come To Thy fi - nal har - vest-home;

All is safe - ly gath - ered in, Ere the win - ter storms be - gin;
Wheat and tares to - geth - er sown, Un - to joy or sor - row grown;
From His field shall in that day All of - fens - es purge a - way;
Gath - er Thou Thy peo - ple in, Free from sor - row, free from sin;

God, our Ma - ker, doth pro - vide For our wants to be sup - plied:
First the blade, and then the ear, Then the full corn shall ap - pear:
Give His an - gels charge at last In the fire the tares to cast;
There, for - ev - er pu - ri - fied, In Thy pres - ence to a - bide:

Come to God's own tem - ple, come, Raise the song of har - vest-home.
Lord of har - vest, grant that we Whole-some grain and pure may be.
But the fruit - ful ears to store In His gar - ner ev - er - more.
Come, with all Thine an - gels, come, Raise the glo - rious har - vest-home. A-men.

WORDS: Henry Alford, 1844   ST. GEORGE'S, WINDSOR
MUSIC: George J. Elvey, 1858   7.7.7.7 D.

Come, Ye Faithful, Raise the Strain 63

1. Come, ye faith-ful, raise the strain Of tri-um-phant glad-ness;
2. 'Tis the spring of souls to-day, Christ hath burst His pris-on,
3. "Al-le-lu-ia!" now we cry To our King Im-mor-tal,

God hath brought His peo-ple forth In-to joy from sad-ness.
And from three day's sleep in death As a sun hath ris-en.
Who, tri-um-phant, burst the bars Of the tomb's dark por-tal;

Now re-joice, Je-ru-sa-lem, And with true af-fec-tion
All the win-ter of our sins, Long and dark, is fly-ing
"Al-le-lu-ia!" with the Son, God the Fa-ther prais-ing;

Wel-come in un-wea-ried strains Je-sus' res-ur-rec-tion.
From His light, to whom we give Laud and praise un-dy-ing.
"Al-le-lu-ia!" yet a-gain To the Spir-it rais-ing. A-men.

WORDS: John of Damascus, 8th century; tr. John M. Neale, 1859
MUSIC: Arthur S. Sullivan, 1872

ST. KEVIN
7.6.7.6 D.

64 From Heaven Above to Earth I Come

1. From heav'n a - bove to earth I come To bear good news to ev - ery home;
2. "To you, this night is born a Child Of Ma - ry, cho - sen moth - er mild;
3. Ah, dear - est Je - sus, ho - ly Child, Make Thee a bed, soft, un - de - filed
4. Glo - ry to God in high - est heav'n, Who un - to man His Son hath giv'n.

Glad ti-dings of great joy I bring, Where-of I now will say and sing:
This lit - tle Child of low-ly birth Shall be the joy of all your earth."
With - in my heart, that it may be A qui - et cham-ber kept for Thee.
While an-gels sing with ten-der mirth, A glad new year to all the earth. A-men.

WORDS: Martin Luther, 1535; tr. Catherine Winkworth, 1855
MUSIC: *Geistliche Lieder*, Leipzig, 1539

VOM HIMMEL HOCH
L.M.

65 How Sweet the Name of Jesus Sounds

1. How sweet the name of Je - sus sounds In a be - liev - er's ear!
2. Dear name! the rock on which I build, My shield and hid - ing - place,
3. Je - sus, my Shep-herd, Broth - er, Friend, My Proph - et, Priest, and King,
4. Weak is the ef - fort of my heart, And cold my warm-est thought;
5. Till then I would Thy love pro - claim With ev - ery fleet - ing breath;

It soothes his sor - rows, heals his wounds, And drives a - way his fear.
My nev - er - fail - ing treas - ury, filled With bound-less stores of grace.
My Lord, my life, my way, my end, Ac - cept the praise I bring.
But when I see Thee as Thou art, I'll praise Thee as I ought.
And may the mu - sic of Thy name Re - fresh my soul in death. A-men.

WORDS: John Newton, 1779
MUSIC: Alexander R. Reinagle, c.1836

ST. PETER
C.M.

Where Cross the Crowded Ways of Life 66

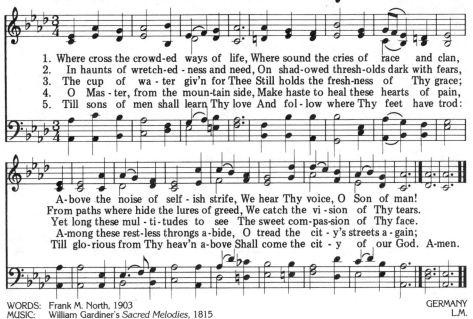

1. Where cross the crowd-ed ways of life, Where sound the cries of race and clan,
2. In haunts of wretch-ed - ness and need, On shad-owed thresh-olds dark with fears,
3. The cup of wa - ter giv'n for Thee Still holds the fresh-ness of Thy grace;
4. O Mas - ter, from the moun-tain side, Make haste to heal these hearts of pain,
5. Till sons of men shall learn Thy love And fol - low where Thy feet have trod:

A-bove the noise of self - ish strife, We hear Thy voice, O Son of man!
From paths where hide the lures of greed, We catch the vi -sion of Thy tears.
Yet long these mul - ti-tudes to see The sweet com-pas-sion of Thy face.
A-mong these rest-less throngs a-bide, O tread the cit - y's streets a - gain;
Till glo-rious from Thy heav'n a-bove Shall come the cit - y of our God. A-men.

WORDS: Frank M. North, 1903
MUSIC: William Gardiner's *Sacred Melodies*, 1815

GERMANY
L.M.

The Lord's My Shepherd, I'll Not Want 67

1. The Lord's my Shep - herd, I'll not want; He makes me down to lie
2. My soul He doth re - store a - gain; And me to walk doth make
3. Yea, though I walk through death's dark vale, Yet will I fear no ill;
4. My ta - ble Thou hast fur - nish - ed In pres - ence of my foes;
5. Good-ness and mer - cy all my life Shall sure - ly fol - low me;

In pas-tures green; He lead - eth me The qui - et wa - ters by.
With - in the paths of right-eous - ness, E'en for His own name's sake.
For Thou art with me, and Thy rod And staff me com - fort still.
My head Thou dost with oil a - noint, And my cup o - ver-flows.
And in God's house for - ev - er - more My dwell -ing place shall be. A-men.

WORDS: Scottish Psalter, 1650; William Whittingham and others; based on Psalm 23
MUSIC: Jessie S. Irvine, 1871; arr. David Grant, 1872

CRIMOND
C.M.

68 O Master, Let Me Walk with Thee

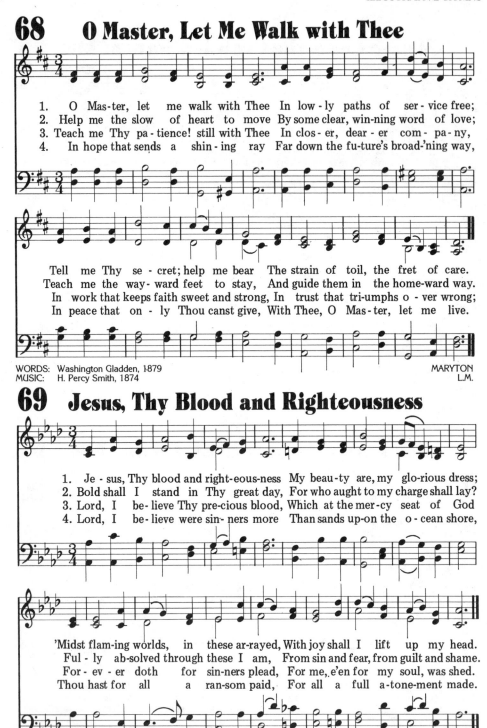

1. O Mas-ter, let me walk with Thee In low-ly paths of ser-vice free;
2. Help me the slow of heart to move By some clear, win-ning word of love;
3. Teach me Thy pa-tience! still with Thee In clos-er, dear-er com-pa-ny,
4. In hope that sends a shin-ing ray Far down the fu-ture's broad-'ning way,

Tell me Thy se-cret; help me bear The strain of toil, the fret of care.
Teach me the way-ward feet to stay, And guide them in the home-ward way.
In work that keeps faith sweet and strong, In trust that tri-umphs o-ver wrong;
In peace that on-ly Thou canst give, With Thee, O Mas-ter, let me live.

WORDS: Washington Gladden, 1879
MUSIC: H. Percy Smith, 1874

MARYTON
L.M.

69 Jesus, Thy Blood and Righteousness

1. Je-sus, Thy blood and right-eous-ness My beau-ty are, my glo-rious dress;
2. Bold shall I stand in Thy great day, For who aught to my charge shall lay?
3. Lord, I be-lieve Thy pre-cious blood, Which at the mer-cy seat of God
4. Lord, I be-lieve were sin-ners more Than sands up-on the o-cean shore,

'Midst flam-ing worlds, in these ar-rayed, With joy shall I lift up my head.
Ful-ly ab-solved through these I am, From sin and fear, from guilt and shame.
For-ev-er doth for sin-ners plead, For me, e'en for my soul, was shed.
Thou hast for all a ran-som paid, For all a full a-tone-ment made.

WORDS: Nikolaus L. von Zinzendorf, 1739; tr. John Wesley, 1740
MUSIC: William Gardiner's Sacred Melodies, 1815

GERMANY
L.M.

Jesus, Lover of My Soul

70

1. Je - sus, Lov - er of my soul, Let me to Thy bos - om fly,
2. Oth - er ref - uge have I none; Hangs my help - less soul on Thee;
3. Thou, O Christ, art all I want; More than all in Thee I find;
4. Plen - teous grace with Thee is found, Grace to cov - er all my sin;

While the near - er wa - ters roll, While the tem - pest still is high;
Leave, ah! leave me not a - lone, Still sup - port and com - fort me.
Raise the fall - en, cheer the faint, Heal the sick, and lead the blind.
Let the heal - ing streams a - bound; Make and keep me pure with - in.

Hide me, O my Sav - ior, hide, Till the storm of life is past;
All my trust on Thee is stayed, All my help from Thee I bring;
Just and ho - ly is Thy name, I am all un - right - eous - ness;
Thou of life the foun - tain art, Free - ly let me take of Thee;

Safe in - to the ha - ven guide; O re - ceive my soul at last!
Cov - er my de - fense - less head With the shad - ow of Thy wing.
False and full of sin I am, Thou art full of truth and grace.
Spring Thou up with - in my heart, Rise to all e - ter - ni - ty.

WORDS: Charles Wesley, 1740
MUSIC: Joseph Parry, 1879

ABERYSTWYTH
7.7.7.7 D.

71 O God of Earth and Altar

1. O God of earth and al - tar, Bow down and hear our cry;
2. From all that ter - ror teach - es, From lies of tongue and pen,
3. Tie in a liv - ing teth - er The prince and priest and thrall;

Our earth - ly rul - ers fal - ter, Our peo - ple drift and die;
From all the eas - y speech - es That com - fort cru - el men,
Bind all our lives to - geth - er, Smite us and save us all;

The walls of gold en - tomb us, The swords of scorn di - vide;
From sale and prof - a - na - tion Of hon - or and the sword,
In ire and ex - ul - ta - tion A - flame with faith, and free,

Take not thy thun - der from us, But take a - way our pride.
From sleep and from dam - na - tion, De - liv - er us, good Lord!
Lift up a liv - ing na - tion, A sin - gle sword to thee. A - men.

WORDS: Gilbert K. Chesterton, 1906
MUSIC: Traditional Welsh melody

LLANGLOFFAN
7.6.7.6 D.

God of Grace and God of Glory   72

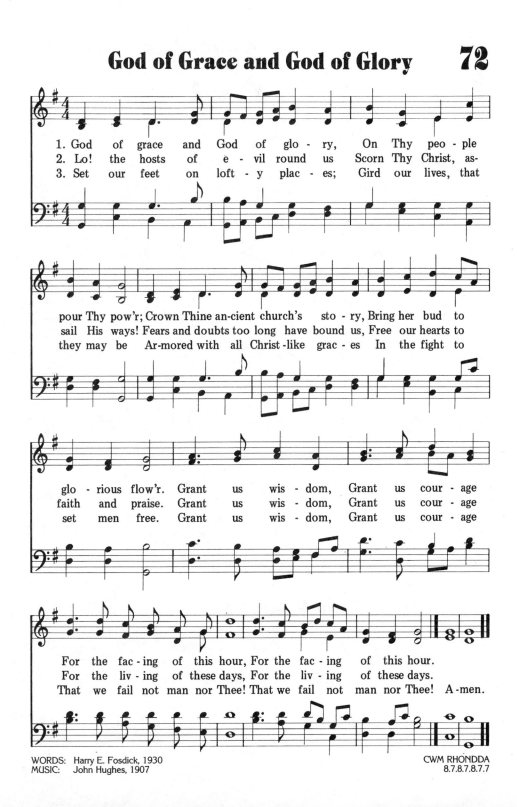

1. God of grace and God of glo - ry, On Thy peo - ple
2. Lo! the hosts of e - vil round us Scorn Thy Christ, as-
3. Set our feet on loft - y plac - es; Gird our lives, that

pour Thy pow'r; Crown Thine an-cient church's sto - ry, Bring her bud to
sail His ways! Fears and doubts too long have bound us, Free our hearts to
they may be Ar-mored with all Christ -like grac - es In the fight to

glo - rious flow'r. Grant us wis - dom, Grant us cour - age
faith and praise. Grant us wis - dom, Grant us cour - age
set men free. Grant us wis - dom, Grant us cour - age

For the fac - ing of this hour, For the fac - ing of this hour.
For the liv - ing of these days, For the liv - ing of these days.
That we fail not man nor Thee! That we fail not man nor Thee! A -men.

WORDS: Harry E. Fosdick, 1930   CWM RHONDDA
MUSIC: John Hughes, 1907   8.7.8.7.8.7.7

73 Lord of Our Life, and God of Our Salvation

1. Lord of our life, and God of our sal - va - tion, Star of our
night, and hope of ev - ery na - tion, Hear and re - ceive thy
Church's sup - pli - ca - tion, Lord God al - might - y.

2. Lord, thou canst help when earth - ly ar - mor fail - eth; Lord, thou canst
save when sin it - self as - sail - eth; Lord, o'er thy rock nor
death nor hell pre - vail - eth; Grant us thy peace, Lord:

3. Peace, in our hearts, our e - vil thoughts as - suag - ing; Peace, in thy
Church, where broth - ers are en - gag - ing; Peace, when the world its
bus - y war is wag - ing; Calm thy foes' rag - ing!

4. Grant us our help till back - ward they are driv - en; Grant them thy
truth, that they may be for - giv - en; Grant peace on earth, or
af - ter we have striv - en; Peace in thy heav - en. A - men.

WORDS: Matthäus von Löwenstern, 1644; tr. Philip Pusey, 1834
MUSIC: *Poiliers Antiphoner*, 1746

ISTE CONFESSOR
11.11.11.5

74 Lift Up Your Voice, Ye Christian Folk

1. Lift up your voice, ye Chris - tian folk, To praise the Ho - ly
2. Lift up your voice! with shout and song Ex - tol his maj - es -

One, Who ran - soms us from Sa - tan's yoke Through
ty, Whose power hath made the fee - ble strong And

Christ, his bless - ed Son. Lo, we who were in
caused the blind to see. And when the sound of

griev - ous state By rea - son of our sin, Our
praise grows dim Still may our lives forth tell, In

heads look up, our fears a - bate, Our tri - umphs now be - gin.
all we do, our love of him Who do - eth all things well.

WORDS: P. H. B. Lyon, 1932   LADYWELL
MUSIC: William H. Ferguson, 1919   C.M.D.

Words from THE RUGBY SCHOOL HYMN BOOK, London, 1932. Used by permission of the author.
Music from THE PUBLIC SCHOOL HYMN BOOK, London, 1919. Music copyright by the Royal School of Church Music, Croydon,
England. Used by Permission.

75   **For All the Saints**

Unison, stanzas 1, 2 and 6.

1. For all the saints who from their la - bors rest, Who Thee by faith be -
2. Thou wast their rock, their fort-ress and their might; Thou, Lord, their cap-tain
6. From earth's wide bounds and o-cean's far-thest coast, Thro' gates of pearl stream

fore the world con-fessed, Thy name, O Je - sus, be for - ev - er blest.
in the well-fought fight; Thou in the dark - ness drear, their one true light.
in the count-less host, Sing - ing to Fa - ther, Son, and Ho - ly Ghost.

(after stanza 6)

Al - le - lu - ia! Al - le - lu - ia! A - men.

Harmony, stanzas 3, 4, 5.

3. O blest com-mun - ion, fel - low - ship di - vine! We fee - bly strug - gle;
4. And when the strife is fierce, the war - fare long, Steals on the ear the
5. The gold - en eve - ning bright-ens in the west; Soon, soon to faith - ful

they in glo - ry shine. Yet all are one in Thee, for all are Thine.
dis - tant tri - umph song, And hearts are brave a - gain and arms are strong.
war - riors com - eth rest; And sweet the calm of Par - a - dise, the blest.

(Sop.) Al - le - lu - ia!
D.C. stanza 6

Al - le - lu - ia! Al - le - lu - ia!

WORDS: William W. How, 1864
MUSIC: Ralph Vaughan Williams, 1906

SINE NOMINE
10.10.10 Alleluias

Music from the ENGLISH HYMNAL by permission of Oxford University Press, London.

Amazing Grace! How Sweet the Sound 76

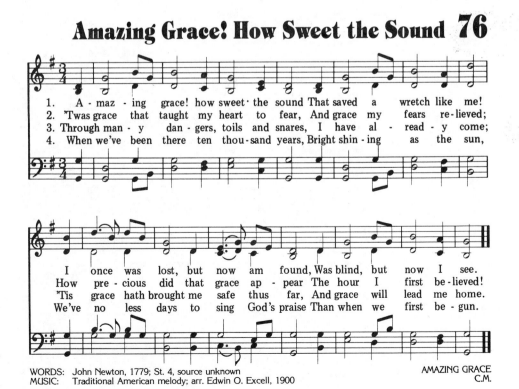

1. A - maz - ing grace! how sweet · the sound That saved a wretch like me!
2. 'Twas grace that taught my heart to fear, And grace my fears re - lieved;
3. Through man - y dan - gers, toils and snares, I have al - read - y come;
4. When we've been there ten thou - sand years, Bright shin - ing as the sun,

I once was lost, but now am found, Was blind, but now I see.
How pre - cious did that grace ap - pear The hour I first be - lieved!
'Tis grace hath brought me safe thus far, And grace will lead me home.
We've no less days to sing God's praise Than when we first be - gun.

WORDS: John Newton, 1779; St. 4, source unknown
MUSIC: Traditional American melody; arr. Edwin O. Excell, 1900

AMAZING GRACE
C.M.

77   Be Thou My Vision

Unison

1. Be Thou my Vi - sion, O Lord of my heart;
2. Be Thou my Wis - dom, and Thou my true Word;
3. Rich - es I heed not, nor man's emp - ty praise,
4. High King of heav - en, my vic - to - ry won,

Naught be all else to me, save that Thou art—
I ev - er with Thee and Thou with me, Lord;
Thou mine in - her - i - tance, now and al - ways;
May I reach heav - en's joys, O bright heav'n's Sun!

Thou my best thought, by day or by night,
Thou my great Fa - ther, I Thy true son;
Thou and Thou on - ly, first in my heart,
Heart of my own heart, what - ev - er be - fall,

Wak - ing or sleep - ing, Thy pres - ence my light.
Thou in me dwell - ing, and I with Thee one.
High King of heav - en, my Treas - ure Thou art.
Still be my Vi - sion, O Rul - er of all. A - men.

WORDS: Irish hymn, c. 8th century; tr. Mary E. Byrne, 1905; versified Eleanor H. Hull, 1912   SLANE
MUSIC: Traditional Irish melody; arr. Donald P. Hustad, 1973   10.10.10.10

Come, All Christians, Be Committed 78

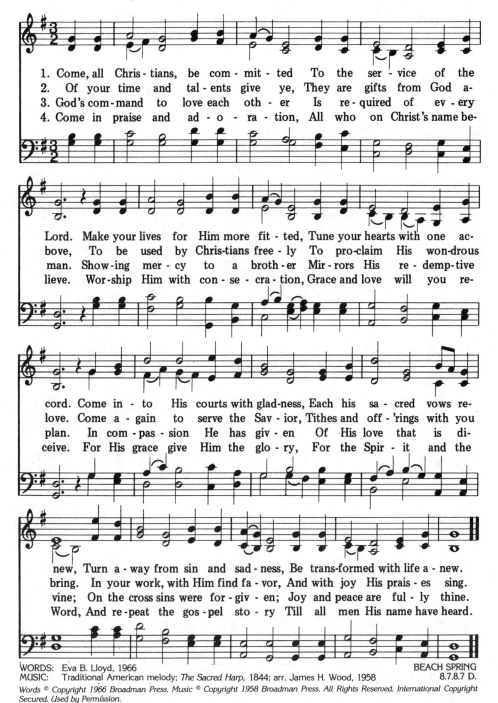

1. Come, all Chris-tians, be com-mit-ted To the ser-vice of the
2. Of your time and tal-ents give ye, They are gifts from God a-
3. God's com-mand to love each oth-er Is re-quired of ev-ery
4. Come in praise and ad-o-ra-tion, All who on Christ's name be-

Lord. Make your lives for Him more fit-ted, Tune your hearts with one ac-
bove, To be used by Chris-tians free-ly To pro-claim His won-drous
man. Show-ing mer-cy to a broth-er Mir-rors His re-demp-tive
lieve. Wor-ship Him with con-se-cra-tion, Grace and love will you re-

cord. Come in-to His courts with glad-ness, Each his sa-cred vows re-
love. Come a-gain to serve the Sav-ior, Tithes and off-'rings with you
plan. In com-pas-sion He has giv-en Of His love that is di-
ceive. For His grace give Him the glo-ry, For the Spir-it and the

new, Turn a-way from sin and sad-ness, Be trans-formed with life a-new.
bring. In your work, with Him find fa-vor, And with joy His prais-es sing.
vine; On the cross sins were for-giv-en; Joy and peace are ful-ly thine.
Word, And re-peat the gos-pel sto-ry Till all men His name have heard.

WORDS: Eva B. Lloyd, 1966
MUSIC: Traditional American melody; *The Sacred Harp*, 1844; arr. James H. Wood, 1958

BEACH SPRING
8.7.8.7 D.

79 O Sing a Song of Bethlehem

1. O sing a song of Beth-le-hem, Of shep-herds watch-ing there,
2. O sing a song of Naz-a-reth, Of sun-ny days of joy,
3. O sing a song of Gal-i-lee, Of lake and woods and hill,
4. O sing a song of Cal-va-ry, Its glo-ry and dis-may;

And of the news that came to them From an-gels in the air:
O sing of fra-grant flow-ers' breath, And of the sin-less Boy:
Of Him who walked up-on the sea And bade the waves be still:
Of Him who hung up-on the tree, And took our sins a-way:

The light that shone on Beth-le-hem Fills all the world to-day;
For now the flowers of Naz-a-reth In ev-ery heart may grow;
For though like waves on Gal-i-lee, Dark seas of trou-ble roll,
For He who died on Cal-va-ry Is ris-en from the grave,

Of Je-sus' birth and peace on earth The an-gels sing al-way.
Now spreads the fame of His dear name On all the winds that blow.
When faith has heard the Mas-ter's word, Falls peace up-on the soul.
And Christ, our Lord, by heav'n a-dored, Is might-y now to save.

WORDS: Louis F. Benson, 1899
MUSIC: Traditional English melody; arr. Ralph Vaughan Williams, 1906

KINGSFOLD
C.M.D.

Music from the ENGLISH HYMNAL by permission of Oxford University Press, London.

From Greenland's Icy Mountains

80

1. From Green-land's i - cy moun-tains, From In - dia's cor - al strand,
2. What though the spic - y breez - es Blow soft o'er Cey-lon's isle;
3. Shall we, whose souls are light - ed With wis - dom from on high,
4. Waft, waft, ye winds, His sto - ry, And you, ye wa - ters, roll,

Where Af - ric's sun - ny foun - tains Roll down their gold - en sand,
Though ev - ery pros-pect pleas - es, And on - ly man is vile?
Shall we to men be - night - ed The lamp of life de - ny?
Till, like a sea of glo - ry, It spreads from pole to pole:

From man-y an an - cient riv - er, From man-y a palm - y plain,
In vain with lav - ish kind - ness The gifts of God are strown;
Sal - va - tion! O sal - va - tion! The joy - ful sound pro - claim,
Till o'er our ran-somed na - ture The Lamb for sin - ners slain,

They call us to de - liv - er Their land from er - ror's chain.
The hea - then in his blind-ness Bows down to wood and stone.
Till earth's re - mot - est na - tion Has learned Mes - si - ah's name.
Re - deem - er, King, Cre - a - tor, In bliss re - turns to reign. A - men.

WORDS: Reginald Heber, 1819
MUSIC: Lowell Mason, 1824

MISSIONARY HYMN
7.6.7.6 D.

81 By Gracious Powers So Wonderfully Sheltered

1. By gra-cious powers so won-der-ful-ly shel-tered,
2. Yet is this heart by its old foe tor-ment-ed,
3. And when this cup you give is filled to brim-ming
4. Yet when a-gain in this same world you give us

and con-fi-dent-ly wait-ing come what may,
still e-vil days bring bur-dens hard to bear;
with bit-ter suf-fering, hard to un-der-stand,
the joy we had, the bright-ness of your Sun,

we know that God is with us night and morn-ing,
O give our fright-ened souls the sure sal-va-tion,
we take it thank-ful-ly and with-out trem-bling,
we shall re-mem-ber all the days we lived through,

and nev-er fails to greet us each new day.
for which, O Lord, you taught us to pre-pare.
out of so good and so be-loved a hand.
and our whole life shall then be yours a-lone.

WORDS: F. Pratt Green, after Dietrich Bonhoeffer
MUSIC: Charles Hubert Hastings Parry, 1904

INTERCESSOR
11.10.11.10

Come Down, O Love Divine 82

1. Come down, O Love di - vine, Seek thou this soul of
2. O let it free - ly burn, Till earth - ly pas - sions
3. And so the yearn - ing strong With which the soul will

mine, And vis - it it with thine own ar - dor glow - ing;
turn To dust and ash - es in its heat con - sum - ing;
long, Shall far out - pass the power of hu - man tell - ing;

O Com - fort - er, draw near, With - in my heart ap - pear,
And let thy glo - rious light Shine ev - er on my sight,
For none can guess its grace, Till he be - come the place

And kin - dle it, thy ho - ly flame be - stow - ing.
And clothe me round, the while my path il - lum - ing.
Where - in the Ho - ly Spir - it makes his dwell - ing. A - men.

WORDS: Bianco da Siena, c. 1367; tr. Richard F. Littledale, 1867   DOWN AMPNEY
MUSIC: Ralph Vaughan Williams, 1906   6.6.11 D.

Music from the ENGLISH HYMNAL by permission of Oxford University Press, London.

83   He Who Would Valiant Be

1. He who would val-iant be 'Gainst all dis-as-ter,
2. Who so be-set him round With dis-mal sto-ries,

Let him in con-stan-cy Fol-low the Mas-ter.
Do but them-selves con-found, His strength the more is.

There's no dis-cour-age-ment Shall make him once re-lent
No foes shall stay his might, Though he with gi-ants fight;

His first a-vowed in-tent To be a pil-grim.
He will make good his right To be a pil-grim.

3. Since, Lord, thou dost defend
Us with thy Spirit,
We know we at the end
Shall life inherit.

Then fancies flee away!
I'll fear not what men say,
I'll labor night and day
To be a pilgrim.

WORDS: John Bunyon, 1684; alt. Percy Dearmer, 1906
MUSIC: English Traditional melody; harm. Ralph Vaughan Williams, 1906

MONKS GATE
6.5.6.5.6.6.6.5

Lead, Kindly Light

84

1. Lead, kind-ly Light, a-mid the en-cir-cling gloom, Lead Thou me on; The night is dark, and I am far from home, Lead Thou me on. Keep Thou my feet; I do not ask to see The dis-tant scene: one step e-nough for me.

2. I was not ev-er thus, nor prayed that Thou Shouldst lead me on; I loved to choose and see my path but now Lead Thou me on. I loved the gar-ish day, and, spite of fears, Pride ruled my will: re-mem-ber not past years.

3. So long Thy power hath blest me, sure it still Will lead me on O'er moor and fen, o'er crag and tor-rent, till The night is gone, And with the morn those an-gel fa-ces smile, Which I have loved long since, and lost a while.

WORDS: John Henry Newman, 1833
MUSIC: William H. Harris, 1932

ALBERTA
10.4.10.4.10.10

Music from ENLARGED SONGS OF PRAISE by permission of Oxford University Press, London.

85 Glorious Things of Thee Are Spoken

1. Glo - rious things of thee are spok - en, Zi - on, cit - y of our God! He whose word can - not be brok - en Formed thee for His own a - bode. On the Rock of A - ges found-ed, What can shake thy sure re - pose? With sal - va - tion's

2. See, the streams of liv - ing wa - ters, Spring - ing from e - ter - nal love, Well sup - ply thy sons and daugh - ters, And all fear of want re - move. Who can faint while such a riv - er Ev - er flows their thirst to as - suage Grace, which, like the

3. Sav - ior if of Zi - on's cit - y I, through grace, a mem - ber am, Let the world de - ride or pit - y, I will glo - ry in Thy name: Fad - ing is the word - ling's pleas - ure, All his boast - ed pomp and show, Sol - id joys and

walls sur - round - ed, Thou mayst smile at all thy foes.
Lord the Giv - er, Nev - er fails from age to age?
last - ing treas - ure None but Zi - on's chil - dren know.

WORDS: John Newton, 1779
MUSIC: Cyril V. Taylor, 1941

ABBOT'S LEIGH
8.7.8.7 D.

Blow Ye the Trumpet, Blow 86

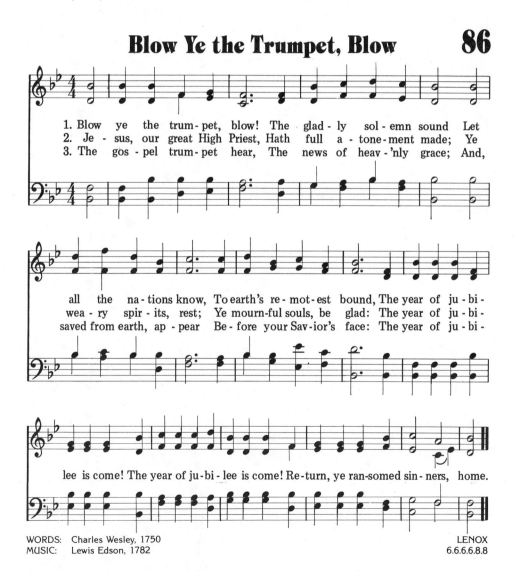

1. Blow ye the trum - pet, blow! The glad - ly sol - emn sound Let
2. Je - sus, our great High Priest, Hath full a - tone-ment made; Ye
3. The gos - pel trum - pet hear, The news of heav - 'nly grace; And,

all the na - tions know, To earth's re - mot - est bound, The year of ju - bi -
wea - ry spir - its, rest; Ye mourn-ful souls, be glad: The year of ju - bi -
saved from earth, ap - pear Be - fore your Sav - ior's face: The year of ju - bi -

lee is come! The year of ju - bi - lee is come! Re - turn, ye ran-somed sin - ners, home.

WORDS: Charles Wesley, 1750
MUSIC: Lewis Edson, 1782

LENOX
6.6.6.6.8.8

87 **Now Thank We All Our God**

Unison

1. Now thank we all our God, With hearts and hands and voic - es, Who won - drous things hath done, In whom His world re - joic - es; Who, from our
2. may this boun - teous God Through all our life be near us, With ev - er - joy - ful hearts And bless - ed peace to cheer us; And keep us
3. praise and thanks to God The Fa - ther now be giv - en, The Son, and Him who reigns With them in high - est heav - en; The one e -

WORDS: Martin Rinkart, 1636; tr. Catherine Winkworth, 1858
MUSIC: Geoffrey Beaumont, 1957
Music Copyright 1957, W. Paxton & Co., Ltd. Used by permission of Mills Music, Inc.

GRACIAS
6.7.6.7.6.6.6.6

88 God, Who Stretched the Spangled Heavens

1. God, who stretched the span-gled heav-ens, In-fi-nite in
2. Proud-ly rise our mod-ern cit-ies, State-ly build-ings,
3. We have ven-tured worlds un-dreamed of Since the child-hood
4. As each far hor-i-zon beck-ons, May it chal-lenge

time and place, Flung the suns in burn-ing ra-diance Through the
row on row; Yet their win-dows, blank, un-feel-ing, Stare on
of our race; Known the ec-sta-sy of wing-ing Through un-
us a-new, Chil-dren of cre-a-tive pur-pose, Serv-ing

si-lent fields of space. We, Your child-ren, in Your like-ness,
can-yoned streets be-low, Where the lone-ly drift un-no-ticed
trav-eled realms of space, Probed the se-crets of the a-tom,
oth-ers, hon-'ring You. May our dreams prove rich with prom-ise,

Share in-ven-tive pow'rs with you: Great Cre-a-tor,
In the cit-y's ebb and flow, Lost to pur-pose
Yield-ing un-im-ag-ined pow'r, Fac-ing us with
Each en-deav-or well be-gun: Great Cre-a-tor,

still cre - a - ting, Show us what we yet may do.
and to mean - ing, Scarce-ly car - ing where they go.
life's de-struc - tion Or our most tri - umph-ant hour.
give us guid - ance Till our goals and Yours are one.

WORDS: Catherine Cameron, 1965
MUSIC: Franz Joseph Haydn, 1797

AUSTRIAN HYMN
8.7.8.7 D.

Let All the World in Every Corner Sing 89

Unison

1. Let all the world in ev - er - y cor - ner sing: My God and King!
2. Let all the world in ev - er - y cor - ner sing: My God and King!

The heav'ns are not too high, His praise may thith - er fly; The
The church with psalms must shout, No door can keep them out; But,

earth is not too low, His prais - es there may grow. Let
more than all, the heart Must bear the long - est part. Let

all the world in ev - er - y cor - ner sing: My God and King!
all the world in ev - er - y cor - ner sing: My God and King! A - men.

WORDS: George Herbert, 1633
MUSIC: Robert G. McCutchan, 1934

ALL THE WORLD
14.12.12.14

90 Sunset to Sunrise Changes Now

Unison

1. Sun - set to sun - rise chang - es now, For
2. E'en though the sun with - holds its light, Lo!
3. Here in o'er-whelm - ing fi - nal strife The

God doth make his world a - new; On the Re - deem - er's
a more heaven - ly lamp shines here, And from the cross on
Lord of life hath vic - to - ry; And sin is slain, and

thorn-crowned brow The won - ders of that dawn we view.
Cal - vary's height Gleams of e - ter - ni - ty ap - pear.
death brings life, And sons of earth hold heaven in fee.

WORDS: Clement of Alexandria, c. 170-220; para. Howard c. Robbins, 1939
MUSIC: *United States Sacred Harmony, 1799*

KEDRON
L.M.

91 God Who Spoke in the Beginning

(♩ = c. 70)

1. God who spoke in the be - gin - ning, form - ing
2. God who spoke through men and na - tions, through e-
3. God whose speech be - comes in - car - nate Christ is

pesante

sim.

rock   and shap - ing spar,   set   all   life   and growth in   mo - tion,
vents long past and gone,   show - ing still   to - day his   pur pose,
ser - vant, Christ is   Lord!   calls us   to   a   life   of   ser - vice,

earth - ly world and   dis - tant star;   He   who calls   the earth to
speaks su - preme - ly through his Son;   He   who calls   the earth to
heart and will   to   ac - tion stirred;   He   who u - ses man's o -

or - der is the ground of what we   are.
or - der gives his word and it   is done.
be - dience has the first and fi - nal   word.

WORDS: Fred Kaan, 1968
MUSIC: Geoffrey Laycock, 1971

VERBUM DEI
8.7.8.7.8.7

92   **In Babylon Town**

1. In Ba-by-lon town
3. Old Ba-by-lon town

By an a-li-en stream   We had sad-ly sat down,   and slept with a
By an a-li-en stream   May be tum-bled all down.   We've no need to

No Pedal

Pedal

dream.   Can you hear   the pipe and drums? Now he comes,   now he
dream.

2. In Beth-le-hem
4. Here now in our

comes.

town   there's no room at the inn,   so she cra-dles him down
town   there is room at the inn,   where we all may sit down

And won-ders be - gin.   *Can you   hear   the pipe and drums?*
His meal to be - gin.

cresc.

cresc.

Now   he comes,   now   he comes.   comes.

WORDS: Hamish Swanston, 1971
MUSIC: Ian Copley, 1971

IN·BABYLON TOWN
5.6.6.5 Ref.

93 I Love Thee, I Love Thee

1. I love Thee, I love Thee, I love Thee, my Lord;
2. I'm hap-py, I'm hap-py, O won-drous ac-count!
3. O Je-sus, my Sav-ior, with Thee I am blest,
4. O, who's like my Sav-ior? He's Sa-lem's bright King;

I love Thee, my Sav-ior, I love Thee, my God;
My joys are im-mor-tal, I stand on the mount;
My life and sal-va-tion, my joy and my rest;
He smiles and He loves me and helps me to sing;

I love Thee, I love Thee, and that Thou dost know;
I gaze on my treas-ure and long to be there,
Thy name be my theme, and Thy love be my song;
I'll praise Him, I'll praise Him with notes loud and clear,

But how much I love Thee my ac-tions will show.
With Je-sus and an-gels and kin-dred so dear.
Thy grace shall in-spire both my heart and my tongue.
While riv-ers of pleas-ure my spir-it shall cheer. A-men.

WORDS: Source unknown
MUSIC: Ingalls' *Christian Harmony*, 1805

I LOVE THEE
11.11.11.11

Joy to the World! The Lord Is Come 94

1. Joy to the world! the Lord is come; Let earth re-
2. Joy to the earth! the Sav-ior reigns; Let men their
3. No more let sins and sor-rows grow, Nor thorns in-
4. He rules the world with truth and grace, And makes the

ceive her King; Let ev-ery heart pre-pare Him room,
songs em-ploy; While fields and floods, rocks, hills, and plains
fest the ground; He comes to make His bless-ings flow
na-tions prove The glo-ries of His right-eous-ness,

And heav'n and na-ture sing, And heav'n and na-ture
Re-peat the sound-ing joy, Re-peat the sound-ing
Far as the curse is found, Far as the curse is
And won-ders of His love, And won-ders of His

1. And heav'n and na-ture sing,

sing, And heav'n, and heav'n and na-ture sing.
joy, Re-peat, re-peat the sound-ing joy.
found, Far as, far as the curse is found.
love, And won-ders, won-ders of His love.

1. And

heav'n and na-ture sing,

WORDS: Isaac Watts, 1719; based on Psalm 98
MUSIC: George Frederick Handel, 1742; arr. Lowell Mason, 1839

ANTIOCH
C.M.

95   O Come, All Ye Faithful

1. O come, all ye faith - ful, joy - ful and tri - um - phant,
2. God of God, and Light of Light be - got - ten,
3. Sing, choirs of an - gels, sing in ex - ul - ta - tion!
4. Yea, Lord, we greet Thee, born this hap - py morn - ing,

O come ye, O come ye to Beth - le - hem!
Lo, He ab - hors not the Vir - gin's womb;
O sing, all ye cit - i - zens of heav'n a - bove;
Je - sus, to Thee be all glo - ry giv'n;

Come and be - hold Him, born the King of an - gels;
Ver - y God, be - got - ten, not cre - a - ted;
Glo - ry to God, all glo - ry in the high - est;
Word of the Fa - ther, now in flesh ap - pear - ing;

Refrain

O come, let us a - dore Him, O come, let us a - dore Him,

O come, let us a - dore Him, Christ the Lord. A - men.

WORDS: Latin hymn; attr. John F. Wade, 1751; tr. Frederick Oakeley, 1841, and others
MUSIC: John F. Wade's *Cantus Diversi*, 1751

ADESTE FIDELES
Irregular meter

To God Be the Glory

96

1. To God be the glo-ry, great things He hath done, So loved He the world that He
2. O per-fect re-demp-tion, the pur-chase of blood, To ev-ery be-liev-er the
3. Great things He hath taught us, great things He hath done, And great our re-joic-ing thro'

gave us His Son, Who yield-ed His life an a-tone-ment for sin, And o-pened the
prom-ise of God; The vil-est of-fend-er who tru-ly be-lieves, That mo-ment from
Je-sus the Son; But pur-er, and high-er, and great-er will be Our won-der, our

Refrain

Life-gate that all may go in.
Je-sus a par-don re-ceives. Praise the Lord, praise the Lord, Let the earth hear His
trans-port, when Je-sus we see.

voice! Praise the Lord, praise the Lord, Let the peo-ple re-joice! O come to the

Fa-ther thro' Je-sus the Son, And give Him the glo-ry, great things He hath done.

WORDS: Fanny J. Crosby, 1875
MUSIC: William H. Doane, 1875

TO GOD BE THE GLORY
11.11.11.11. Ref.

97 Hail, Thou Once Despised Jesus

1. Hail, Thou once de - spis - ed Je - sus, Crowned in mock-er - y a King!
2. Je - sus, hail! en - throned in glo - ry, There for - ev - er to a - bide;
3. Wor - ship, hon - or, power and bless-ing Thou art wor - thy to re - ceive;

Thou didst suf - fer to re - lease us; Thou didst free sal - va - tion bring.
All the heaven - ly hosts a - dore Thee, Seat - ed at Thy Fa - ther's side:
Loud - est prais - es, with - out ceas - ing, Meet it is for us to give.

Hail, Thou ag - o - niz - ing Sav - ior, Bear - er of our sin and shame!
There for sin - ners Thou art plead - ing; There Thou dost our place pre - pare:
Help, ye bright an - gel - ic spir - its, Bring your sweet - est, no - blest lays;

By Thy mer - its we find fa - vor; Life is giv - en through Thy name.
Ev - er for us in - ter - ced - ing, Till in glo - ry we ap - pear.
Help to sing our Sav - ior's mer - its; Help to chant Im - man - uel's praise. A - men.

WORDS: John Bakewell, 1757
MUSIC: *Christian Lyre*, 1831

PLEADING SAVIOUR
8.7.8.7 D.

Awake, Awake to Love and Work   98

Unison

1. A - wake, a - wake to love and work, The lark is in the
2. Come, let thy voice be one with theirs, Shout with their shout of
3. To give and give, and give a - gain, What God hath giv - en

sky, The fields are wet with dia - mond dew, The
praise; See how the gi - ant sun soars up, Great
thee; To spend thy - self nor count the cost, To

worlds a - wake to cry Their bless - ings on the
Lord of years and days! So let the love of
serve right glo - rious - ly The God who gave all

|1,2 |3

Lord of life, As he goes meek - ly by.
Je - sus come And set thy soul a - blaze:
worlds that are, And all that are to be.

WORDS: G. A. Studdert-Kennedy, 1921   MORNING SONG
MUSIC: John Wyeth's *Repository of Sacred Music, Part Second*, 1813;   8.6.8.6.8.6
       harm. Carlton R. Young, 1964

Music © Copyright 1964 Broadman Press. All Rights Reserved. Used by Permission.

99 **Come, Come, Ye Saints**

1. Come, come, ye saints, no toil nor la - bor fear; But with joy
2. The world of care is with us ev - 'ry day; Let it not
3. We'll find the rest which God for us pre -pared, When at last

wend your way. Tho hard to you the jour - ney may ap - pear,
this ob -scure: Here we can serve the Mas - ter on the way,
he will call; Where none will come to hurt or make a - fraid,

Grace shall be as your day. We have a liv - ing
And in him be se - cure. Gird up your loins; fresh
He will reign o - ver all. We will make the air with

Lord to guide, And we can trust him to pro - vide; Do
cour - age take; Our God will nev - er us for - sake; And
mu - sic ring, Shout prais - es to our God and King; O

this, and joy your hearts will swell: All is well! All is well!
so our song no fear can quell: All is well! All is well!
how we'll make the cho-rus swell: All is well! All is well!

WORDS: William Clayton, 1846; alt. Joseph F. Green, 1960
MUSIC: Adapt. J. T. White's *The Sacred Harp*, 1844

ALL IS WELL
10.6.10.6.8.8.8.6

Words © Copyright 1960 Broadman Press. All Rights Reserved. Used by Permission.

My Song Is Love Unknown 100

Unison

1. My song is love un-known, My Sav-ior's love to me,
2. He came from his blest throne, Sal-va-tion to be-stow:
3. Some-times they strew his way, And his sweet prais-es sing;
4. In life, no house, no home My Lord on earth might have;
5. Here might I stay and sing, No sto-ry so di-vine;

Love to the love-less shown, That they might love-ly be. O who
But men made strange, and none The longed-for Christ would know. But O
Re-sound-ing all the day Ho-san-nas to their King. Then "Cru-
In death, no friend-ly tomb But what a strang-er gave. What may
Nev-er was love, dear King, Nev-er was grief like thine! This is

am I, That for my sake My Lord should take Frail flesh and die.
my friend, My friend in deed, Who at my need His life did spend!
ci-fy!" Is all their breath, And for his death They thirst and cry.
I say? Heav'n was his home: But mine the tomb Where-in he lay.
my friend, In whose sweet praise I all my days Could glad-ly spend.

WORDS: Samuel Crossman, 1664
MUSIC: James Bigelow, 1962

ROBERTSON
6.6.6.6.4.4.4.4

Music © Copyright 1962 by James Bigelow. All Rights Reserved. Used by Permission.

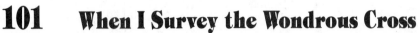

101   When I Survey the Wondrous Cross

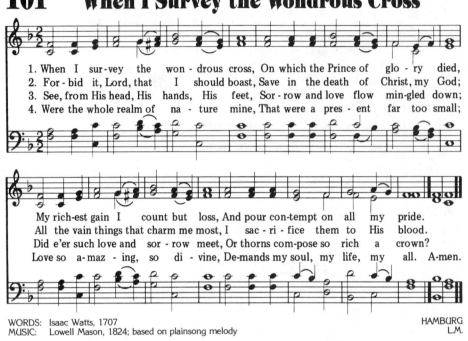

1. When I sur-vey the won-drous cross, On which the Prince of glo-ry died,
2. For-bid it, Lord, that I should boast, Save in the death of Christ, my God;
3. See, from His head, His hands, His feet, Sor-row and love flow min-gled down;
4. Were the whole realm of na-ture mine, That were a pres-ent far too small;

My rich-est gain I count but loss, And pour con-tempt on all my pride.
All the vain things that charm me most, I sac-ri-fice them to His blood.
Did e'er such love and sor-row meet, Or thorns com-pose so rich a crown?
Love so a-maz-ing, so di-vine, De-mands my soul, my life, my all. A-men.

WORDS: Isaac Watts, 1707   HAMBURG
MUSIC: Lowell Mason, 1824; based on plainsong melody   L.M.

102   Jerusalem, My Happy Home

1. Je-ru-sa-lem, my hap-py home, When shall I come to thee?
2. O hap-py har-bor of the saints, O sweet and pleas-ant soil!
3. Thy saints are crowned with glo-ry great; They see God face to face;
4. There Da-vid stands with harp in hand As mas-ter of the choir:
5. Je-ru-sa-lem, my hap-py home, Would God I were in thee!

When shall my sor-rows have an end? Thy joys when shall I see?
In thee no sor-row may be found, No grief, no care, no toil.
They tri-umph still, they still re-joice: Most hap-py is their case.
Ten thou-sand times that man were blest That might this mu-sic hear.
Would God my woes were at an end, Thy joys that I might see!

WORDS: "F.B.P.," 16th century; based on anonymous hymn   LAND OF REST
MUSIC: Traditional American melody; arr. Annabel M. Buchanan, 1938   C.M.

My Hope Is Built on Nothing Less 103

1. My hope is built on noth-ing less Than Je - sus' blood and right-eous-ness;
2. When dark-ness veils His love - ly face, I rest on His un - chang-ing grace;
3. His oath, His cov - e - nant, His blood Sup - port me in the whelm-ing flood;
4. When He shall come with trum - pet sound, O may I then in Him be found;

I dare not trust the sweet-est frame, But whol - ly lean on Je - sus' name.
In ev - ery high and storm - y gale, My an - chor holds with - in the veil.
When all a - round my soul gives way He then is all my hope and stay.
Dressed in His right - eous - ness a - lone, Fault - less to stand be - fore the throne.

Refrain

On Christ the sol - id Rock I stand; All oth - er ground

is sink - ing sand, All oth - er ground is sink - ing sand.

WORDS: Edward Mote, 1834
MUSIC: William B. Bradbury, 1863

SOLID ROCK
L.M. Ref.

104   How Firm a Foundation

1. How firm a foun - da - tion, ye saints of the Lord,
2. "Fear not, I am with thee; O be not dis - mayed,
3. "When through the deep wa - ters I call thee to go,
4. "When through fier - y tri - als thy path - way shall lie,
5. "The soul that on Je - sus hath leaned for re - pose,

Is laid for your faith in His ex - cel - lent Word!
For I am thy God, and will still give thee aid;
The riv - ers of sor - row shall not o - ver - flow;
My grace, all suf - fi - cient, shall be thy sup - ply:
I will not, I will not de - sert to his foes;

What more can He say than to you He hath said,
I'll strength - en thee, help thee, and cause thee to stand,
For I will be with thee, thy trou - bles to bless,
The flame shall not hurt thee; I on - ly de - sign
That soul, though all hell should en - deav - or to shake,

To you who for ref - uge to Je - sus have fled?
Up - held by my right - eous, om - nip - o - tent hand.
And sanc - ti - fy to thee thy deep - est dis - tress.
Thy dross to con - sume, and thy gold to re - fine.
I'll nev - er, no, nev - er, no, nev - er for - sake!" A - men.

WORDS: Rippon's *Selection of Hymns*, 1787
MUSIC: Traditional American melody; Caldwell's *Union Harmony*, 1837

FOUNDATION
11.11.11.11

Were You There?

105

1. Were you there when they cru - ci - fied my Lord? (Were you there?)
2. Were you there when they nailed Him to the tree? (Were you there?)
3. Were you there when they pierced Him in the side? (Were you there?)
4. Were you there when they laid Him in the tomb? (Were you there?)
5. Were you there when He rose up from the dead? (Were you there?)

Were you there when they cru - ci - fied my Lord? (Were you there?)
Were you there when they nailed Him to the tree? (Were you there?)
Were you there when they pierced Him in the side? (Were you there?)
Were you there when they laid Him in the tomb? (Were you there?)
Were you there when He rose up from the dead? (Were you there?)

Oh!

Some-times it caus - es me to trem-ble, trem-ble,
(5. Some-times I feel like shout-ing glo - ry, glo - ry,)

trem-ble, Were you there when they cru - ci - fied my Lord? (Were you there?)
trem-ble, Were you there when they nailed Him to the tree? (Were you there?)
trem-ble, Were you there when they pierced Him in the side? (Were you there?)
trem-ble, Were you there when they laid Him in the tomb? (Were you there?)
glo - ry! Were you there when He rose up from the dead? (Were you there?)

WORDS and MUSIC: Traditional Spiritual

WERE YOU THERE?
Irregular meter

106 Brethren, We Have Met to Worship

1. Breth-ren, we have met to wor-ship   And a-dore the Lord our God;
2. Breth-ren, see poor sin-ners round you Slum-ber-ing on the brink of woe;
3. Sis-ters, will you join and help us? Mo-ses' sis-ter aid-ed him;
4. Let us love our God su-preme-ly, Let us love each oth-er too;

Will you pray with all your pow-er, While we try to preach the Word?
Death is com-ing, hell is mov-ing, Can you bear to let them go?
Will you help the trem-bling mourn-ers Who are strug-gling hard with sin?
Let us love and pray for sin-ners, Till our God makes all things new.

All is vain un-less the Spir-it Of the Ho-ly One comes down;
See our fa-thers and our moth-ers, And our chil-dren sink-ing down;
Tell them all a-bout the Sav-ior, Tell them that He will be found;
Then He'll call us home to heav-en, At His ta-ble we'll sit down;

Breth-ren, pray, and ho-ly man-na   Will be show-ered all a-round.
Breth-ren, pray, and ho-ly man-na   Will be show-ered all a-round.
Sis-ters, pray, and ho-ly man-na   Will be show-ered all a-round.
Christ will gird Him-self, and serve us With sweet man-na all a-round.

WORDS: George Atkins?   HOLY MANNA
MUSIC: William Moore's *Columbian Harmony*, 1825   8.7.8.7 D.

When I Can Read My Title Clear 107

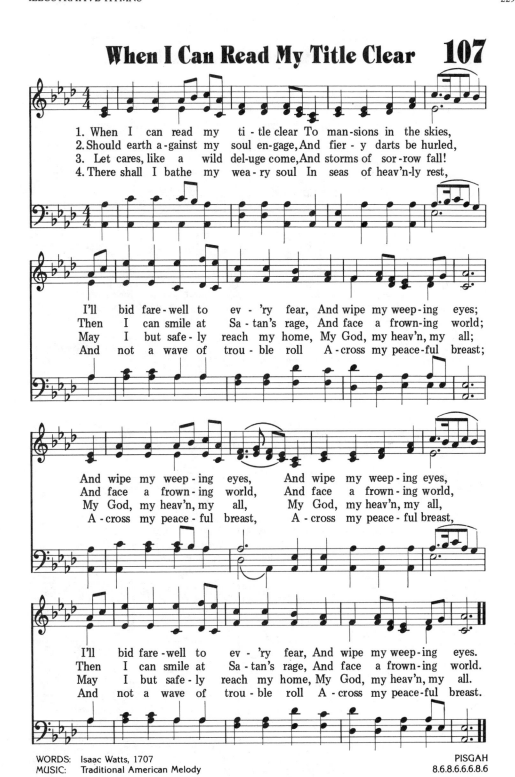

1. When I can read my ti-tle clear To man-sions in the skies,
2. Should earth a-gainst my soul en-gage, And fier-y darts be hurled,
3. Let cares, like a wild del-uge come, And storms of sor-row fall!
4. There shall I bathe my wea-ry soul In seas of heav'n-ly rest,

I'll bid fare-well to ev-'ry fear, And wipe my weep-ing eyes;
Then I can smile at Sa-tan's rage, And face a frown-ing world;
May I but safe-ly reach my home, My God, my heav'n, my all;
And not a wave of trou-ble roll A-cross my peace-ful breast;

And wipe my weep-ing eyes, And wipe my weep-ing eyes,
And face a frown-ing world, And face a frown-ing world,
My God, my heav'n, my all, My God, my heav'n, my all,
A-cross my peace-ful breast, A-cross my peace-ful breast,

I'll bid fare-well to ev-'ry fear, And wipe my weep-ing eyes.
Then I can smile at Sa-tan's rage, And face a frown-ing world.
May I but safe-ly reach my home, My God, my heav'n, my all.
And not a wave of trou-ble roll A-cross my peace-ful breast.

WORDS: Isaac Watts, 1707
MUSIC: Traditional American Melody

PISGAH
8.6.8.6.6.6.8.6

108 O for a Thousand Tongues to Sing

1. O for a thou-sand tongues to sing My great Re-deem-er's praise,
2. Je-sus! the name that charms our fears, That bids our sor-rows cease,
3. He breaks the power of can-celed sin, He sets the pris-oner free;
4. Hear Him, ye deaf; His praise, ye dumb, Your loos-ened tongues em-ploy;
5. My gra-cious Mas-ter and my God, As-sist me to pro-claim,

The glo-ries of my God and King, The tri-umphs of His grace.
'Tis mu-sic in the sin-ner's ears, 'Tis life and health and peace.
His blood can make the foul-est clean; His blood a-vailed for me.
Ye blind, be-hold your Sav-ior come; And leap, ye lame, for joy.
To spread thro' all the earth a-broad, The hon-ors of Thy name. A-men.

WORDS: Charles Wesley, 1739
MUSIC: Carl G. Gläser, 1784-1829; arr. Lowell Mason, 1839

AZMON
C.M.

109 In Christ There Is No East or West

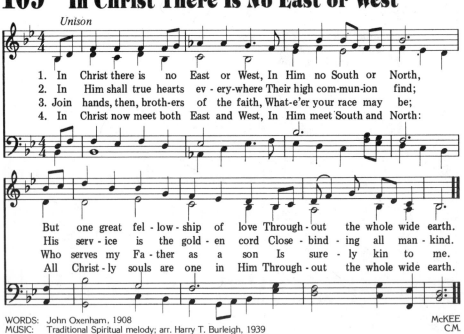

Unison

1. In Christ there is no East or West, In Him no South or North,
2. In Him shall true hearts ev-ery-where Their high com-mun-ion find;
3. Join hands, then, broth-ers of the faith, What-e'er your race may be;
4. In Christ now meet both East and West, In Him meet South and North:

But one great fel-low-ship of love Through-out the whole wide earth.
His serv-ice is the gold-en cord Close-bind-ing all man-kind.
Who serves my Fa-ther as a son Is sure-ly kin to me.
All Christ-ly souls are one in Him Through-out the whole wide earth.

WORDS: John Oxenham, 1908
MUSIC: Traditional Spiritual melody; arr. Harry T. Burleigh, 1939
Words used by permission of Desmond Dunkerly.

McKEE
C.M.

Great Is Thy Faithfulness 110

1. Great is Thy faith-ful-ness, O God my Fa-ther, There is no shad-ow of
2. Sum-mer and win-ter, and springtime and har-vest, Sun, moon and stars in their
3. Par-don for sin and a peace that en-dur-eth, Thy own dear pres-ence to

turn-ing with Thee; Thou chang-est not, Thy com-pas-sions they fail not;
cours-es a-bove Join with all na-ture in man-i-fold wit-ness
cheer and to guide; Strength for to-day and bright hope for to-mor-row,

Refrain

As Thou hast been Thou for-ev-er wilt be.
To Thy great faith-ful-ness, mer-cy and love. Great is Thy faith-ful-ness!
Bless-ings all mine, with ten thou-sand be-side!

Great is Thy faith-ful-ness! Morn-ing by morn-ing new mer-cies I see; All I have

need-ed Thy hand hath pro-vid-ed—Great is Thy faith-ful-ness, Lord, un-to me!

WORDS: Thomas O. Chisholm, 1923
MUSIC: William M. Runyan, 1923

FAITHFULNESS
11.10.11.10. Ref.

111 Sing Them Over Again to Me

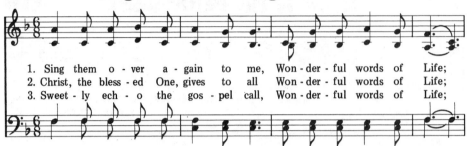

1. Sing them o-ver a-gain to me, Won-der-ful words of Life;
2. Christ, the bless-ed One, gives to all Won-der-ful words of Life;
3. Sweet-ly ech-o the gos-pel call, Won-der-ful words of Life;

Let me more of their beau-ty see, Won-der-ful words of Life.
Sin-ner, list to the lov-ing call, Won-der-ful words of Life.
Of-fer par-don and peace to all, Won-der-ful words of Life.

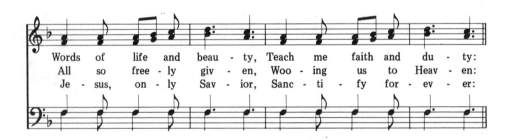

Words of life and beau-ty, Teach me faith and du-ty:
All so free-ly giv-en, Woo-ing us to Heav-en:
Je-sus, on-ly Sav-ior, Sanc-ti-fy for-ev-er:

Refrain

Beau-ti-ful words, won-der-ful words, Won-der-ful words of Life. Life.

WORDS and MUSIC: Philip P. Bliss, 1874   WORDS OF LIFE
                                                         8.6.8.6.6.6 Ref.

Lord Christ, the Father's Mighty Son 112

(Unison or Harmony)

1. Lord Christ, the Fa-ther's might - y Son, whose work up - on the
2. To make us one your prayers were said. To make us one you
3. Lord Christ, for-give us, make us new! What our de - signs could
4. We will not ques-tion or re - fuse the way you work, the

cross was done to give and re - ceive, make all our
broke the bread for all to re - ceive. Its piec - es
nev - er do your love can a - chieve. Our prayers, our
means you choose, the pat - tern you weave, but re - con -

scat - tered church - es one that the world may be - lieve.
scat - ter us in - stead: how can oth - ers be - lieve?
work, we bring to you that the world may be - lieve.
cile our war - ring views that the world may be - lieve.

*Small notes for organ only.

WORDS: Brian Wren
MUSIC: John Wilson

EAST MEADS
8 8 5.8 6.

113 Farther Along

1. Tempt - ed and tried we're oft made to won - der Why it should be thus
2. When death has come and tak - en our loved ones, It leaves our home so
3. Faith - ful till death said our lov - ing Mas - ter, A few more days to
4. When we see Je - sus com-ing in glo - ry, When He comes from His

all the day long, While there are oth - ers liv - ing a - bout us,
lone - ly and drear; Then do we won - der why oth - ers pros - per,
la - bor and wait; Toils of the road will then seem as noth - ing,
home in the sky; Then we shall meet Him in that bright man-sion,

Refrain

Nev - er mo - lest - ed tho in the wrong.
Liv - ing so wick - ed year af - ter year. Far - ther a - long we'll
As we sweep thru the beau - ti - ful gate.
We'll un - der-stand it all by and by.

know all a - bout it, Far - ther a long we'll un - der-stand why; Cheer up, my

broth-er, live in the sun-shine, We'll un-der-stand it all by and by.

WORDS: W. B. Stevens, 1937   **STAMPS**
MUSIC: W. B. Stevens, arr. J. R. Baxter, Jr., 1937   10.9.10.9 Ref.

Let Us with a Gladsome Mind   114

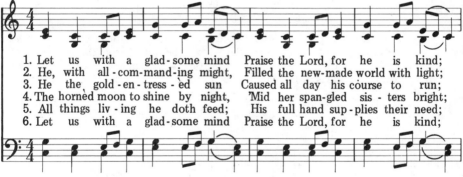

1. Let us with a glad-some mind   Praise the Lord, for he is kind;
2. He, with all-com-mand-ing might,   Filled the new-made world with light;
3. He the gold-en-tress-ed sun   Caused all day his course to run;
4. The hornèd moon to shine by night,   'Mid her span-gled sis-ters bright;
5. All things liv-ing he doth feed;   His full hand sup-plies their need;
6. Let us with a glad-some mind   Praise the Lord, for he is kind;

For his mer-cies aye en-dure, Ev-er faith-ful, ev-er sure.

WORDS: Based on Psalm 136; John Milton, 1645, alt.   **CHINESE MELODY**
MUSIC: Arr. Bliss Wiant, 1936   7.7.7.7

115 O Zion, Haste

1. O Zi - on, haste, thy mis - sion, high ful - fill - ing, To tell to
2. Be - hold how man - y thou-sands still are ly - ing, Bound in the
3. Pro - claim to ev - 'ry peo - ple, tongue, and na - tion That God, in
4. Give of thy sons to bear the mes - sage glo - rious; Give of thy

all the world that God is Light; That he who made all na - tions
dark - some pris - on house of sin, With none to tell them of the
whom they live and move, is Love: Tell how he stoop'd to save his
wealth to speed them on their way; Pour out thy soul for them in

is not will - ing One soul should per - ish, lost in shades of night.
Sav - ior's dy - ing, Or of the life he died for them to win.
lost cre - a - tion, And died on earth that man might live a - bove.
pray'r vic - to - rious; And all thou spend - est Je - sus will re - pay.

Refrain

Pub - lish glad ti - dings, ti - dings of peace,

Ti - dings of Je - sus, re - demp-tion and re - lease.

WORDS: Mary Ann Thompson, 1868   TIDINGS
MUSIC: James Walch, 1875   11.10.11.10 Ref.

We Praise You, O God, Our Redeemer 116

1. We praise you, O God, our Re - deem - er, Cre - a - tor,
2. We wor - ship you, God of our fa - thers, we bless you;
3. With voic - es u - nit - ed our prais - es we of - fer,

In grate - ful de - vo - tion our trib - ute we bring.
Through life's storm and tem - pest our Guide have you been.
And glad - ly our song of true wor - ship we raise;

We lay it be - fore you, we kneel and a - dore you,
When per - ils o'er - take us, es - cape you wilt make us,
Our sins now con - fess - ing, we pray for your bless - ing,

We bless your ho - ly name, glad prais - es we sing.
And with your help, O Lord, life's bat - tles we win.
To you, our great Re - deem - er, ev - er be praise. A - men.

WORDS: Julia C. Cory, 1902
MUSIC: Netherlands Folk Song, 1626; arr. Edward Kremser, 1877

KREMSER
12.11.12.11

117 Lord, I Want to Be a Christian

1. Lord, I want to be a Chris-tian In - a my heart, in - a my
2. Lord, I want to be more lov - ing In - a my heart, in - a my
3. Lord, I want to be more ho - ly In - a my heart, in - a my
4. Lord, I want to be like Je - sus In - a my heart, in - a my

heart, Lord, I want to be a Chris - tian In - a my heart.
heart, Lord, I want to be more lov - ing In - a my heart.
heart, Lord, I want to be more ho - ly In - a my heart.
heart, Lord, I want to be like Je - sus In - a my heart.

Refrain

In - a my heart,   In - a my heart,
       In - a my heart,   In - a my heart,

Lord, I want to be a Chris - tian In - a my heart.
Lord, I want to be more lov - ing In - a my heart.
Lord, I want to be more ho - ly In - a my heart.
Lord, I want to be like Je - sus In - a my heart.

WORDS and MUSIC: Traditional Spiritual

I WANT TO BE A CHRISTIAN
Irregular meter

Give to the Winds Your Fears 118

1. Give to the winds your fears, Hope, and be un - dis-mayed;
2. Still heav - y is your heart? Still sink your spir - its down?
3. Far, far a - bove your thought His coun - sel shall ap - pear,

God hears your sighs and counts your tears, God shall lift up your head,
Cast off the weight, let fear de - part, And ev - ery care be gone.
When ful - ly He the work has wrought That caused your need-less fear.

Through waves and clouds and storms He gen - tly clears the way;
He ev - ery - where has sway And all things serve His mind;
Leave to His sov - ereign will To choose and to com - mand:

Wait for His time, so shall the night Soon end in joy - ous day.
His ev - ery act pure bless-ing is, His path un - sul - lied light
With won - der filled, you then shall own How wise, how strong His hand. A-men.

WORDS: Paul Gerhardt, 1653; tr. John Wesley, 1937; based on Psalm 37
MUSIC: George J. Elvey, 1868

DIADEMATA
S.M.D.

119 O Jesus Christ, to Thee May Hymns Be Rising

1. O Je-sus Christ, to thee may hymns be ris - ing
2. Grant us new cour - age, sac - ri - fi - cial, hum - ble.
3. Show us thy Spir - it, brood - ing o'er each cit - y,

In ev - ery cit - y for thy love and care;
Strong in thy strength to ven - ture and to dare;
As thou didst weep a - bove Je - ru - sa - lem,

In - spire our wor - ship, grant the glad sur - pris - ing
To lift the fall - en, guide the feet that stum - ble,
Seek - ing to gath - er all in love and pit - y,

That thy blest Spir - it brings men ev - ery - where.
Seek out the lone - ly and God's mer - cy share.
And heal - ing those who touch thy gar - ment's hem.

WORDS: Bradford Gray Webster, 1954
MUSIC: Daniel Moe, 1957

CITY OF GOD
11.10.11.10

Rise to Greet the Sun

120

1. Rise to greet the sun   Red in the east-ern sky,
2. May this day be blest,   Trust-ing in Je-sus' care,

Like a glo-rious bride-groom   His joy-ous race to run.
Heart and mind il-lu-mined   By heav-en's ra-diance fair.

Fly-ing birds in heav-ens high, Fra-grant flowers a - bloom
Thanks for rai-ment un - a-dorned, Rice and whole-some   food;

Tell the gra-cious Fa-ther's nigh, Now His work as-sume.
These the Lord in mer-cy   gives, Nev-er - fail-ing good.   A-men.

WORDS: T. C. Chao, 1936; tr. Bliss Wiant, 1946   LE P'ING
MUSIC: Chinese Folk melody; adapt. Hu Te-an, ?; arr. Bliss Wiant, 1946   5.6.6.6.7.5.7.5

121 Our Father God, Thy Name We Praise

1. Our Fa-ther God,   thy   name   we   praise,   To
2. Touch, Lord,   the   lips   that   speak   for   thee;   Set
3. As   with   our   breth-ren   here   we   meet,   Thy

thee   our hymns   ad - dress - ing,   And   joy-ful-ly   our
words   of   truth   be - fore   us,   That   we   may grow   in
grace   a - lone   can   feed   us.   As   here   we   gath - er

voic-es raise   Thy   faith-ful-ness   con - fess - ing;   As -
con-stan - cy,   The   light   of   wis - dom   o'er   us.   Give
at   thy feet   We   pray that thou   wilt   heed   us.   The

sem - bled   by   thy grace,   O   Lord,   We   seek fresh   guid - ance
us   this day   our   dai - ly bread;   May   hun - gry   souls   a -
pow'r   is thine,   O   Lord di - vine,   The   king - dom   and   the

from thy Word; Now grant a - new thy bless - ing.
gain be fed; May heav'n - ly food re - store us.
rule are thine. May Je - sus Christ still lead us! A - men.

WORDS: Matt. 6:9-13; Anabaptist *Ausbund*, 16th century, tr. Ernest A. Payne, 1960   MIT FREUDEN ZART
MUSIC: Bohemian Brethren *Kirchengesänge*, 1566   8.7.8.7.8.8.7
Words used by permission of Ernest A. Payne.

The Bread of Life for All Men Broken 122

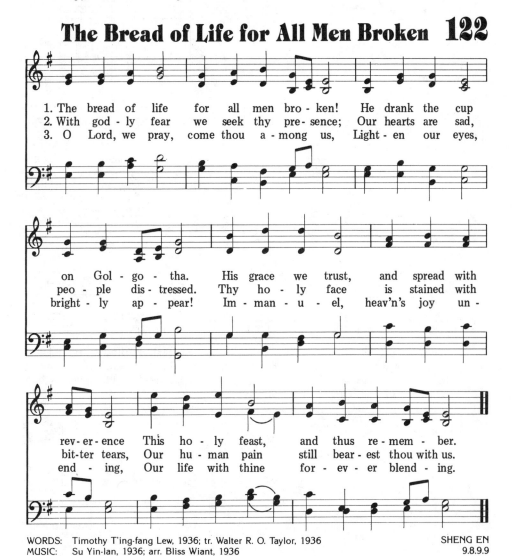

1. The bread of life for all men bro - ken! He drank the cup
2. With god - ly fear we seek thy pre - sence; Our hearts are sad,
3. O Lord, we pray, come thou a - mong us, Light - en our eyes,

on Gol - go - tha. His grace we trust, and spread with
peo - ple dis - tressed. Thy ho - ly face is stained with
bright - ly ap - pear! Im - man - u - el, heav'n's joy un -

rev - er - ence This ho - ly feast, and thus re - mem - ber.
bit - ter tears, Our hu - man pain still bear - est thou with us.
end - ing, Our life with thine for - ev - er blend - ing.

WORDS: Timothy T'ing-fang Lew, 1936; tr. Walter R. O. Taylor, 1936   SHENG EN
MUSIC: Su Yin-lan, 1936; arr. Bliss Wiant, 1936   9.8.9.9

123   **Tell Out, My Soul**

1. Tell out, my soul, the great-ness of the Lord! Un - num - bered
2. Tell out, my soul, the great-ness of His Name! Make known His
3. Tell out, my soul, the great-ness of His might! Pow'rs and do-
4. Tell out, my soul, the glo - ries of His word! Firm is His

bless-ings give my spir - it voice; Ten - der to me the
might, the deeds His arm has done; His mer - cy sure, from
min - ions lay their glo - ry by. Proud hearts and stub - born
prom - ise, and His mer - cy sure. Tell out, my soul, the

prom-ise of His word; In God my Sav - ior shall my heart re - joice.
age to age the same; His ho - ly Name, the Lord, the might - y one.
wills are put to flight, The hun-gry fed, the hum-ble lift - ed high.
great-ness of the Lord To chil-dren's chil-dren and for - ev - er-more!

WORDS: Timothy Dudley-Smith, 1961; based on Luke 1:46-55   WOODLANDS
MUSIC: Walter Greatorex, 1916   10.10.10.10

Sing a New Song to the Lord 124

1. Sing a new song to the Lord, He to whom wonders belong!
2. Now to the ends of the earth See His salvation is shown;
3. Sing a new song and rejoice, Publish His praises abroad!
4. Join with the hills and the sea Thunders of praise to prolong!

Rejoice in His triumph and tell of His pow'r—
And still He remembers His mercy and truth,
Let voices in chorus, with trumpet and horn,
In judgment and justice He comes to the earth—

O sing to the Lord a new song!
Unchanging in love to His own.
Resound for the joy of the Lord!
O sing to the Lord a new song!

WORDS: Timothy Dudley-Smith, 1971; based on Psalm 98
MUSIC: David G. Wilson, 1973

CANTATE DOMINO
7.7.11.8

125 Built on the Rock the Church Doth Stand

1. Built on the Rock the church doth stand, E - ven when stee - ples are fall - ing; Crum-bled have spires in ev - ery land, Bells still are chim - ing and call - ing, Call - ing the young and old to rest, But a - bove all the soul dis-tressed, Long-ing for life ev - er - last - ing.

2. Sure - ly in tem - ples made with hands, God the most high is not dwell - ing; High a - bove earth His tem - ple stands, All earth - ly tem - ples ex - cel - ling. Yet He whom heav'ns can - not con - tain Chose to a - bide on earth with men, Built in our bod - ies His tem - ple.

3. We are God's house of liv - ing stones, Built for His own hab - i - ta - tion; He fills our hearts, his hum - ble thrones, Grant-ing us life and sal - va - tion; Were two or three to seek His face, He in their midst would show His grace, Bless-ings up - on them be - stow - ing.

4. Now we may gath - er with our King E'en in the low - li - est dwell - ing; Prais - es to Him we there may bring, His won-drous mer - cy forth - tell - ing. Je - sus His grace to us ac - cords; Spir - it and life are all His words; His truth doth hal - low the tem - ple. A - men.

WORDS: Nicolai F. S. Grundtvig, 1837; tr. Carl Doving, 1909;   KIRKEN DEN ER ET
           adapt. Fred C. M. Hansen, c.1927   8.8.8.8.8.8.8.8
MUSIC: Ludvig M. Lindeman, 1840

Thanks to God for My Redeemer 126

1. Thanks to God for my Re-deem-er, Thanks for all Thou dost pro-vide!
2. Thanks for prayers that Thou hast an-swered, Thanks for what Thou dost de-ny!
3. Thanks for ros-es by the way-side, Thanks for thorns their stems con-tain!

Thanks for times now but a mem-'ry, Thanks for Je-sus by my side!
Thanks for storms that I have weath-ered, Thanks for all Thou dost sup-ply!
Thanks for homes and thanks for fire-side, Thanks for hope, that sweet re-frain!

Thanks for pleas-ant, balm-y spring-time, Thanks for dark and drear-y fall!
Thanks for pain and thanks for plea-sure, Thanks for com-fort in de-spair!
Thanks for joy and thanks for sor-row, Thanks for heav'n-ly peace with Thee!

Thanks for tears by now for-got-ten, Thanks for peace with-in my soul!
Thanks for grace that none can meas-ure, Thanks for love be-yond com-pare!
Thanks for hope in the to-mor-row, Thanks thro' all e-ter-ni-ty!

WORDS: August L. Storm, 1891; tr. Carl E. Backstrom, 1931
MUSIC: John A. Hultman, 1891

TACK, O GUD
8.7.8.7 D.

127 New Songs of Celebration Render

Unison

1. New songs of cel - e - bra - tion ren - der To Him who
2. Joy - ful - ly, heart - i - ly re - sound - ing, Let ev - ery
3. Riv - ers and seas and tor - rents roar - ing, Hon - or the

has great won - ders done; Awed by His love His foes sur - ren - der
in - stru - ment and voice Peal out the praise of grace a - bound - ing,
Lord with wild ac - claim; Moun - tains and stones, look up a - dor - ing

And fall be - fore the Might - y One. He has made known His
Call - ing the whole world to re - joice. Trum - pets and or - gans
And find a voice to praise His Name. Righ - teous, com - mand - ing,

great sal - va - tion Which all His friends with joy con - fess; He has re -
set in mo - tion Such sounds as make the heav - ens ring: All things that
ev - er glo - rious, Prais - es be His that nev - er cease: Just is our

vealed to ev-ery na-tion His ev-er-last-ing right-eous-ness.
live in earth and o-cean Make mu-sic for your Might-y King.
God, whose truth vic-to-rious Es-tab-lish-es the world in peace.

WORDS: Erik Routley, 1974; based on Psalm 98
MUSIC: Louis Bourgeois, 1543; harm. by Erik Routley

RENDEZ À DIEU
9.8.9.8 D.

Words Copyright © 1974 by Hope Publishing Company. All Rights Reserved.
Music Copyright © 1977 by Hope Publishing Company. All Rights Reserved.

All Who Love and Serve Your City 128

Unison

1. All who love and serve your cit - y, all who
2. In your day of loss and sor - row, in your
3. In your day of wealth and plen - ty, wast - ed
4. For all days are days of judg - ment, and the
5. Ris - en Lord, shall yet the cit - y be the

bear its dai - ly stress, All who cry for peace and
day of help-less strife, Hon - or, peace, and love re -
work and wast-ed play, Call to mind the word of
Lord is wait-ing still, Draw-ing near to those who
cit - y of de-spair? Come to-day, our Judge, our

jus - tice, all who curse and all who bless.
treat - ing, seek the Lord, who is your life.
Je - sus, "Work ye yet while it is day."
spurn him, of-f'ring peace from Cal-v'ry's hill.
Glo - ry; be its name "The Lord is there!"

WORDS: Erik Routley
MUSIC: Peter Cutts

BIRABUS
87.87.

Words Copyright © 1969 by Galliard Ltd. All Rights Reserved. Used by Permission of Galaxy Music Corporation, N.Y., sole U.S. agent.
Music Copyright © 1969 by Hope Publishing Co., Carol Stream, IL 60188. All Rights Reserved.

129 Let Us Talents and Tongues Employ

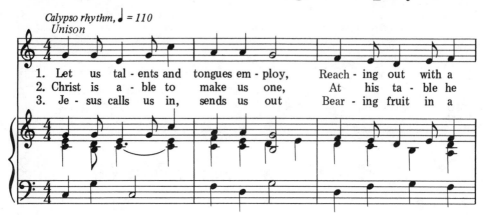

Calypso rhythm, ♩ = 110
Unison

1. Let us tal - ents and tongues em - ploy, Reach - ing out with a
2. Christ is a - ble to make us one, At his ta - ble he
3. Je - sus calls us in, sends us out Bear - ing fruit in a

shout of joy: Bread is bro - ken, the wine is poured,
sets the tone, Teach - ing peo - ple to live to bless,
world of doubt, Gives us love to tell, bread to share:

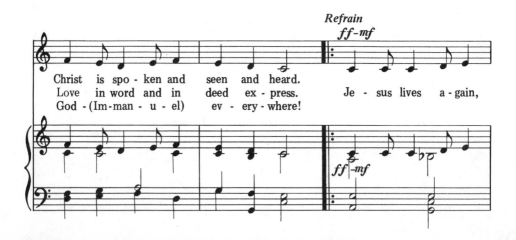

Christ is spo - ken and seen and heard.
Love in word and in deed ex - press.
God - (Im-man - u - el) ev - ery - where!

Refrain
ff–mf

Je - sus lives a - gain,

ff–mf

earth can breathe a-gain, Pass the Word a-round: loaves a - bound!

WORDS: Fred Kaan   LINSTEAD
MUSIC: Jamaican Folk Song, adapted by Doreen Potter   L.M. Ref.

Copyright © 1975 by Hope Publishing Company, Carol Stream, IL 60188. International Copyright Secured. All Rights Reserved.

Free to Be Me   130

Unison

1. Free to be me, God, I real-ly am free; Free to be-
2. Free-dom, pos-ses-sion that makes me like you, Fright-ens me,
3. Free to live ful-ly, to fol-low your way, Give my-self

come what you want me to be; Free to de-cide wheth-er
God, when its mean-ing seeps through; Bless-ing or curse, Lord, con-
whol-ly, to die ev-ery day; Free to be real, God, to

I should be lord, Or be your slave and o-bey your word.
demned to be free? Free, but re-spon-si-ble, free to be me.
strip off my mask, Be your cre-a-tion, it's all that I ask.

WORDS: Kate Wilkins Woolley, 1970   CHISLEHURST
MUSIC: William L. Hooper, 1970   10.10.10.10

Copyright © 1970 Broadman Press. All Rights Reserved. Used by Permission.

131 From Thee All Skill and Science Flow

Unison

1. From thee all skill and sci - ence flow, All pit - y, care, and love,
2. And has - ten, Lord, that per - fect day When pain and death shall cease,

All calm and cour - age, faith and hope: O pour them from a - bove;
And thy just rule shall fill the earth With health and light and peace,

And part them, Lord, to each and all, As each and all shall need,
When - ev - er blue the sky shall gleam, And ev - er green the sod,

To rise like in - cense, each to thee, In no - ble thought and deed.
And man's rude work de-face no more The par - a - dise of God. A-men.

WORDS: Charles Kingsley, 1871
MUSIC: Katherine K. Davis. 1964

MASSACHUSETTS
C.M.D.

Music Copyright © 1964 by Abingdon Press. Used by Permission.

Praise the Lord

132

WORDS: Psalm 113:1-2 (st. 1); Marjorie Jillson (st. 2-4), 1973
MUSIC: Heinz Werner Zimmermann, 1973

CARPENTER 1970
Irregular meter

133   Christ Is the World's Light

Unison

1. Christ is the world's light; Christ and none oth - er;
2. Christ is the world's peace: Christ and none oth - er;
3. Christ is the world's life, Christ and none oth - er;
4. Give God the glo - ry, God and none oth - er;

Born in our dark - ness, He be - came our broth - er.
No one can serve Him and de - spise an - oth - er.
Sold once for sil - ver, mur - dered here, our broth - er—
Give God the glo - ry, Spir - it, Son and Fa - ther;

If we have seen Him, we have seen the Fa - ther:
Who else u - nites us, one in God the Fa - ther?
He, who re - deems us, reigns with God the Fa - ther:
Give God the glo - ry, God in Man my broth - er:

Glo - ry to God on high!
Glo - ry to God on high!
Glo - ry to God on high!
Glo - ry to God on high! A - men.

WORDS: Fred Pratt Green, 1968
MUSIC: Melody from *Paris Antiphoner*, 1681; harm. *Cantate Domino*, 1980

CHRISTE SANCTORUM
10.11.11.6

Christ, upon the Mountain Peak 134

Unison

1. Christ, up - on the moun - tain peak stands a - lone
2. Trem - bling at his feet we saw Mo - ses and
3. Swift the cloud of glo - ry came, God pro - claim-
4. This is God's be - lov - ed Son! Law and pro -

in glo - ry blaz - ing; Let us, if we
E - li - jah speak - ing. All the pro - phets
ing in its thun - der Je - sus as his
phets fade be - fore him; First and last and

dare to speak, with the saints and an - gels
and the law shout through them their joy - ful
Son by name! Na - tions, cry a - loud in
on - ly one, let cre - a - tion now a -

praise him. Al - le - lu - ia!
greet - ing. Al - le - lu - ia!
won - der Al - le - lu - ia!
dore him. Al - le - lu - ia!

WORDS: Brian Wren
MUSIC: Peter Cutts

SHILLINGFORD
7 8.7 8. Alleluia

135 When in Our Music God Is Glorified

1. When in our mu-sic God is glo-ri-fied, And ad-o-
2. How of-ten, mak-ing mu-sic, we have found A new di-
3. So has the Church, in lit-ur-gy and song, In faith and
4. And did not Je-sus sing a Psalm that night When ut-most
5. Let ev-ery in-stru-ment be tuned for praise! Let all re-

ra-tion leaves no room for pride, It is as though the whole cre-
men-sion in the world of sound, As wor-ship moved us to a
love, through cen-tu-ries of wrong, Borne wit-ness to the truth in
e-vil strove a-gainst the Light? Then let us sing, for whom he
joice who have a voice to raise! And may God give us faith to

a-tion cried Al-le-lu-ia! Al-le-lu-ia! Al-le-lu-ia!
more pro-found Al-le-lu-ia! Al-le-lu-ia! Al-le-lu-ia!
ev-ery tongue, Al-le-lu-ia! Al-le-lu-ia! Al-le-lu-ia!
won the fight: Al-le-lu-ia! Al-le-lu-ia! Al-le-lu-ia!
sing al-ways Al-le-lu-ia! Al-le-lu-ia! Al-le-lu-ia!

WORDS: Fred Pratt Green, 1972   CELEBRATION '85
MUSIC: Milburn Price, 1985   10.10.10.4

Creating God, Your Fingers Trace 136

1. Cre-at-ing God, your fin-gers trace The bold de-signs of farth-est space; Let sun and moon and stars and light And what lies hid-den praise your might.
2. Sus-tain-ing God, your hands up-hold Earth's mys-teries known or yet un-told; Let wa-ter's fra-gile blend with air, En-a-bling life, pro-claim your care.
3. Re-deem-ing God, your arms em-brace All now de-spised for creed or race; Let peace, de-scend-ing like a dove, Make known on earth your heal-ing love.
4. In-dwell-ing God, your gos-pel claims One fam-i-ly with a bil-lion names; Let ev-ery life be touched by grace Un-til we praise you face to face.

WORDS: Jeffery Rowthorn (b. 1934), alt.
MUSIC: Reginald Sparshatt Thatcher (1888-1957)

WILDERNESS
L.M.

137 Peace in Our Time, O Lord

1. Peace in our time, O Lord; for this we pray: May ev-ery
(2.) heart, O Lord; for this I pray: May I know

na - tion know peace as the way; May no more
calm - ness now in ev - ery way; Help me to

sons be killed in bat-tle's fray, May each one know the
trust in you each ur-gent day, That I may be as-

truth of peace your way. 2. Peace in my
sured of peace your way.

WORDS: Betty Jo Corum, 1971
MUSIC: Milburn Price, 1971

PAX IAM
10.10.10.10

From Shepherding of Stars 138

1. From shep - herd - ing of stars that gaze Toward
2. Your shep - herd King from star - lit hall Bends
3. This night your King brings from a - far The
4. He shep - herds from the this - tled place The
5. Em - brace the Christ child, and with songs Bind

heav'n - ly fields of light, I come with tid - ings to a - maze You
down to wea - ry lands, Lies man - gered low in cat - tle stall. Go
vir - gin's lul - la - by, The Wise Men's faith, a guid - ing star, And
flocks by thick - ets torn; His pierc - ed hands heal all your race Sore
up the hearts of men. To shep - herd - heal - er - king let throngs Sing

watch - ers in the night, You watch - ers in the night.
touch his in - fant hands, Go touch his in - fant hands.
love from God Most High, And love from God Most High.
wound - ed by the thorn, Sore wound - ed by the thorn.
glo - ri - as a - gain, Sing glo - ri - as a - gain.

WORDS: F. Samuel Janzow, 1969
MUSIC: Richard W. Hillert, 1969

SHEPHERDING
8.6.8.6.6

139 When the Church of Jesus

Unison

1. When the church of Je - sus Shuts its out - er door,
2. If our hearts are lift - ed Where de - vo - tion soars
3. Lest the gifts we of - fer, Mon - ey, tal - ents, time,

Lest the roar of traf - fic Drown the voice of prayer:
High a - bove this hun - gry Suf - f'ring world of ours:
Serve to salve our con - science To our se - cret shame:

May our prayers, Lord, make us Ten times more a - ware
Lest our hymns should drug us To for - get its needs,
Lord, re - prove, in - spire us By the way you give;

That the world we ban - ish Is our Chris - tian care.
Forge our Chris-tian wor - ship In - to Chris - tian deeds.
Teach us, dy - ing Sav - ior, How true Chris - tians live.

WORDS: F. Pratt Green, 1960
MUSIC: Ralph Vaughan Williams, 1925

KING'S WESTON
11.11.11.11

God Has Spoken by His Prophets 140

Unison

1. God has spo-ken by his proph-ets, Spo-ken his un-chang-ing Word;
2. God has spo-ken by Christ Je-sus, Christ, the ev-er-last-ing Son,
3. God is speak-ing by his Spir-it, Speak-ing to the hearts of all,

Each from age to age pro-claim-ing God, the one, the righ-teous Lord.
Bright-ness of the Fa-ther's glo-ry, With the Fa-ther ev-er one;
In the age-less Word ex-pound-ing God's own mes-sage for us all.

In the world's de-spair and tur-moil, One firm an-chor holds us fast:
Spo-ken by the Word In-car-nate, God of God, be-fore time was;
Through the rise and fall of na-tions One sure faith yet stand-ing fast;

God is king, his throne e-ter-nal; God the first, and God the last.
Light of light to earth de-scend-ing, He re-veals our God to us.
God a-bides, his Word un-chang-ing; God the first, and God the last.

WORDS: George W. Briggs, 1952, alt.
MUSIC: Derek Holman, 1971

CARN BREA
8.7.8.7. D.

141 I Come with Joy

Unison

1. I come with joy to meet my Lord, For - giv - en,
2. I come with Chris - tians far and near To find, as
3. As Christ breaks bread and bids us share, Each proud di -
4. And thus with joy we meet our Lord. His pres - ence,
5. To - geth - er met, to - geth - er bound, We'll go our

loved and free, In awe and won - der to re - call His
all are fed, The new com - mun - i - ty of love In
vi - sion ends. The love that made us, makes us one, And
al - ways near, Is in such friend - ship bet - ter known; We
dif - f'rent ways, And as His peo - ple in the world, We'll

life laid down for me, His life laid down for me.
Christ's com - mun - ion bread, In Christ's com - mun - ion bread.
stran - gers now are friends, And stran - gers now are friends.
see and praise Him here; We see and praise Him here.
live and speak His praise, We'll live and speak His praise.

WORDS: Brian A. Wren, 1968
MUSIC: American melody;
        arr. Austin C. Lovelace, 1977

DOVE OF PEACE
8.6.8.6.6

We Meet You, O Christ

Unison

1. We meet you, O Christ, in man-y a guise:
2. In mil-lions a-live, a-way and a-broad,
3. We hear you, O Man, in ag-o-ny cry.
4. You choose to be made at one with the earth;

your im-age we see in sim-ple and wise.
in-volved in our life you live down the road.
For free-dom you march, in ri-ots you die.
the dark of the grave pre-pares for your birth.

You live in a pal-ace, ex-ist in a shack.
Im-pris-oned in sys-tems, you long to be free.
Your face in the pa-pers we read and we see.
Your death is your ris-ing, cre-a-tive your word:

We see you, the gar-dener, a tree on your back.
We see you, Lord Je-sus, still bear-ing your tree.
The tree must be plant-ed by hu-man de-cree.
the tree springs to life and our hope is re - stored.

WORDS: Fred Kaan
MUSIC: Basque Carol, harm. by George Mims

NORMANDY
10 10.11 11.

143 Thank You, God, for Water, Soil and Air

$\dot{} = 66$

Unison

1. Thank   you, God,   for
2. Thank   you, God,   for
3. Thank   you, God,   for
4. Thank   you, God,   for
5. Thank   you, God,   for

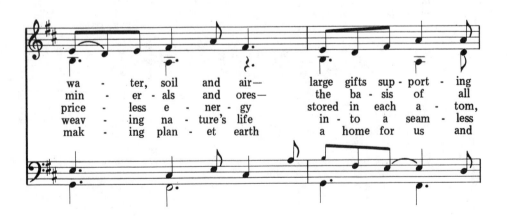

wa - ter, soil and air—   large gifts sup - port - ing
min - er - als and ores—   the ba - sis of   all
price - less e - ner - gy   stored in each a - tom,
weav - ing na - ture's life   in - to a   seam - less
mak - ing plan - et earth   a home for us   and

ev - ery-thing that lives.   For - give   our spoil - ing and   a - buse of
build - ing, wealth and speed.   For - give   our reck - less plun - der-ing and
ga - thered from the   sun.   For - give   our greed and care - less-ness of
robe,   a   frag - ile whole.   For - give   our haste that tam - pers un - a -
a - ges yet   un - born.   Help us to share, con - sid - er, save and

them.   Help   us   re - new   the   face   of the
waste.   Help   us   re - new   the   face   of the
power.   Help   us   re - new   the   face   of the
wares.   Help   us   re - new   the   face   of the
store.   Come and   re - new   the   face   of the

1, 2, 3, 4   5

earth.
earth.
earth.
earth.

rit.

earth.

rit.

WORDS: Brian Wren
MUSIC: Erik Routley

ALTHORP
9 10.10 9.

144   **Now the Silence**

Now the si - lence, Now the peace, Now the emp - ty hands up-

lift - ed; Now the kneel - ing, Now the plea, Now the Fa - ther's

arms   in wel - come; Now the hear - ing, Now the pow'r,

Now   the ves - sel brimmed for pour - ing;

Now the bod - y, Now the blood, Now the joy - ful

cel - e - bra - tion; Now the wed - ding, Now the songs,

Now the heart for - giv - en leap - ing; Now the Spir - it's

vis - i - ta - tion, Now the Son's e - piph - a - ny,

Now the Fa - ther's bless - ing. Now. Now. Now.

WORDS: Jaroslav J. Vajda
MUSIC: Carl F. Schalk

NOW
Irregular

145 Like the Murmur of the Dove's Song

1. Like the mur-mur of the dove's song, Like the chal-lenge of her
2. To the mem-bers of Christ's Bo-dy, To the branch-es of the
3. With the heal-ing of di-vi-sion, With the cease-less voice of

flight, Like the vig-or of the wind's rush, Like the
Vine, To the Church in faith as-sem-bled, To her
prayer, With the power to love and wit-ness, With the

new flame's ea-ger might: Come, Ho-ly Spir-it, come.
midst as gift and sign: Come, Ho-ly Spir-it, come.
peace be-yond com-pare: Come, Ho-ly Spir-it, come.

*Phrase 1 of each stanza may be sung by one group, with a contrasted group singing phrase 2, and all joining for the final phrase.

WORDS: Carl P. Daw, Jr., 1982   BRIDEGROOM
MUSIC: Peter Cutts, 1969   8.7.8.7.6

Words Copyright © 1982 by Carl Daw, Jr. Used by Permission.
Music Copyright © 1969 by Hope Publishing Company. All Rights Reserved.

Awake, O Sleeper, Rise from Death 146

1. A - wake, O sleep - er, rise from death, And Christ shall
2. To us on earth he came to bring From sin and
3. There is one Bo - dy and one hope, One Spir - it
4. Then walk in love as Christ has loved, Who died that
5. For us Christ lived, for us he died And con-quered

give you light, So learn his love— its length and
fear re - lease, To give the Spir - it's u - ni -
and one call, One Lord, one Faith, and one Bap -
he might save; With kind and gen - tle hearts for -
in the strife. A - wake, a - rise, go forth in

breadth,   Its   full - ness, depth,   and   height.
ty,   The   ver - y   bond   of   peace.
tism,   One   Fa - ther   of   us   all.
give   As   God   in   Christ   for - gave.
faith,   And   Christ   shall   give   you   life.

WORDS: F. Bland Tucker, 1980
MUSIC: Max Miller, 1984

MARSH CHAPEL
C.M.

147   Because I Have Been Given Much

Unison

1. Be - cause I have been giv - en much, I too must give;
2. Be - cause I have been shel - tered, fed, By thy good care,
3. Be - cause love has been lav - ished so Up - on me, Lord,

Be - cause of thy great boun - ty, Lord, Each day I live,
I can - not see an - oth - er's lack And I not share
A wealth I know that was not meant For me to hoard,

I shall di - vide my gifts from thee With ev - ery broth - er
My glow - ing fire, my loaf of bread, My roof's safe shel - ter
I shall give love to those in need, Shall show that love by

that I see Who has the need of help from me.
o - ver - head, That he too may be com - fort - ed.
word and deed: Thus shall my thanks be thanks in - deed.

WORDS: Grace Noll Crowell, 1936
MUSIC: Phillip Landgrave, 1974

SEMINARY
8.4.8.4.8.8.8

Jesus, Friend of Thronging Pilgrims 148

Unison

1. Je - sus, friend of throng - ing pil - grims, As of those who
2. Thou didst know the mar - ket plac - es And the streets in
3. Send thy ser - vants to the high-ways Where are heard the
4. By thy pow'r be streets trans - fig - ured, Haunts of sin be

walk a - lone, Look up - on our crowd - ed cit - ies
days of yore; Thou couldst see be - neath the plea - sures
dole - ful cries; Call a - gain the hun - gry mass - es
pur - i - fied; Rich and poor be found in con - cord,

With com - pas - sion from thy throne; Lov - ing Shep - herd,
Bro - ken hearts and spir - its sore; Gra - cious Heal - er,
To the feast that sat - is - fies; For the sup - per,
Zi - on's courts their hope and pride; Lord of cit - ies,

Lov - ing Shep - herd, Move a - mong us as thine own.
Gra - cious Heal - er, How we need thy touch once more!
For the sup - per Now is spread be - fore their eyes.
Lord of cit - ies, Here make heal - ing peace a - bide.

WORDS: W. Nantlais Williams, 1954   ERIN
MUSIC: Paul Langston, 1974   8.7.8.7.8.7

149 What Does the Lord Require?

WORDS: Micah 6:8; Albert F. Bayly
MUSIC: Erik Routley, 1969

SHARPTHORNE
6.6.6.6.3.3.6

How Gracious Are Thy Mercies, Lord 150

1. How gra-cious are thy mer-cies, Lord, They hal-low all my days;
2. How love-ly are thy mer-cies, Lord, The earth, the sky, the sea,
3. How ten-der are thy mer-cies, Lord, Thy grace when days are long,

Thy gifts of ten-der-ness and love In-spire my heart to praise.
For all things good and beau-ti-ful I of-fer praise to thee.
And in the lone-ly mid-night hour Thy pre-cious gift of song.

The grow-ing mir-a-cle of faith As-sures me I am thine;
For clouds by day and stars by night, For blos-soms frail and fair,
When I ap-proach the gates of death And life is at an end,

Oh, praise thy name that I can share This fel-low-ship di-vine!
For all thy glo-rious hand-i-work My heart is moved to prayer.
Thy pres-ence will sus-tain me still, My Sav-ior and my Friend!

WORDS: Sybil Leonard Armes, 1964
MUSIC: Traditional English melody; arr. Ralph Vaughan Williams, 1906

KINGSFOLD
Irregular meter

151 We Would See Jesus; Lo! His Star

Unison

1. We would see Je - sus; lo, his star is shin - ing
2. We would see Je - sus; Ma - ry's Son most ho - ly,
3. We would see Je - sus; on the moun - tain teach - ing,
4. We would see Je - sus; in the ear - ly morn - ing,

A - bove the sta - ble while the an - gels sing;
Light of the vil - lage life from day to day;
With all the lis - t'ning peo - ple gath - ered round;
Still as of old he call - eth "Fol - low me";

There in a man - ger on the hay re - clin - ing;
Shin - ing re - vealed thro' ev - ery task most low - ly;
While birds and flow'rs and sky a - bove are preach - ing
Let us a - rise, all mean - er ser - vice scorn - ing;

Haste, let us lay our gifts be - fore the King.
The Christ of God, the life, the truth, the way.
The bless - ed - ness which sim - ple trust has found.
Lord, we are thine, we give our - selves to thee.

WORDS: J. Edgar Park, 1913
MUSIC: William J. Reynolds, 1974

MORA PROCTOR
11.10.11.10

Rejoice, Ye Pure in Heart 152

1. Re - joice, ye pure in heart! Re - joice, give thanks, and sing! Your glo - rious ban - ner wave on high, The cross of Christ your King.
2. With all the an - gel choirs, With all the saints of earth, Pour out the strains of joy and bliss, True rap - ture, no - blest mirth.
3. Yes, on through life's long path, Still chant - ing as ye go, From youth to age by night and day, In glad - ness and in woe.
4. Then on, ye pure in heart! Re - joice, give thanks, and sing! Your glo - rious ban - ner wave on high, The cross of Christ your King.

Refrain

Ho - san - na, Ho - san - na, Ho - san - na, Re - joice, give thanks and sing.

WORDS: Edward H. Plumptre, 1865
MUSIC: Richard Dirksen, 1974

VINEYARD HAVEN
S.M. Ref.

153 I Am the Bread of Life

1. ___ I am the Bread of life.   You who
2. The bread that___ I will give   Is my
3. Un - less___ you eat   Of the
4. ___ I am· the Res - ur - rec - tion,___
5. Yes, Lord,___ I be - lieve   That___

come to me shall not   hun - ger;___ And who be -
flesh for the life of the world,___ And if you
flesh of the Son of   Man___ And ___
I___ am the   life.___ If you be -
you___ are the   Christ,___ The ___

lieve in me shall not thirst.   No one can come to
eat___ of this bread,   You shall___ live for-
drink___ of his blood,   And drink___ of his
lieve___ in___ me,   E - ven___ though you
Son___ of___ God.   Who___ have

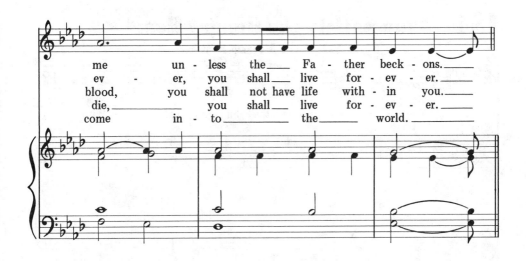

me   un - less   the____ Fa - ther   beck - ons.____
ev - er,   you   shall____ live   for - ev - er.____
blood,   you   shall   not have life   with - in   you.____
die,____   you   shall____ live   for - ev - er.____
come   in - to____   the____ world.____

Refrain
Harmony

And I will raise   you up,   and I will raise   you

up,   And I will raise   you up   on the last   day.

WORDS: John 6; Suzanne Toolan, SM, b. 1927   BREAD OF LIFE
MUSIC: Suzanne Toolan, SM, b. 1927   Irregular with Ref.

154 You Satisfy the Hungry Heart
(The Gift of Finest Wheat)

Unison

You sat-is-fy the hun-gry heart With

gift of fin-est wheat; Come give to us, O

sav-ing Lord, The bread of life to eat.

Harmony

1. As when the shep - herd calls his sheep, They
2. With joy - ful lips we sing to you Our
3. Is not the cup we bless and share The
4. The mys - t'ry of your pres - ence, Lord, No
5. You give your - self to us, O Lord; Then

know   and   heed his voice;   So when you   call   your
praise   and   grat - i - tude,   That you should count us
blood   of   Christ out-poured? Do not one   cup,   one
mor -   tal   tongue can tell: Whom all the   world can
self -   less let   us   be,   To serve each   oth - er

D.C.

fam - 'ly, Lord, We   fol - low and re - joice.
wor - thy, Lord, To   share   this heav'n - ly food.
loaf, de - clare Our one - ness in the Lord?
not con - tain   Comes in   our hearts to dwell.
in your name   In   truth   and char - i - ty.

WORDS: Omer Westendorf, b. 1916   BICENTENNIAL
MUSIC: Robert E. Kreutz, b. 1922   C.M. with Ref.

155 Jesus Comes Today

1. Je - sus comes to - day! Pre - pare to meet your God! No Pres - i - den - tial cav - al - cade en - cir - cles him with might; the shep - herds kiss a work - er's child who loves till all are rec - on - ciled: Pre - pare to meet your God.

2. Jesus comes today!
   Prepare to meet your God!
      No massed Convention roars its praise
      to hail the new messiah;
      love has no powers to lay aside
      so crowds will have him crucified:
      Prepare to meet your God!

3. Jesus comes today!
   Prepare to meet your God!
      No Primaries can pave his way
      to be the people's choice;
      he chooses us, and calls our name,
      and life can never be the same:
      Prepare to meet your God!

WORDS: Brian Wren, b. 1936
MUSIC: Peter Cutts, b. 1937

PREPARATION
Irregular meter

INDEX OF ILLUSTRATIVE HYMNS

(First column lists hymn first line; second, hymn number; third, tune name)

God who spoke in the beginning	91	VERBUM DEI
God, who stretched the spangled heavens	88	AUSTRIAN HYMN
Great is thy faithfulness	110	FAITHFULNESS
Hail, thou once despised Jesus	97	PLEADING SAVIOUR
Hark, the herald angels sing	61	MENDELSSOHN
He who would valiant be	83	MONKS GATE
Hope of the world, thou Christ	34	VICAR
How firm a foundation	104	FOUNDATION
How gracious are your mercies, Lord	150	KINGSFOLD
How sweet the name of Jesus sounds	65	ST. PETER
I am the Bread of Life	153	BREAD OF LIFE
I come with joy	141	DOVE OF PEACE
I love thee, I love thee	93	I LOVE THEE
If you will only let God guide you	19	NEUMARK
In Babylon town	92	IN BABYLON TOWN
In Christ there is no east or west	109	MCKEE
Jerusalem, my happy home	102	LAND OF REST
Jerusalem the golden	60	EWING
Jesus comes today	155	PREPARATION
Jesus, friend of thronging pilgrims	148	ERIN
Jesus, lover of my soul	70	ABERYSTWYTH
Jesus makes my heart rejoice	32	HAYN
Jesus, priceless treasure	17	JESU, MEINE FREUDE
Jesus shall reign where'er the sun	38	DUKE STREET
Jesus, still lead on	35	SEELENBRÄUTIGAM
Jesus, the very thought of thee	28	KING'S NORTON
Jesus, thou joy of loving hearts	55	QUEBEC
Jesus, thy blood and righteousness	69	GERMANY
Joy to the world	94	ANTIOCH
Lead, kindly Light, amid the encircling gloom	84	ALBERTA
Let all the world in every corner sing	89	ALL THE WORLD
Let us talents and tongues employ	129	LINSTEAD
Let us with a gladsome mind	114	CHINESE SONG
Lift up your voice, ye Christian folk	74	LADYWELL
Like the murmur of the dove's song	145	BRIDEGROOM
Lo, how a Rose e'er blooming	16	ES IST EIN' ROS' ENTSPRUNGEN
Lord Christ, the Father's mighty Son	112	EAST MEADS
Lord, I want to be a Christian	117	I WANT TO BE A CHRISTIAN
Lord Jesus, think on me	39	SOUTHWELL
Lord of our life, and God of our salvation	73	ISTE CONFESSOR
My hope is built on nothing less	103	SOLID ROCK
My song is love unknown	100	ROBERTSON
New songs of celebration render	127	RENDEZ A DIEU
Now thank we all our God	87	GRACIAS
Now the silence	144	NOW
O come, all ye faithful	95	ADESTE FIDELES
O come, O come, Emmanuel	57	VENI EMMANUEL

O for a closer walk with God	27	CAITHNESS
O for a thousand tongues to sing	108	AZMON
O gladsome light, O grace	43	NUNC DIMITTIS
O God of earth and altar	71	LLANGLOFFAN
O Jesus Christ, to thee may hymns	119	CITY OF GOD
O Master, let me walk with thee	68	MARYTON
O Morning Star, how fair and bright	10	WIE SCHÖN LEUCHTET
O Sacred Head, now wounded	12	PASSION CHORALE
O sing a song of Bethlehem	79	KINGSFOLD
O Splendor of God's glory bright	1	SPLENDOR PATERNAE
O Zion, haste, thy mission high fulfilling	115	TIDINGS
Of the Father's love begotten	3	DIVINUM MYSTERIUM
Open now the gates of beauty	26	UNSER HERRSCHER
Our Father God, thy name we praise	121	MIT FREUDEN ZART
Out of the depths I cry to you	6	AUS TIEFER NOT
Peace in our time, O Lord	137	PAX IAM
Praise the Lord	132	CARPENTER 1970
Praise to the Lord, the Almighty	24	LOBE DEN HERREN
Print thine image pure and holy	46	PSALM 42
Redeemed, how I love to proclaim it	53	ADA
Rejoice, ye pure in heart	152	VINEYARD HAVEN
Rise, my soul, and stretch thy wings	47	AMSTERDAM
Rise to greet the sun	120	LE P'ING
Sing a new song to the Lord	124	CANTATE DOMINO
Sing praise to God who reigns above	30	MIT FREUDEN ZART
Sing them over again to me	111	WORDS OF LIFE
Spread, O spread, thou mighty word	29	GOTT SEI DANK
Stand up, and bless the Lord	22	OLD 134TH
Sunset to sunrise changes now	90	KEDRON
Tell out, my soul	123	WOODLANDS
Thank you, God, for water, soil, and air	143	ALTHORP
Thanks to God for my Redeemer	126	TACK, O GUD
The bread of life for all men broken	122	SHENG EN
The church's one foundation	59	AURELIA
The day of resurrection	58	LANCASHIRE
The day thou gavest, Lord, is ended	33	LES COMMANDEMENS DE DIEU
The God of Abraham praise	49	LEONI
The head that once was crowned with thorns	23	ST. MAGNUS
The Lord's my shepherd, I'll not want	67	CRIMOND
To God be the glory	96	TO GOD BE THE GLORY
Unto us a boy is born	14	PUER NOBIS
Wake, awake for night is flying	11	WACHET AUF (Nicolai)
Wake, awake for night is flying	12	WACHET AUF (Nicolai/Bach)
We meet you, O Christ	142	NORMANDY
We praise you, O God, our Redeemer	116	KREMSER
We would see Jesus; lo, his star is shining	151	MORA PROCTOR
"Welcome, happy morning!" age to age	56	FORTUNATUS
Were you there?	105	WERE YOU THERE?
What does the Lord require	149	SHARPTHORNE
When all thy mercies, O my God	42	TALLIS' ORDINAL

INDEX OF ILLUSTRATIVE HYMN TUNES

(The numbers refer to hymns for which tunes are used)

General Index